LONG TAKE

LONG TAKE

Akira Kurosawa

TRANSLATED BY

Anne McKnight

University of Minnesota Press
Minneapolis
London

Published by the University of Minnesota Press
111 Third Avenue South, Suite 290
Minneapolis, MN 55401-2520
http://www.upress.umn.edu

ISBN 978-1-5179-0328-2 (hc)
ISBN 978-1-5179-0329-9 (pb)

A Cataloging-in-Publication record for this book is available from the Library of Congress.

Printed in the United States of America on acid-free paper

34 33 32 31 30 29 28 27 26 10 9 8 7 6 5 4 3 2

"You must explain."

"I won't. Sleeping or dreaming, the dreamer must accept his dreams."

—Death replies to Orpheus, in *Orpheus*,
directed by Jean Cocteau (Kurosawa film no. 20)

CONTENTS

NOTE ON JAPANESE NAMES AND TERMS

With the exception of Akira Kurosawa, I have preserved Japanese name order, which puts the family name first (as in Mifune Toshirō).

Transliteration follows the moderated Hepburn style, with macrons for long vowels except for *ii.* Macrons are not used here in commonly known Japanese words (such as Tokyo).

Some words that have precise definitions and a heavy conceptual weight (such as *subjectivity*) have been transliterated and also appear with their original kanji characters. In this case, "subjectivity" would follow the format "subjectivity (shutaisei, 主体性)" or alternatively, "hiroba (forum, 広場)."

Film titles are listed according to the title by which they are most searchable in the United States. For example, Satyajit Ray's 1955 film is referred to as *Pather Panchali.*

TRANSLATOR'S INTRODUCTION

Cinephilia, Silent Cinema, and the First Person

Anne McKnight

For many viewers in the mainland United States, over the nearly six decades and thirty films of his career as a director, Akira Kurosawa was the point of entry into Japanese cinema. His debut on the world stage was made possible by a fluke, brokered by an Italian scholar turned language teacher, Giuliana Stramiglioni. Stramiglioni imported postwar Italian films to Japan, including the neorealist cinema that emerged from barely postwar Italy, when its rubble and black markets must have resonated with the Tokyo of the Occupation era. While U.S. authorities focused on Japanese film as something to democratize and purge of its feudal remnants, her office submitted the 1950 film *Rashomon* to the festival without even telling Kurosawa.[1]

Though it was widely regarded in Japan "as an incomprehensible film during its production and after its release," as Mitsuhiro Yoshimoto reminds us, the film won the Golden Lion, the most prestigious prize at Venice.[2] This was followed by a special Oscar for the best foreign-language picture. These unexpected successes launched Kurosawa into the main arena of world cinema.

We can see the afterlives of Kurosawa's films in works from the *Star Wars* saga to the spaghetti Western *A Fistful of Dollars* and the Indian Hindi-language blockbuster *Sholay*. His works have decisively shaped what it means to be a cinephile—a lover of rain and torpid heat onscreen, of the Surrealist touch brought into postwar Tokyo, of art films, of Japanese movies, a lover of cinema itself. But much less is known about the films from Japan and from around the world that Kurosawa himself admired, loved, and metabolized into his own work. His earlier memoir *Something Like an Autobiography* (1983) gives a glimpse into his early viewing world in a chronicle of films he saw.[3] But this list is nested in a footnote and trails off in the silent era. The memoir itself ends just as Kurosawa's career is launched into a different world with the release and export of *Rashomon,* though Kurosawa was writing during the production of *Kagemusha,* in 1980, just as he began working with international coproductions. One is left feeling there is much more to be said.

This book is an attempt to extend the earlier chronicle, and to flesh out the ways in which Kurosawa watched and absorbed cinema, at times parlaying it into his own work. *Long Take* includes a list of one hundred of Kurosawa's favorite films, along with conversations he had with editors and two key interlocutors—film director Yamada Yōji and fiction writer and playwright Inoue Hisashi. The conversations are framed by his daughter, Kazuko, who assembled and arranged the film list, in two short essays that follow the conversations. Her work as medium and amanuensis enables us to open our frames of reference and to read the films in new ways, seeing what Kurosawa took from other works, what he left behind, and how he regards his place in cinema.

Unlike the New Wave filmmakers who broke through a generation later, such as Ōshima Nagisa and Matsumoto Toshio, Kurosawa steered clear of issues other directors argued loudly about. He often shut down probing questions by ascribing things to chance—claiming not to know how he ended up in film or where the title of his most renowned film came from. Kurosawa also claimed to dislike films that wore their theory proudly (rikutsu-poku eiga, 理屈っぽく映画) and said, somewhat shockingly and with some shade, that he never really watched Godard. This differed from the active polemics of later filmmakers who made their positions clear in debates, essays, manifestos, and editorial positions about politically invested, avant-garde filmmakers such as Luis Buñuel and Alain Resnais.[4]

As film historian Christian Keathley notes, "The cinephiles' dialogue, which leads ultimately to revaluation and reassessment of cinema, is legitimized in large part through critical writing."[5] The critical affections of cinephiles reshuffle the deck of cultural reference points as they filter, argue, and interpret films. As this reshuffling moves from paper into conversation or into the production process, cinephiles weigh the material differently so that its values are differently distributed. Kurosawa was not very invested in the critical writings that shaped cinephilia. If we look for cinephilia only in written polemics, it can be hard to suss out his take on films because he insisted for the most part that they do the talking for themselves. The essays and dialogues in this volume demonstrate Kurosawa's active process of cinephilia by mapping the coordinates of his ideal cinema—the list of one hundred films shows him appreciating, but also evaluating, sorting, and commenting. As we look at the materials his cinephilia transfers from silent film, non-Western modern cinemas and directors, and independent cinema, we can clear a different place for Kurosawa in world cinema—beyond the important but not exclusive connections to both Old and New Hollywood.

Kurosawa didn't leave behind a written record of positions and polemics giving himself a self-authorized place in film history. From a certain point of view, the missing context leaves a lot of room for debate about where to place his films in Japan's highly internationalized history of film forms. The blurriness of the background that audiences and filmmakers would most like to hear about directly impacts the difficulty of translating Kurosawa speaking. The conversations in these chapters take place among editors and old friends who share many unspoken artistic and political contexts and do not need to explain the obvious. On occasions when Kurosawa does go on record about other films and filmmakers, he offers boilerplate praise like "amazing" (subarashii, 素晴らしい), "stunning" (sugoi, すごい), or "well done" (umai, 上手い). These words are evocative and authoritative, cementing his own fluency in examples of world cinema: Kurosawa knows what's what and is confident about his place in it. But these words also camouflage the actual referent, and in English translation without context, can easily sound repetitive, or lazy and vague.

Given the breadth of his viewing and interaction with other world filmmakers, Kurosawa's speech is conspicuously lacking in the technical vocabulary we often associate with connoisseurship or appreciation. And the vagueness of his language for appreciation is intriguingly at odds with clarity and intensity of his memory for specific moments, themselves traces of cinephilia that serve as points of reference for real life—for example, the way John Ford bids farewell to Kurosawa as he enters an elevator reprises the rhythm and choreography of Ford's film *Horse Soldiers.*

Most resonant but cryptic is "fascinating" (omoshiroi, 面白い), a word he frequently uses in his characteristic gruff, short sentences—ones that often end in particles that anticipate agreement with his conversation partner and steer the conversation one way (toward assumed agreement, in the case of "ne"), or deliver new and highly opinionated information, steering the conversation another way (in the case of "yo"). In these conversations, "fascinating" can mean surprising or entertaining, but may also refer to something that captures your attention because it is unexpected but leads to a deeper aesthetic insight.[6] In *Long Take,* "fascinating" can refer to out-and-out suspense films like *The French Connection* or to dishy anecdotes in a biography of John Ford. But it also may point to Dostoevsky's musings on dreams or a philosophy of craft where you "do your best in your work as an artisan." These cryptic turns of phrase basically allow Kurosawa to chart his own folksy-seeming but highly plotted sense of judgment. Paying attention to these blurry words not only helps *us* see how Kurosawa sees his place in film history but also helps us see his assessment of other films.

English-language scholarship might trace such moments of cinephilia back through their etymology, to locate a specific kind of spectatorship—seeing something "amazing" or "wonderful," as in *It's a Wonderful Life,* a miracle to behold. But each Japanese word is more open about the emotion or affect the film might evoke, and we need to do more than project our own gloss onto what "amazing" or "fascinating" might mean. My method in translating involved tracking down and watching all the films Kurosawa refers to in his list and, in passing, locating the "fascinating" scenes he mentions in often throwaway and effusive contexts, reading through the criticism in English and Japanese (and French, where appropriate), and connecting his critical reactions—"fascinating," "amazing," "stunning," "wonderful"—to specific scenes to find patterns.

My title *Long Take* comes from the fact that the essays and dialogues in this volume were published over a period of decades, and further show the sweep of Kurosawa's lifetime of viewing almost a century of cinema.[7] The list and these translated conversations that survey his career offer a fuller context of how Kurosawa wrote himself into world cinema history through watching the films he loved and talking about them.[8]

Kurosawa's cinephilia—love of cinema as film and as an institution that could be better than it is—is conveyed in the sheer variety and magnitude of references he translates to screen, captured in these conversations through references to specific films, as well as discussions of research and participation in film festivals. The patterns of praise from this large sample of a hundred films foreground three elements in particular that put Kurosawa in a new light: the tool kit of silent cinema; the value and inspiration he finds in non-Western filmmakers; and the emotional adjacency Kurosawa idealizes when director, camera, actor, and spectator all align in their uncoordinated performance, as in a spontaneous movement. This is a different model of viewing than identification, which makes the moviegoer an atomized receiver rather than part of a system that includes filmmaker, film, and audience in shared space and time. Art objects, most especially film, serve as reference points for life—the choreography of moments, but also ideal forms of behavior by those in power, such as teachers and those with class privilege, like samurai. Related is the stubborn—and sometimes, on set, explosive—commitment to reproducing the world of research in the world of the set, so that screenwriters, cinematographers, and lacquerists alike are held to high standards of performance.

The status of film as a socially marginal entertainment in early twentieth-century Japan meant that it was not Kurosawa's class destiny to be a cinephile. His love of films was fostered by men in his family who ignored the bad reputation of film that moralizers bruited about in the 1910s. Though "a strict man of military background," Kurosawa's father took him to theaters that screened Japanese, Russian, European, and Hollywood cinemas almost in real time, and even to theaters, which were still tinged with leftover premodern loucheness and ill repute.[9]

Distribution of European films in Tokyo introduced Expressionism and other avant-garde movements as well as experiments in sound film and musicals that came out of the German studio system in the late 1920s and early 1930s. These films would have shown Kurosawa that sound cinema offered an immense playbook beyond naturalistic sound, a theme he discusses at length in several of this volume's conversations. Erik Charell's *Congress Dances* (1931, no. 8) used the first recorded orchestra in cinema history. G. W. Pabst's musical adaptation of the socialist musical *Threepenny Opera* (1931, no. 9) featured music by Kurt Weill based on a play by Bertolt Brecht and used songs as both performance and as anatomies of the power struggles between the police and underworld of the film's London setting. The cultural weight of classical music as an art enjoyed by the masses is felt in these films, as it is in many other films of the 1940s and 1950s. The populist reach of classical music is even apparent in *Godzilla* (no. 34), in which a young couple, a nurse and a salvage company employee, have to abandon their date-night plans for a string quartet concert because of Godzilla's looming attack.

While these performances are not directly planted into Kurosawa's works, we can see their traces in films where recorded song is a driving force of the story. An eighteen-minute sequence in *One Wonderful Sunday* (1947) is a striking example. A penniless young couple can't afford to enjoy indoor spectacles and are forced to wander the outdoors and invent their own entertainment on their rainy day off. As the man's frustration mounts, the couple enters an abandoned amphitheater, and as a gesture of love to his fiancée, the man air-conducts a performance of Schubert's *Unfinished Symphony*, as a hostile wind whips: "You can create worlds in your dreams, right?"

His confidence in sustaining the illusion flags, and seeing his despair in the face of such hostility, the young woman breaks in to address the audience, beseeching the spectators directly. Her face is lit like a silent picture, and the camera zooms in as she lashes back, addressing "everyone" in the audience, asking for their support on behalf of all the broke young lovers like them, "freezing in the cold winds of the world." Her fiancé resumes, and the soundtrack picks up the shared illusion of their empty orchestra (literally, kara-oke, in the modern turn of phrase we would use). The young woman's Brechtian moment of direct address crystallizes through heartfelt emotion, rather than the blunt and knowing analytic of Pabst's narrator, but the framing, the lighting, and the role of song resonate strongly.

Similarly, if more subtly, song connects to a retro form of social critique in the most energetic scene in Kurosawa's last film, *Maadadayo* (1993). This scene features a group of suited men dancing through a banquet hall singing as they celebrate their annual reunion with their former teacher. The song is based on a familiar song sung by strolling medicine peddlers, wounded veterans of the 1904–5 Russo-Japanese War who would make a living selling medicine dressed in uniform and singing the refrain while walking and playing the accordion.[10] The film treats the song as a *kaeuta* (changing song, 替え歌)—a parody that swaps out parts of a song's lyrics with topical references, while keeping the melody. In the original version, each verse of the song substitutes a different example of the ills the medicine will cure in the struggling everyperson's human body.

In *Maadadayo,* the lyrics reference the ills and foolishness plaguing the social body that is in dire need of healing. The weight of critique falls on the bosses who yammer about democracy all the while stacking

In *One Wonderful Sunday,* Masako, part of a young couple, implores the audience, many of whom must have been broke or young themselves, to support the lovers to achieve their dreams of housing, unalienated labor, and access to art for the masses.

the deck, and on the yes-men who support them, just as Pabst's film equates the criminal underworld with the aboveboard world of banking. The eternal return of foolishness is formally signaled by adding stanzas and references to daily life. This makes for a song that is joyful but can extend itself to touch on everyday people's suffering. In his last film, *Maadadayo,* song does what Kurosawa films aspire to do overall—latch on to elements of preexisting reality and daily life, articulate them through a living communal set piece, and give everyone in the room a simultaneous experience of this heightened reality.

Because it presents a fantasy of unending change and spontaneity, the set piece of song in *Maadadayo* effectively reconciles a conflict between performance and recorded sound. Performance can maintain its spontaneity, while recording preserves it. The tension between ephemeral performance and recorded sound had a personal resonance for Kurosawa, as well as marking a major shift in mass entertainment. Kurosawa's brother Heigo performed in cinemas as an up-and-coming *benshi,* or film narrator, in the competitive performance culture of prewar urban Tokyo, working under the most celebrated *benshi* of the era, Tokugawa Musei. The *benshi* rivaled the films themselves in popularity, and many people came expressly to hear the performance of their favorite narrator, whose cover versions of the stories framed and embellished the films, both Japanese and foreign.[11] The acceptance of recorded music in film set in motion a gradual replacement of the storytelling culture of the *benshi,* making way for a modern studio system separate from live performing arts. The exact reasons are unclear, but Heigo committed suicide just as the vocation of *benshi* came under surveillance by the Japanese state due to their ability to improvise potentially subversive comments. After some failed strikes, *benshi* were automated out of existence by theaters that introduced sound film.

Heigo ushered Kurosawa into the age of modern media by feeding him books published by the new paperback industry that sparked a "one-yen boom" in pocket books. The series included fiction writers such as Leo Tolstoy and Natsume Sōseki, writers whose works would later shape Kurosawa's films. Literary historian Nate Shockey calls this autodidact culture "a radical publishing experiment and a protracted plan to popularize philosophy for mass consumption."[12] Not just philosophy, but translations of religious texts, scientific texts, and eventually series of world literature in translation appeared and were read by many who, like Kurosawa, did not go to college but learned through apprenticeship. (Kurosawa left formal education after middle school, the equivalent of today's high school; he was the only non-college graduate in his entering "class" as an assistant director.)

Olga Solovieva's eye-opening book on Kurosawa's deep engagement with Russian literature and utopian thought notes, "Kurosawa knew not only the Japanese, Russian, and Western cultural canons but also understood how individual works within those canons relate to each other. His cinematic adaptations, as well as his autobiography, are rich in play with Russian and other literary allusions."[13] The 1991 roundtable included in this volume gives us insights to Kurosawa's literary debts to Russian literature beyond the familiar canon. It's well known that Kurosawa credits Tolstoy's *War and Peace* as the basis of the script for *Seven Samurai,* a statement he repeats here. But in this roundtable, as well as in the production notes for *Seven Samurai,* he mentions a 1926 novel by the proletarian writer Alexander Fadeyev as an equally key source. Kurosawa read Fadeyev's novel *The Rout* after it was translated into Japanese by the leading proletariat critic Kurahara Korehito as part of the one-yen pocket book explosion.

In his translator's introduction, Kurahara positions *The Rout* as the story of "the closest partisan war to us."[14] The novel depicts a group of partisans—"without a single protagonist"—made up of Russians, Ukrainians, and an ethnically Jewish leader, female and male, miners and farmers, all committed to free love and revolution against the ruling class in the wake of the Russo-Japanese War of 1904–5, the war that launched Japan into the first ranks of imperial nations. Kurahara's praise for the novel comes from the way the richness of the "scene to scene" everydayness and characters take over from what might otherwise be judged for its "impoverished" plot.[15] Kurahara praises the novel as an exceptional proletarian novel that is actually entertaining in its use of multiple protagonists with differentiated characterization in their collective, rather than being a mere diagram for action.[16] Idealizing Russian history and cultural forms at the expense of his own nation's history of glory and empire building put Kurahara in a rare, and soon to be banned, position. As Kurosawa discusses in the roundtable "*Seven Samurai,* Redux," in this volume, the sense of everydayness and highly episodic storytelling found in *The Rout* are also characteristic of *Seven Samurai.*

A second likeness of *The Rout* to *Seven Samurai* is that both texts feature an ensemble of wildly disparate partisans fighting against a decadent enemy. In *Seven Samurai,* this ensemble would be the outlaw bandits, or *nobushi,* where *bushi* is an actual position in the social order that refers to samurai. These outlaws are the doppelgängers of the samurai employed by the village, examples of the marauding outlaws that the seven samurai (or six plus Mifune's character) could have become if they had banded together to plunder the farmers rather than defend them.

As we hear in reference to *Seven Samurai* and other films in this collection, Kurosawa is a director who puts unusual pressure on the scenario to do the heavy lifting of making a good film. His investment in the written word is thus no surprise, and the conversations in this volume bring up multiple connections to Russian utopian literature and thought. But his list of one hundred turns up a truly unexpected debt to literature. In fact, a full sixty of the works on the list were turned into films from literary fiction, serial novels, or narrative newspaper features.

The genre of Japanese writing in vogue when Kurosawa was most steeped in reading and viewing in the 1920s was "I-fiction" (shishōsetsu, 私小説). I-fiction is writing often in first-person voice but sometimes in the third person. I-fiction contains elements that purport to present a veiled version of the author's life, though in practice details of description, interior monologue, and consciousness may be camouflaged or embellished and an independent narrative voice might interpret the character through free indirect style. Whether or not I-fiction is strictly true, it is always a virtuoso display where style; observation of self, other, and world with different degrees of tone and proximity; and granular details of consciousness are prized over structure and narrative development. Small details of I-fiction—even, or perhaps especially, fabulated ones—heighten the impression of authenticity as well as a proximity to a highly expressive narrating voice. The seemingly radical first-person narratives of *Rashomon*, for example, would not seem new to anyone who was trained by modernist literature to read fragmented or competing versions of the same event.

In fact, Kurosawa references the willfully constructive dimension of I-fiction when he defines what a film is in this volume. It is an animate object that assembles many details and parts from different literal species of sources, but in the end when it is assembled can only be itself. The example refers to a story by Shiga Naoya, one of the founders of I-fiction:

> Here's an interesting story for you. Shiga Naoya has a short story called "Bear," and there is a passage where the narrator's son appears. That part is an essay the son writes about a dog called Bear. The son writes, "My dog looks like a bear, but this part looks like a *tanuki,* and this part looks like a *kitsune,*" and he keeps saying how many things his dog looks like, on and on. And then at the very end he says, "Well, actually he's a dog, so he looks most of all like a dog" (laughs). And that's also how I think about film. Sometimes in films there are elements like literature, like theater, parts that are like painting, musical elements, there are various kinds of elements. But, well, actually it's a movie.[17]

This anecdote is a way of illustrating how film is made of multiple materials, some adapted from others (like dogs called Bear), but when put together it has an aesthetic status, and a life of its own, that transcends them all.

Put in context, film was able to adapt materials from other modes of first-person expression. The mutually reinforcing first-person expressions found in fiction and silent film of the 1920s give a vast repertoire for showing the vivid interior life of a character within a larger narrated frame. A large cluster of films on the list came from a silent cinema toolbox Kurosawa would screen every time he began making a film. These films were laden with innovative methods for close-ups, micro movements of things in motion, and constructivist montage such as we see in later films like *Rashomon*.

A good example of such a film is Jean Epstein's *The Fall of the House of Usher* (no. 5). *Usher* is connected to Kurosawa not only through the attachment to Poe—one of Kurosawa's scripted but unmade films was based on Poe's short story "The Masque of the Red Death"—but also through the use of experimental technique in the service of characterization. The story is adapted from Poe's gothic story about a traveler who visits a friend who resides in a decrepit mansion and tries to cheer him up by playing the guitar. The mood darkens as it becomes clear his friend has imprisoned his own sister and gets even bleaker when the friend confesses that he thinks the house is alive. In the performance, the movements of the actor and vibrations of the guitar playing precede the shots of ocean and trees and are depicted in a closer shot, so the performance seems to be the sound source whose actions cause the movement of the sea outside the house, as the sequence bounces from guitar to sea to trees, a symbiotic relation of movement that connects three separate spaces through a synesthesia, converting music into motivation, just as in Kurosawa's example.

The expressive powers of close-up and micro movement were conveyed most clearly in writing by the director Jean Epstein, who along with Louis Delluc was one of the main theorists of the expressive possibilities of silent film and the basis of early French discourses on cinephilia. The term Epstein advocated, after Delluc put the word on the critical map, was *photogénie*—the quality of being filmic that emerges when the camera changes reality into something radically new. Kurosawa's cinephilia took these techniques and transposed them into postwar cinema.

The radically new place Kurosawa takes micro movements and the expressiveness of sound is the male body, dramatized most clearly in *Rashomon*. Black-and-white dappled textures on natural surfaces transfer onto the body of Mifune Toshirō while he lies, as Moeko Fujii notes, "supine" under a tree, in a pose that invites new modes of appreciation.[18] Kurosawa's use of the telephoto lens collapses multiple planes into a single surface visible in fine detail bringing together the background of

Playing the guitar conjures an entire landscape in *The Fall of the House of Usher*, as hands transform guitar sounds into literal wind and, in turn, ocean waves sound like the wind.

a tree and Mifune's face and torso in medium close-up. This sequence in *Rashomon* is the crystallization of *photogénie* and the techniques of subjective narrative that Kurosawa absorbed in the 1920s.

Mifune's character, a self-described thief and rapist, dozes while at times he watches an elegant lady being led by a nobleman on a horse through the forest. Over two minutes, a drama plays out whose unfolding in real time takes far less than the two minutes of the sequence itself. Rather than overlap or contradict, the sequence treats time as a three-dimensional volumetric space that can be represented from numerous possible angles—and as with the interiority of a character, experiential time overrides real time. As we watch the character, a series of shots from his point of view track the lady coming closer and then receding away, with a repetition and intermittent celestina that signals we are seeing the thief/rapist's story through his subjective telling of it. The close-up on Mifune allows us to see his every movement—the looks that cross his face as he dreams or watches or plots; his fingers scratching himself or fanning away a fly; the left nipple and distinct beads of sweat that glisten as his chest breathes up and down.

This was one of the sequences that made Mifune the "face" of Japanese cinema when *Rashomon* broke through. His photogenic quality displaced the earlier Japanese male protagonist, Hayakawa Sessue, the example around whom Epstein and Delluc developed their own ideas. Hayakawa had been the example of the initial articulation of *photogénie*: "pure *photogénie*, cadenced movement."[19] Most reviews of the time cast Mifune's acting as primitive or animal-like, or stressed the "indeterminacy" of guilt or innocence. When we look again through the lens of I-fiction and the debates on *photogénie* that underpinned film aesthetics of the 1920s, we get a different view.

While Mifune's character may be cruel and predatory, the expression casts him as all too human, and the very embodiment of the humanist depiction of a vivid and aleatory interior life.[20] Kurosawa notes Mifune's capacity to convey a density of information that far outstripped other actors' abilities to express a role: "the ordinary Japanese actor might need ten feet of film to create an impression; Mifune needed only three feet. The speed of his movements was such that he said in a single action what took ordinary actors three separate movements to express."[21] The notion of the actor as a volumetric space in motion found a heightened expression in Mifune.

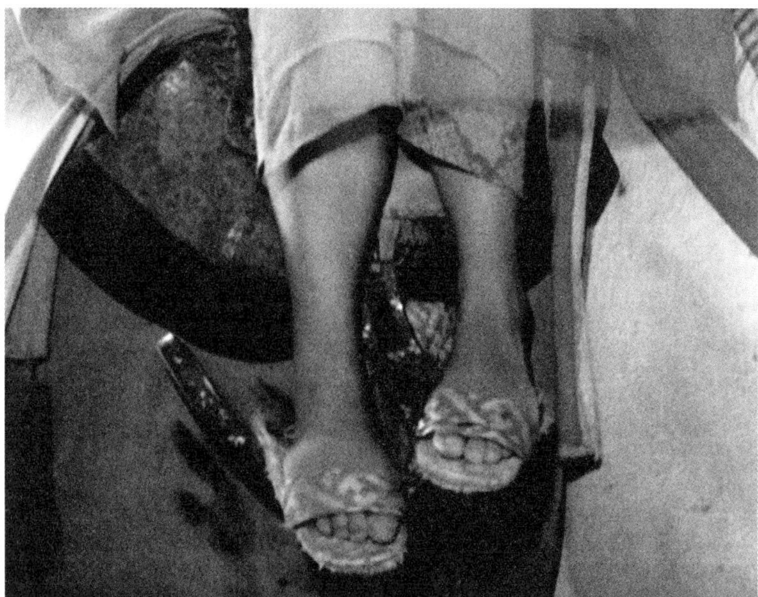

Mifune's head and torso are captured in granular detail, as is the tree. A later shot in the same sequence dramatizes the shot of the lady's feet with a celestina that connects the two shots and follows on Mifune's gaze.

In 1920s Japan, new modes of self-expression fanned out from the burgeoning magazine industry, and the first-person voice began to go beyond interviews and first-person fiction. The result is a highly expressive "self" of each person distributed across media in an increasingly familiar and mass-mediated set of genres—primarily, those that emphasized the recorded voice of an illusory faithfulness to a fictional "voice." This voice bridged from fiction to nonfiction, and from oral to written formats. Less hierarchical than interviews, the conversations that came into their own as a genre are called *taidan*. These are recorded conversations between two people that range freely and often wildly across topics. Although the conversations were later edited, the genre allows people from various cultural scenes to be matchmade in order to produce interesting conversations. These conversations might joke or go off topic in ways infrequently seen in scripted interviews, similar to the telltale detail in a fiction piece.

For example, in the 1987 *taidan* (conversation) with Inoue Hisashi, the writer asks Kurosawa about the famous last scene of *Seven Samurai*, in which a mud-ridden plain and driving rain present massive difficulties for all the samurai and bandits. During the shoot, Kurosawa reveals, the crew all had to wear boots day after day, and his feet were so perpetually soaked in rain and mud that all his toenails died and fell off. The bravado and endurance of this effort throws shade on Hollywood Westerns, with which *Seven Samurai* is often compared. Due to the constant California sun, Kurosawa says, Hollywood directors have it easy. Because they don't have to bother with weather and are not required to have the same ingenuity and work ethic as the Japanese cast and crew—or even the horses, actually—who slog through the labor of a film set day after day in the mud, sacrifice their toenails, and still pull off one of the greatest battle scenes in film history.

Zadankai are the same as *taidan* but involve more than two people; this term referring to a conversation with multiple people was actually coined by the magazine *Bungei shunjū*, where the conversations in this volume were first published. Because of the improvised dynamic that allows for digression, *taidan* and *zadankai* are important venues for distributing a director's "voice," their language, and opinions. Conversations show how they embed themselves in cultural conversations with long-term friends and their own points of reference. *Taidan* and *zadankai* give especially valuable insights into the creative work of directors like Kurosawa who do not regularly publish essays and who tend to avoid critical language, stressing entertainment value and back-stories at the expense of theory. And each interview offers a differently distributed self—not only the films that resonated with Kurosawa, but a different sense of how Kurosawa sees his work within world cinema alongside these films.

The Structure and the List

Opening the third part of this book, "Remembering Kurosawa," is a record of Kurosawa's cinephilia as seen in a list of one hundred of his favorite films. These are films he might screen in a hypothetical theater, preserved as an archive of styles and models for filmmakers to come. We might imagine his theater as a combination of Japan's National Film Archive, which holds about forty thousand Japanese films, and the archive of films preserved by Martin Scorsese's Film Foundation, mentioned in "Kurosawa's One Hundred Films," the essay that immediately precedes the list.

The list of one hundred was compiled by Kurosawa's daughter, Kazuko, from conversations and interviews she absorbed beginning in childhood. She recounts this history in one of two essays that close this collection. Her first memory has her as a three-year-old saying good night to the adults as they pass her around, from lap to lap, while they dine and drink and tell stories. She recalls: "I also remember bringing beer around to everyone at the dinners. At the beginning I could only hold two at a time, but my child's mind aspired to hold four, and then it became six, counting higher as I grew older." After more than a decade of caretaking for her mother, Kazuko would join the production staff during the making of *Dreams* (1990), working for the legendary costumer Wada Emi. As an adult, she worked as her father's sounding board and caretaker while serving as the go-to person for damage control after his on-set explosions.

It is Kazuko who established the framework of dreams for this collection. The volume of interviews and conversations was published one year after Kurosawa's death, with two essays and the dream-related title contributed by Kazuko. The list of films she assembled gives an integrity to the story of her father's life even though the interviews have a gap of fifteen years in the middle. As Kazuko writes in her essay "Dreaming It Forward," she spent many years talking about dreams with her father over dinner, and he appeared in her dreams after his death. In Kurosawa world, the conceit of the dream is that the past can erupt at any given moment into the living present, and you have a relation to it because it is already living.

The fantasy of the everlasting conversation—connecting past and present, living and dead, sleeping and waking—might make us wonder what it means to present the arc of a chronology without noting all the loss that surely inhabits it. Only 20 percent of films from the early Hollywood studio era remain, and surely viewing experiences that should be viewable are lost. And only 2 percent of Japanese films from the prewar era remain, owing to the bombing and conflagrations of war, as well as postwar neglect by studios that failed to preserve their films. Perhaps these works might be found lying in Russian archives or excavated from someone's garage and put on eBay, as has happened to other Japanese films and recordings long assumed to be lost to the fortunes of time and war. But the message of this book is that the archive is dependent on memory where history fails, and that observers of a life often preserve memories its participants cannot see or put into words. Kazuko's arrangement and narration are as much an ethnographic endeavor as they are an homage. The cultural weight of dreams can be seen in classical works of Japanese literature and theater, but here it is filtered through a modern sensibility constructed in the 1920s and made legible through the list.

The films on the list are arranged in chronological order. The earliest experiments of film beginning in 1895 do not have a place in the list. Nor will we find the canonical epic melodramas of *The Birth of a Nation* or *The Cheat* (both 1915). Instead, listed first is a melodrama from 1919, emerging from the moment where film begins to aspire to the status of art, and a culture of cinephilia emerges as cinema becomes an object of discourse in the press and among critics, all the while the state keeps an eye on its potential powers.[22]

The D. W. Griffith melodrama *Broken Blossoms* (1919) features a young girl (Lillian Gish), abused by her boxer father and befriended by a "Chinese" man, Richard Barthelmess, who plays his meekly adoring role in yellowface costume, motivated by a humanist spiritualism and a circumspect desire to protect Gish's character while remaining constantly by her side. This kindly, protective man from the "East" confronts the brutal patriarch, but ends up killing himself. *Broken Blossoms* is known for the terrifying closet scene—reprised in the "Here's Johnny" scene of *The Shining*—where the viewer viscerally feels the claustrophobia of Gish's character being attacked by her hatchet-wielding father as she hides in a closet. If Kurosawa overlooked the trees of Orientalist plot in order to immerse in the forest of Griffith's artistic innovation, the effect of audiences experiencing viscerally the vivid interior life of a character on screen in real time seemed to have stuck. Kurosawa returns multiple times in this volume to his point about an ideal audience experiencing an adjacent experience of a character's emotional life.[23]

The focus on the child in the first film adds an unexpected contrast to the theme of adult suffering and agency in Kurosawa's critically acclaimed films. We see a string of works featuring children: the avant-garde child from *Composition Class* (no. 17) or *Pather Panchali* (no. 37) or *The 400 Blows* (no. 43) and *Stowaway in the Sky* (no. 48). Each of these child characters is able, unlike adults, to tune into and explore possibilities of joy and the connection to history and cosmologies. This link is especially true in Kurosawa's late films such as *Dreams* and *Rhapsody in August* in which children are connectors between local and cosmological life. The child-centered films contrast to the adults we see from *The Cabinet of Dr. Caligari* (no. 2) and *Dr. Mabuse the Gambler* (no. 3) to *Purple Noon* (no. 49) and *In the Heat of the Night* (no. 59) who struggle with corruption, betrayal, and duplicity.

Another subset of the list, musicals, appears beginning in the early days of sound. In Japan, sound did not erupt into the process of filmmaking with a single film like *The Jazz Singer*; it happened over time and through many debates about the transformation of cinema from a performance art into a process of mechanical reproduction. As Paul Anderer notes, "Amazingly, a dwindling number of silents were still being produced in Japan the year Kurosawa joined the industry, in 1936. Only come 1937, the year of the Marco Polo Bridge incident, and the beginning of the total war between Japan and China, would the last Japanese silent film be made, after which the voice of the *benshi* would be irrevocably silenced."[24] Although made in color, the motion and dynamism that recall the micro movements and gradations of silent film contain images so mesmerizing that Kurosawa dropped them almost literally into his own work, as discussed in this volume. We see this with the famous underwater plants in Tarkovsky's *Solaris* (no. 66). In *Solaris,* the plants bridge the journey back to earth for the main character, the astronaut Chris;

in *Dreams,* strikingly similar undulant plants furnish a bridge between worlds and generations, life and death in a rural village. After this last scene, the credits roll over a close-up over the same plants that strongly recalls this scene in *Solaris,* so key to transitioning between worlds, both visually and metaphysically. This list will skip wartime and propaganda cinema, but later, Kurosawa's participation in Cold War film festivals and state-sponsored culture extended avant-garde legacies from Russia and enabled new contacts with filmmakers from France, India, Iran, and Taiwan that were unthinkable to most American filmmakers. Added to this was a long relation to Hollywood films from the days of silent Westerns to the age of special effects.

Three interviews and two roundtable conversations that feature Kurosawa follow the list and give backstories to many of the entries. The interviews were conducted by an editor of the magazine *Bungei shunjū* (Literary arts of the season). *Bungei shunjū* is a publishing house with a major monthly founded in 1923 that publishes many prize-winning literary works and sponsors the Akutagawa Prize, arguably the most significant prize in Japanese literary culture; apart from literature, it publishes essays and interviews with established cultural figures from film and other arts, and is a general barometer for national prestige culture.

The first interview appeared in *Bungei shunjū* in 1970, shortly after Kurosawa's disastrous foray into the Hollywood coproduction of *Tora! Tora! Tora!,* a film about Pearl Harbor. Film historian Markus Nornes notes that the filmmakers had high hopes of "reconciling the relationship of the United States and Japan, two short decades after the occupying forces executed the defendants of the Tokyo Trial."[25] But the production foundered when Kurosawa was fired by the film's producer Twentieth Century–Fox.

The interview appeared several months before the release of the independently produced *Dodes'ka-den,* an experiment on a financial as well as an artistic front. Kurosawa mortgaged his house to finance its production, and *Dodes'ka-den* was also his first fully color film. This interview gives insight into the toll the changing landscape of studio production took on established filmmakers. Kurosawa expresses frustration not just that budgets were cut in response to filmgoers' shift to watching television, but also that financing was extended to directors Kurosawa considered to be "salarymen" who were lacking in creative vision as well as creative control. As Alex Zahlten writes, "Indeed, even today it

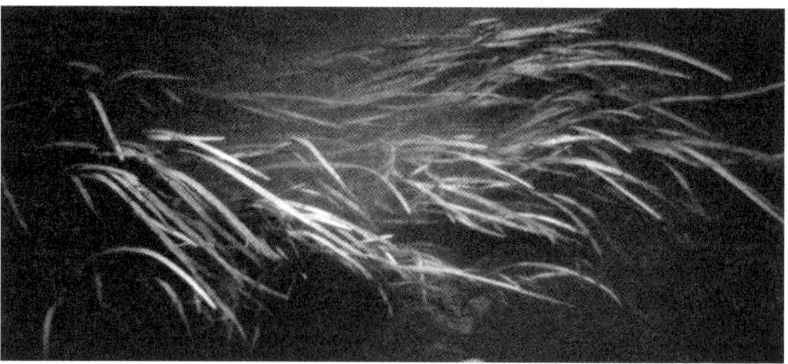

On the left, the camera pulls in on undulant plants in Tarkovsky's *Solaris.*

The protagonist lays flowers at a memorial to a village elder in the last episode of Kurosawa's *Dreams,* a sequence that ends with a close-up of undulant plants that transposes the *Solaris* image into a celebration of death as a part of a well-lived life.

is official policy in many companies to recruit employees from sections unrelated to film to be producers, or to favor new recruits with no formal film education, to ensure a 'business perspective' rather than an 'art perspective.' "[26]

Kurosawa further laments the impact of such business decisions on cinephilia. The bland nature of movies such "salarymen" made in exchange for more steady financing fails to inspire a new generation of young cineastes. He idealizes the independent energies of New American Cinema directors such as John Cassavetes and producers such as

Joseph E. Levine, who were able to see beyond valuing films only for their commercial potential and find ways to finance productions that valued the labor and creativity of cast and crew. A surprising number of independently produced New Wave pictures appear in the early 1960s, as does an undertow of noir and suspense films.[27] Though Kurosawa tried to go in the direction of independent financing in what he felt to be the soul-crushing studio system, *Dodes'ka-den* failed at the box office, decimating his personal finances. The compound stresses of the film's critical and financial failure probably provoked Kurosawa to attempt suicide in 1971.

The second interview in the book takes place in 1987, picking up after fifteen years. The Japanese translation of the John Ford biography *Pappy* is published and offers an occasion to delve into Kurosawa's admiration for John Ford Westerns and his knowledge of the Hollywood studio system, as well as the real-life encounters he had with Ford. The interview conveys Kurosawa's granular knowledge of the Ford stable of actors, for example, Native American rodeo star Ben Johnson and his "poetic" riding style. Also on display is the affinity Kurosawa feels with Ford as a spoke in the wheel of the studio machine, and head of an idealized family of actors. Kurosawa's commentary on Ford's bullying is both dumbstruck and committed to insisting that there is a directorial logic behind it.

On one hand, Kurosawa's justification of Ford's violence is shocking. What also stands out as Kurosawa recounts his encounters with Ford is the sheer poignance of a world-historical director such as Kurosawa reading the latest translations to further his understanding of an elder director he respects. All the while one suspects that while John Ford may have summoned Kurosawa to a fancy hotel in Tokyo, commanded a bottle of whiskey from the "boy," and forced Kurosawa to drink while his teetotaling self looked on, John Ford never read a book about Akira Kurosawa. This asymmetry of knowledge where American studio directors are all output and no input makes it all the more important to listen to Kurosawa's "voice."

The 1985 success of *Ran* followed by the 1990 success of *Dreams* brought Kurosawa back on line in the international arena thanks to the financing leveraged by George Lucas and Steven Spielberg that had begun with *Kagemusha* (1980). A roundtable with writer Inoue Hisashi in 1990, just after *Dreams* came out, looks retrospectively at Kurosawa's place on the world stage. Inoue was a highly regarded playwright and novelist, extremely funny with acutely political readings of Japanese history. He wrote major works about the effects of the atomic bomb and life during the U.S. Occupation, including *The Face of Jizō,* about a young librarian in Hiroshima whose father was killed by the atomic bomb dropped on Hiroshima on August 6, 1945. Mourning him gets in her way of starting a romance, until he visits her in a dream and encourages the courtship.

The conversation with Inoue is useful in two ways. He witnesses Kurosawa's role in the global scene. And, perhaps more importantly, his glee at reversing the master–servant relation of the Occupation is palpable. While being slightly mortified at his own national pride, Inoue delights in seeing Kurosawa given an Academy Honorary Award in Hollywood by George Lucas and Steven Spielberg. For him and many of his generation, this would have represented a belated and probably triumphant reversal of positions. At the same time he celebrates Kurosawa's world-historical position, his own work about a daughter who receives her father's blessing after his death resonates strongly with this volume.

As a writer of both theater and fiction, Inoue is keenly aware of the tools a writer can borrow from, and he situates Kurosawa for us in these frames. Inoue's placing of *Dreams* in the context of I-fiction and Noh theater expands our understanding of the range of materials Kurosawa employed. Noh is a stately and abstract genre of premodern theater that has a fixed stage design and a fixed set of roles. It formerly enjoyed royal patronage and was the performing art attended by samurai. A typical play involves a *shite,* the lead character of the play, whose story is drawn out by the *waki,* or supporting character. In the 1990 *taidan,* Inoue likens one episode of *Dreams* to *mugen* Noh, a phantasmal subset of Noh where the entire play is a dream or illusion seen by the *waki.* In episode 4, the "I" character, acting as the *waki,* draws out the story of a ghostly soldier who refuses to go to the land of the dead. The components of the landscape are modern, set right after the Pacific War—a tunnel, some trees and houses—but the layout resembles the major landmarks of a Noh stage.

The overall story arc of *Dreams* follows I-fiction by having the main "I" character in the film age chronologically over the course of the film, though taking on different forms. He ages from boy to man and is always an observer to something otherworldly. Inoue develops the association with first-person fiction by noting the epigraph to each episode of *Dreams*: a simple black screen on which is written "This is what I saw in my dream" (kon'na yume o mita, こんな夢を見た). As almost every Japanese reader would know, this is the opening line of each episode of novelist Natsume Sōseki's 1908 series of fantastical short stories *Ten Nights of Dreams* (Yume jū'ya, 夢十夜). Each episode has a different time period and different setting. They are united by the fact that, like *Dreams,* each episode involves the main character's encounter with a personage later revealed to be a phantom. An intensely emotional connection with a memory structures the dream. The conversation with Inoue also probes politics in a discussion of Kurosawa's scathing depiction of a nuclear meltdown in one episode of *Dreams.* It gives the backstory to the seventh episode in *Dreams,* which depicts a mass of nuclear refugees in the wake of a garish and terrifying power-plant meltdown.

This book's original Japanese title was *Dreams Are Forms of Genius* (Yume wa tensai de aru, 夢は天才である). It remediates the title of a 1906 novella called *Clouds Are Forms of Genius* (Kumo wa tensai de aru, 雲は天才である). Here the term "genius" is different from the way the term is often applied to Kurosawa himself—someone with exceptional mental powers who is bound to rise above the system. But it actually comes from the phrase "tensai education" (tensai kyōiku, 天才教育), a pedagogical style used by Kurosawa's childhood art teacher that encouraged free expression of a child's own gifts. The character "天," *ten,* refers to a cosmology, closely allied to the nature resident in all things, the higher order that would link to the expression of the child's gifts; it also forms part of words for the Milky Way, astronomy and ceiling lights. It links the force of creativity to a higher order not of achievement or hierarchy, like awards given at school or film industry events, but of anarchist-tinged freedom and shared possession of life's powers and resources.

The writer of *Clouds Are Forms of Genius* was Ishikawa Takuboku (1886–1912), a poet, fiction writer, and socialist-leaning sometime teacher who died at the early age of twenty-six. The story is written in the style of I-fiction, exploiting its free-flowing, spontaneous, and emotionally raw prose, from the point of view of an underpaid substitute teacher, modeled on Takuboku, in a struggling rural town. This teacher is proudest of the time he spends with students after hours, apart from classes, when he can teach as he likes. He passionately wants to provide the spark for "youthful fireworks filled with red-blooded oil." This figural language, along with other figures of arrows, bombs, tinderboxes, and Jacobins, suggests potentially volatile revolution as well as the

Kurosawa with Nakano Toshihiko and Baishō Mitsuko on the set of the first episode of *Dreams,* "The Foxes' Wedding." Courtesy of Kurosawa Production Co., Ltd.

transformation of life's potential into beauty and surprise with the mind and body as its fuel.[28] The narrator clashes with the principal who rules over the school by insisting that "a true educator must follow the regulations to the letter and has to make sure the lessons follow the prescribed form in an ideal way with zero deviation." His mandate of top–down principles is drawn from the state-mandated Imperial Rescript on Education and stipulates that education should build discipline and strong citizens with these talents and bodies, rather than fostering the students' inner lives or connections to each other and the cosmos.

Takuboku's story drew not only on his own experience as a teacher, but also on an emerging idiom for leftist cultures of action and political passion that connected Japan to theories of social justice and mutual aid from elsewhere in the world, especially Russia, and would infuse attempts to join art and politics for generations to come. The narrator's connection with his students flowers from a school song he composes, which the children spontaneously sing. But hearing the song, the principal's face is "like a raging forest fire." The principal and his minions crack down on the song and chase away the children. The song's message is revived when a disheveled traveler bearing a cryptic letter of introduction from a friend of the teacher drifts into the school. The stranger shares a long backstory about a mutual friend that supports the values the narrator and children share, and links to the "genius" of their mutual friend. The title of Kurosawa's original book takes Takuboku's idiom of "cloud" and transposes it into "dream"—a system of language, events, and affections that link the natural, political, and human worlds, as well as a call for nontraditional presences of creative life within large institutions such as the studio system.

The update of Takuboku's image of free creativity from cloud to dream suggests we should take note of the philosophies of education found in the Russian source texts, as well as the communally oriented nature of dreams in Kurosawa's work. Takuboku was well read in Tolstoyan thought based on translations in the *Commoners' Newspaper*, as well as other more mainstream venues; the most famous translations, including "Bethink Yourselves!" (1904), delinked Russian thought about transnational popular democracy from the idea of a state. Takuboku's critique in the story of the suffocating powers of educational institutions and turn to aesthetics as a medium for communication and freedom contains strong echoes of this era's use of Tolstoy. This traveler, metaphorized as a cloud, and the source of inspiration, could have arrived from many of the Russian literary texts that Kurosawa first read as a youth, bringing with him Tolstoy's free education, Fadeyev's multiethnic partisanship and homoerotic joy, and a general view of art as a creative power that can bring a different shared world into being through representation.[29]

The next conversation comes from the following year, 1991. A Kurosawa retrospective broadcast on television, his former archenemy, affords a chance for a roundtable on *Seven Samurai* with Inoue, joined by director Yamada Yōji. Yamada models a different career trajectory for a successful director of the same generation. Yamada is the director of the Tora-san series, the longest-running series not only in Japanese cinema but in the entire world. Tora-san is a hapless but large-hearted bachelor who returns to his neighborhood after twenty years of wandering, a cycle of restlessness and return that is reprised with each film. When he first comes back home, there is a strong suggestion he has been involved with the yakuza or is otherwise not quite socialized, but he gets taken back into the neighborhood anyway, after some social awkwardness. In the first episode, Tora-san arrives back home and wants to show off his success to his old friends and neighbors, a performance that ends up trying to grift them as he reintroduces himself—just as his long-separated, much more responsible sister walks into the scene. In a later episode, Tora-san's sister becomes engaged. He is on his best behavior at the family celebration, but accidentally gets so drunk that his wild toasts send the meal into chaos and the marriage almost falls off the rails. In episodes of the series that follow, Tora-san gets restless, goes on the road, falls in love, has his heart broken, and returns home. The franchise allowed Yamada to make his peace with the studio system so effectively that Tora-san kept the Shōchiku studio alive even as the whole system unraveled. That series's success subsidized Yamada's more independent films, such as *A Distant Cry from Spring* (no. 79).

The comedic frame of Tora-san draws on a long history of performance that draws details out of daily life to turn the mundane into an epic. This style is characteristic of *rakugo,* a kind of bare-bones vaudeville in which a single storyteller will hold an audience rapt through a long absurd story with lots of comic digressions. *Sun in the Last Days of the Shogunate* (no. 40) contains a well-known *rakugo* set piece called "Saheiji Overstays," about a young man who can't pay his bill in the pleasure quarters and is given jobs to do to work off his debt. He ends up making

In this scene from *Our Lovable Tramp,* the first in the Tora-san series, Tora-san (Atsumi Kiyoshi) returns to his neighborhood and is trying to hawk trinkets to friends and relatives when his sister returns.

himself so useful to the house that they finally pay him to leave. The *rakugo* sensibility is designed to clue the audience into much more about the machinations of the story than a character so that they can enjoy anticipating story elements that might spin delightfully out of control.

That same sensibility is found in the scene of *The Hidden Fortress* in which Mifune Toshirō's character argues with a checkpoint guard. His real crime is smuggling a princess past the checkpoint, but he argues about a piece of gold with the guard, who wants to keep it after inspecting it; the argument gives the princess a chance to cross the checkpoint and steal away.

This sensibility of long, winding stories is also found in perhaps the most underknown part of Kurosawa's list, the Japanese comedies. It was only after Itami Jūzō, the son of the director of number 14 on the list, Itami Mansaku's comedy *Capricious Young Man,* introduced his 1985 comedy *Tampopo* to the art film circuit that filmgoers recognized Japanese films could be comedies as well as brimming with tragedy and gravitas found in films on the international art circuit. An exceptionally fine comedy is Yamanaka Sadao's *Tange Sazen—The Million-Ryō Pot* (no. 13). The story is partly inspired by René Clair's *Le million,* about a winning lottery ticket that goes astray. Yamanaka's version features a hideous "old pot with monkey drawings" that a lord is given, which he regifts to his brother in the capital. It turns out that the pot is decorated with a map that reveals the location of a huge sum of money buried by his own lord. The film is a long, picaresque attempt through many blunders to trick the younger brother into giving the pot back without alerting anyone else to its value.

Mifune distracts the checkpoint guard in *The Hidden Fortress* with a stick in which he "finds" a piece of gold.

The comedies are just one context for Kurosawa's works that the list of a hundred films brings to our attention. When Kurosawa weighs in on what is likely to create a new generation of cinephiles, he mentions two things: a vibrant exhibition culture and a financing structure that allows filmmakers to have creative control outside of a "salaryman" structure. There is no way he would know that the next Japanese cineaste to win the Caméra d'Or at Cannes would be female and would have her own issues with on-set explosions, or that coproduction would become a norm, when it was a completely outlier thing to do when he made *Dersu Uzala* and *Dreams.*[30] The hundred-year span of the films Kurosawa would show in his imaginary movie theater invites us to see his films anew, in dialogue with the images, song, recording technology, jokes, and stories of a century of film.

I
Kurosawa Speaks

To Spark a New Golden Age (1970)

In this essay, Kurosawa casts a look back at the circumstances of shooting *Seven Samurai,* on the occasion of its broadcast on television as part of a Kurosawa retrospective. At the same time, he turns a cinephile's eye to films from New American Cinema and the French Nouvelle Vague that transformed the creative world of filmmaking, and he worries about how to create a cinephile culture in Japan while looking for new models for film financing.

The Akira Kurosawa series that's now running on television brought up all kinds of emotions for me; most of all, I recognize how time has passed. My greatest hope for the series is that young people will be able to see my works. To see films they hardly have a chance to watch, like *No Regrets for Our Youth* and *One Wonderful Sunday. No Regrets for Our Youth* is from 1946, and—you understand—people born that year would now be twenty-three.

In the Pouring Rain

I'm going to bet that *Seven Samurai* had the most viewers in the series this time around too. In the 1950s, it didn't take a special effort to assemble the people and the materials for a film like that. But think about actors today. I bet they couldn't keep up with the kind of hard physical working conditions we worked under.

We shot the very last scene, where the bandits attack the village, in about a week, in the pouring rain, in the dead of winter. I think I was soaking wet from morning to night.

At that time, there were rice fields in front of the Tōhō studio in Kinuta, where there's an apartment complex now. A huge snowstorm had just dumped a lot of snow, and it was incredibly muddy. We were ready to shoot a particular scene, but the fields had gotten all wet and on top of that it was cold. You would never know by looking at it on the screen, but it was sleeting off and on. In the middle of all of that, Mifune-chan was for all intents and purposes pretty much naked. When the actors had breaks, they would jump into the bath to warm themselves up. I remember wearing a raincoat and being all wet. It was a miracle I didn't catch my death of cold.

The mud in that particular area of Kinuta is a real challenge. Once you put on rubber boots that come all the way up to your belly, and wade in the mud up to your thighs, you can't even move. In a battle scene, I'd be standing there as the horses raced up to me. I'd have to gauge their speed and then quickly yell "cut" and get out before they flattened me. The lighting people and props people would come running, and it would take the whole bunch of them to yank me out of my boots. Mud is really something, I tell you. It really got in everywhere. All my toenails ended up turning black and falling off.

But strangely it didn't really hurt. We were really behind schedule, which got us into trouble with the studio. But if we had shot the very last scene any sooner, chances are the studio would have said we had enough footage and would have called it quits. So I decided not to shoot the last scene till the very end, that last battle scene. But they ordered me to edit and then show them the footage that we had already shot. The studio people were really steamed. So I left out the battle scene, edited it, and showed it to them. Mifune-chan yells, "They're here! They're here," and the bandits are barreling toward him. And right there—it ended. When I told them I hadn't shot a single frame to follow that, they backed off, and told me to shoot as much as I wanted to finish it.

There's a moment in the last scene where Shimura Takashi weeps, and when we were just about to shoot it, it started snowing again. That caused a huge mess, but we managed to work it out, and finally we wrapped it up in a week. It took about a year and a half from the time we started. Thinking back on it, it was something of a miracle that we were able to shoot that kind of a production in that amount of time.

It's hard to tell if should chalk it up to being broke or if we were just clueless back in those days. But there was a hill nearby, and we decided to construct a village at the foot of it. We could have just rented out the whole thing. We only used a part of it, and other parts were planted with wheat and some vegetables, and we had the feeling we couldn't let it go

Kurosawa and the ensemble of *Seven Samurai* on the muddy set. Courtesy of Kurosawa Production Co., Ltd.

wild. The mentality of life during wartime was probably still affecting us: the feeling that you don't do damage to very valuable agricultural crops.

So, what happened was that to finish this scene we had to move from Nagaoka to Gotemba, about twenty-six miles away. At the time, the traffic situation was just horrible. It would take us a whole day to move in a big convoy. These days, it's almost impossible to shoot a *jidai-geki* on location. Wherever you go, the roads are asphalt, or when you go to shoot an old temple you find a TV antenna sticking out. Even way out in the middle of nowhere, there is always some modern-looking building getting in the way. Japan is running out of room.

There's only a little bit of room left at the foot of Mount Fuji where the horses can run freely. Something happened between the time we made *Throne of Blood* in 1957 and *The Hidden Fortress* in 1958.

The most dramatic change is that there are no more horses that can run like that. You have to train the horses used in battle scenes as an ensemble. With horses these days, when you give them the signal to "go!" they all start charging in their own directions. Even if *that* doesn't happen, sometimes they start fighting and kicking each other. In the old days, they used horses that had been trained in groups by the army, and for a while even in the postwar era these horses were around; people used them as workhorses on farms. These days, people use mechanical tractors because they are cheaper than keeping horses. In the old days, it was easy to get together six hundred horses, and now we have a hard time getting our hands on ten.

And that's why there's almost none of the land left where you could make so-called action dramas. The horses and the land are gone, and it's such a small country, Japan.

The New York School and the Nouvelle Vague

When television got to be popular, it hit American movies, especially Hollywood, pretty hard. It took some time for the Japanese film industry to get to the same point. The time lag means that we didn't have to follow exactly in the same tracks.

As American cinema started to slump, I would try to urge the studio heads in Japan that they had to rethink everything or they were headed for trouble as well. They didn't budge, so today, the movies are falling into the same kind of mess as happened in Hollywood, and it's really unclear how they're going to pull themselves out of it. They're headed for the bottom.

Here and there they came up with some measures to stave off part of the damage. But it was the same problem the Japanese army had on the Chinese continent—which is that each unit forged ahead on its own, in all different directions, and they just got swallowed up by the landscape. They just lost track of who was in charge, and how to work toward a common goal; they just lost track of everything.

That sort of messiness is also terrible for a production. So now the first priority is to bring together all these loose ends to bring some consistency to the process. The television and film industry people should get together and figure out their collective issues. They should work with the actors. They should figure out how to allocate the crew and actors, and how to move forward. That's the most important thing to figure out, in my view. There is only a small pool of actors, and the same goes for directors and art directors—the pool of people in the whole industry is quite small. People just keep getting in each other's way and dragging each other down because they get panicked about the shortage of staff. Television and film should not be at each other's throats. Theater and film managed to work things out after all.

American film really hit the skids, and now it's on the way back up. So we should be paying attention to what they did to get things back up and running again.

To put it bluntly, they were able to bounce back because they gave the artists a lot of room to move creatively, make their own decisions. They let the directors do what directors do and gave them free rein. The studio didn't force things to go in a particular direction, and in exchange for being hands-off they agreed that their investment in the film would be more modest. They left the creative control to the filmmakers, and these filmmakers turned out to make incredibly original films. This approach made it possible for things like the New York School to emerge from what seemed to be out of nowhere. The scale was small, but independent productions like *The Graduate* and *The Fixer* came out, and they raised the bar for American film in a significant way.

The kinds of ambitious Hollywood pictures that attract huge audiences in places like Japan don't have the same draw in their home country of the United States. But when we think about worldwide box office returns, or what I guess we could call returns from developed countries, the earnings tend to be good, and a lot of the overall revenue comes from that kind of film, as they become mini blockbusters.

The situation with the Japanese studios now is that filmmakers' autonomy has been almost completely taken away. From screenwriters to directors, they're all kept on a tight leash by the studio and basically treated like salarymen.

Those who can't stand being turned into salarymen will split off from the studio, and when they leave they also leave behind their financing, so they won't be able to make the kind of pictures they want to make.

The "star production" model was a workaround that actors developed, and it made some headway in creating conditions for film production outside of the studio system.[1] There are many examples of that model. But such a system has to build in support for the next generation of young new filmmakers. And that's connected to support for creative control in the filmmaking process. So it's crucial to value the creativity of these directors, people who are in the best position to make the decisions that affect their own filmmaking.

When they show my pictures at places like the Cinémathèque in France, lots of young people show up. After the screenings they surround me and ask me lots of questions. When I see that kind of excitement for cinephile culture it makes me think a lot of good filmmakers will come out of that scene. In fact, it already produced the Nouvelle Vague of people like François Truffaut and Jean-Luc Godard.

In America I get envious seeing how moviegoers—especially young people—go to see the interesting new works coming out. I'm also envious of how these films are a big topic of conversation when intellectuals get together. Young people—like between seventeen and twenty-five—are obsessed with new movies. The next generation of leading filmmakers is going to come out of that space. I just don't feel that same kind of enthusiasm in Japan.

But in any case, the way young people think and feel is changing all the time. Their minds are so dynamic, so much in flux. They're quite bored with the filmmaking style of our generation; they find it slow and tedious. When my series was on TV, I listened to some young people talk about what they thought, and they made some points that surprised me. They were really taken with the parts that we threw together on the spot, since we were often working on the fly and with such a low budget. But they found the shots done in an old style too long and just boring. Their ideas really made me rethink things.

Lately people are giving me a hard time about keeping up with the times. They get on me for staying inside and reading all day, and tell me I should get out of the house and go to Roppongi or Shinjuku or someplace. But when I get there, it's so crowded with young people, and I don't really get it anymore. I get intimidated going into those spaces by myself.

I don't really go to these areas so often, but in the evenings sometimes I go out to see a movie in Shinjuku, and it feels a bit uncanny to me. These people with purple hair, you don't know if they're boys or girls, Japanese people or what. It's not like I've tried to talk to them, but when they're standing right up next to me, I just can't help thinking what in the world is going on here. If I complain about it afterward, someone will scold me and tell me this scene is totally normal and if I think it's weird, I need to get with the times.[2]

I have to admit that filmmakers of my generation might be cutting themselves off from reality a bit too much. I really should get out and figure out what young people are thinking, what they're doing—it's part of my job as a filmmaker.

The Charm of the TV Commercial

The moviemaking process is changing a lot these days. I also have a sense that scenario writing itself has changed. Newer people start off by writing a series of highlights, set piece scenes, and then go on to make the story by connecting those scenes. You don't get the feeling that they map out the structure in advance and then stick to it.

Along those lines, as you can see with Dustin Hoffman in *Midnight Cowboy* (1969), his performance isn't exactly "acting" as I know it. Somehow the realness of his Ratso Rizzo character got stuck in my head; there's something unforgettable about it. Seeing his performance made me realize that maybe the very concept of what it means to "act" is changing too.

We should do a better job of keeping up with all these shifts. Lately I've realized how filmmakers of my generation don't seem committed to learning new things, seeking out the new.

These days I see a lot of intriguing commercials on TV. I happened to see the ones that won the Cannes Lions International Festival of Creativity before the prizes were announced. There was one for an organization that helps children with neurological disorders.

It starts with a man making a phone call to his mother. He tells her his child has been born. It's a boy. Physically, he's in great shape, but something seems wrong. He seems to have some neurological damage. He thinks it's better his wife shouldn't see him, and he'll call again soon. Then the man hangs up the phone and starts to think. This is all shot in a close-up; only the position of the camera moves. When a child is born, everybody gives the father a cigar, it seems. Another man stands. The man from the phone silently offers the other man a cigar. That man gives the other one a slap on the shoulder and congratulates him. The first man lets down his shoulders like he's defeated and walks away. Suddenly the screen freezes, and a voice-over announces that the organization exists and people should use it—it is there to help people, and we should all help each other. And that was the end.

That commercial packed in all the storytelling of a typical feature film in a fraction of the time. I thought it was wonderful.

That time I saw a lot of other commercials; there are so many clever ones. The advertising industry gives you responsibility as a director quite early in your career, so it seems commercials are quite popular with young people, and it forces them to work with a lot of new technology. They have very little time to get their point across, and they have to use this time to get the most impact. I imagine that one of these days some exciting new film directors will come out of the commercial scene.

I wonder why young Japanese people gave up on the film world. When I started in the studio system, people like Naruse Mikio and Yamanaka Sadao were already in the pipeline and there were so many cinephiles. When I was applying for jobs, there were five positions for assistant director but five hundred applicants.

These days Japanese film is on the downswing, so there aren't so many cinephiles, though I think there are still a lot of people who enjoy film. But the big problem for new people is how to get financing, how to make films. You're really lost once you take away the Big Five and television.[3] It's our responsibility as senior filmmakers with experience in the industry to create opportunities for young filmmakers.

Fighting with the Fans

When I see a good movie, it challenges me to push my own work to the same level and brings out my competitive spirit. But when I see a bad movie, or one that's sloppily made, it just ruins my desire to create. Sometimes, you run across these films.

One director that's really challenged me lately, maybe because I know him, is Lindsay Anderson, especially *if. . . .* (1968). And then there's *The Fixer* and *Midnight Cowboy,* that I just mentioned.

I haven't really watched Jean-Luc Godard's films. Claude Lelouche's *A Man and a Woman* (1966) was really fantastic, but his later works just seem to retrace the same story of *A Man and a Woman.*

There's one other film I love that was a real missed opportunity. Tony Richardson has a film called *The Charge of the Light Brigade* (1968), right.[4] I adore that movie; I think it's a masterpiece. But it only lasted in the theaters for a week and then it just vanished. The battle scenes are amazing, and that distinctive kind of English humor is great. The whole thing was great, but for some reason almost no one came to see it. Tony Richardson is one of the most gifted filmmakers working today; there's got to be a way to market it more creatively. I'm guessing the publicity people didn't really get the film. In Japanese it was called *A Faraway Battlefield.* The title makes it sounds like a romance taking place on a battlefield. Faraway?!? The original title is *The Charge of the Light Brigade.*

The billboards also feature an image of a couple posed in a kiss. No wonder the viewers have totally different expectations. And they get mad, thinking they've been had, ripped off. I actually got into a fight with a woman sitting next to me in the theater.

She kept muttering about things she didn't like, and I would keep thinking "This is great!" and at some point she started to complain really loudly. I had to ask her to be quiet, and she flounced out, tossing off her last complaint: "That last scene makes no sense!" I was so crushed.

What was strange was that Sergei Bondarchuk's *War and Peace* (1967) covers the same territory, but it was very popular with filmgoers. In contrast to Richardson's war scenes, which capture the period feeling quite well, the war depicted in *War and Peace* was utterly incoherent. So bad you couldn't even tell who Napoleon was. He makes Napoleon and Andrei Bolkonsky look exactly the same and ride the same type of white horse. On top of the fact that it's almost impossible to bring Tolstoy's *War and Peace* to the screen, it's hard to figure out where the film is coming from. The film is held together by three main families: the house of Bolkonsky, the house of Bezukhov, and the house of Rostov. But the house of Rostov almost completely disappears. The tension between those three houses doesn't hold up.

Anyway, I felt bad for Tony Richardson. And something similar happened with the reception of *The 400 Blows*. A shame, because it is Truffaut's best work. But it completely flopped in Japan. Clearly this was because of the title. Just because there's a child in it, they called it *The Adults Just Don't Understand*. People see the title and think they already know the film, so they don't go to see it. Another film I really admired was *The Graduate*. It was produced by Joseph E. Levine, or actually his company. It was a huge risk for them that led to an incredible box office hit. The return from that one hit was enough to allow Levine to parlay his company into a bona fide production studio, which up to that time had only produced and distributed films. The ups and downs in the American film world are extreme like that. If you make a picture and you screw up the release, your fortunes can drop like a rock, but they can also rise just as high when you get it right. There is nothing like that in Japan.

Leading the Vanguard of Production

Partly that's because in America, a film needs financing from a bank. A film is in reality its own business, and it acts like a business. In Japan the financing is decided within the studio, and each production moves ahead at its own pace. This mode of financing causes a lot of stress and conflict, as you might imagine.

With the way things are, if things don't shift over to the American system of financing, Japanese cinema is never going to evolve.

The group we started, the Four Knights Club (Yonki no kai), will be devoted to this kind of film financing, acting like a bank.[5]

Let me explain our thinking a bit more. For starters, we think it is a scandal that four of the most established veterans of filmmaking—Kinoshita Keisuke, Ichikawa Kon, Kobayashi Masaki, and myself—aren't able to make films and have more or less fallen into silence.

No matter how hard it is, we have to take the lead and do whatever it takes to get our films made. Of course, they have to be good films—but the most important thing is, first and foremost, to make them. For us as filmmakers to stay silent at this moment would be criminal. The four of us banded together because each of us still has a lot of films to make, and because we get along.

We also hope that all kinds of veterans working in the industry—not just directors, but also cinematographers and the art and music departments—will put their weight behind this launch and turn it into a full-fledged production movement. Another reason we started this group is that once the four of us are up and running, we'll be able to support new, young people making independent works.

We've already set some things up, but at the end of the day, we need a vision to make good films. Really cutting-edge works. If that doesn't happen, there's no point in creating this club.

Right now in the film world it's really hard to make films because of the limited amount of financing. Even if you have a script in hand, you're constantly worried that if you add in the scenes you want here or there, you won't have enough money to finish it. In the past you could write a script without calculating that kind of thing. Labor was also cheaper. These days, a novice carpenter will cost you five thousand yen a day. Someone who can barely hammer a nail.

These are the kinds of things that get in your way as you are trying to make a film. We need to break this structure down so that we can make something new.

Then, as I mentioned earlier, we need to be able to make movies by borrowing money directly from a bank. This also has advantage of clarifying who has the financial responsibility. The way things have worked till now, there is no real responsibility. The production is bleeding into the red everywhere, but who really has responsibility for that deficit and who should decide what to do? There's no one on the hook there. In a sense that means there's actually no producer. It's really dysfunctional.

If you're a top director overseas, your compensation is decided through a percentage system. If your film is a huge hit, your cut ends up being very substantial. I've heard that a director like Frankenheimer can make one or two million dollars from one film.[6] These directors live in houses you wouldn't believe, and lead lives you also wouldn't believe. That's just unthinkable for us. We're not seeking that kind of money; we just want to be able to eat.

More than anything we want to be able to spend money on production, but every year the budgets get smaller. At the same time, the number of employees grows larger at each studio, and every year they want pay raises. The aggregate amount of money each studio has is not increasing much, but the indirect costs keep increasing, and production is stuck with what's left. It's not just production costs that are affected, it's also the directors. They're not actually put to work on projects—it's more like they're running out the clock at each company.

Because the studios are focused on the financial end, trying to eke out a profit, they don't really pay much attention to the films' contents. It's a vicious cycle of budgets that drop, creating the conditions for lousy content.

While we say we want to restore things to the way they were in the so-called Golden Age of studio film, we know that just one strategy alone can't reform the whole system. We want to make bank financing a priority—but of course we're not urging everyone to go and quit the studios all at once. We think the problem needs to be solved in stages.

It's precisely because things have reached this state that we—as the people who made this first move—have such a responsibility. If we fail, of course, that kind of financing will be ruined for others. Another thing we want to shift is the release date. So what we're saying is we want to decide on release dates at a point in the production where it doesn't force us to rush production just to meet an arbitrary date. In the case of the Big Five, the release date is set even before shooting begins, and that means not only do you have to work fast but you can't make any changes along the way.

Tora! Tora! Tora! and Me

You want to know about *Runaway Train* and *Tora! Tora! Tora!*, I imagine. The weekly tabloids have printed all kinds of speculations, haven't they, and it's kind of hard for me to wade into all of that.[7]

What finally tore apart the production of *Runaway Train* was the script—the one we wrote and the one from the American writer were totally at odds. The Americans thought we would use their script, and for me that was impossible.

The stories weren't actually all that far apart. The part that clashed was that the American side wanted to introduce all the main characters and their backstories *before* the runaway train took off. Then only after that exposition would the train go out of control.

My approach was different. I wanted to have the engine lose control, then introduce a man who was on board the train by chance. That's how it should start. And then the people in the control room or in the company's office would desperately try to stop the train. Once the train leaves, *then* for the first time the people would be introduced and the drama would start. Developing the characters first just doesn't make any sense.

One more point of disagreement hinged on how to shoot the runaway train. For me, five minutes of screen time meant only shooting for five minutes. The way I make movies, for the most part screen time is the same as real time. I don't manipulate time to make it appear differently on screen. But the American scenario crammed twenty-five minutes of action into five minutes of screen time. Our way of working was just fundamentally different. The American writer's thinking and mine were just too far apart. That's where the lack of compatibility came in.

The problem with *Tora! Tora! Tora!* really came down to who had the right to edit. It's a pretty delicate task to narrate the outbreak of war between the United States and Japan in a coproduction between those two countries. The basic plan was to combine film from two directors, one from each "side"; so it would have been out of the question for me to have no right to edit. Editing can make or break a movie. If the editing had gotten across a message about "that sneaky bastard Yamamoto Isoroku and his surprise attack," I would have jumped off the top of the Twentieth Century-Fox building and killed myself.

People from both sides went back and forth about the final edit, and at last agreed that I would okay it once it was finished to my satisfaction. I told them that part would absolutely have to be in the written contract, or it wouldn't work. But even at the very end, they didn't include that condition.

There were a lot of delicate areas because the film told the story of the war from both sides, and especially because the Americans are very conscious of the massive damage they suffered at Pearl Harbor. Our side didn't have the right to final edit, so we couldn't do our job. That's what was behind that fiasco.

The American who introduced me to the project suggested that I could just get started, and that somehow it would all work out. I could get things rolling, then cut out midway, and it would be fine. It would be fine if I just rubber-stamped it, and they could use my name. That was quite a clever plan that guy came up with . . .[8] And that's how it all happened; I suppose the details will all come out at some point.

Reading John Ford (1987)

Kurosawa muses on the life and works of director John Ford, on the occasion of the publication of the biography *Pappy* in Japanese translation in 1987. He focuses on specific Ford films, with a granular recall of many, as well as identifying strongly with the camaraderie on Ford's set and the frictions between Ford and the studios.

KUROSAWA This book, *Pappy,* tells the story of John Ford while it's also, in a way, telling the story of Hollywood. Here's how it breaks down the Hollywood part. There was a period at the beginning when the role of the director was pretty minimal in contrast to the actor, who was the star. Next came the director era. During that phase, the director was at the center of filmmaking. And then came the era when people who had experience in the industry became producers, and the time came when they were at the center of filmmaking. And then I suppose came an era when industry people were commercial through and through. They didn't come up making films. Then the era shifted to capitalists who made films and considered film a commercial business. I found it quite fascinating how these shifts are described throughout the book, with a lot of nuance.[1]

BUNGEI SHUNJŪ EDITOR The writer is John Ford's grandson, and so you can read it as a biography of a great film director at the same time you can also read it as a history of Hollywood...

KUROSAWA Exactly. John Ford lived a long time right in the thick of all that history. Through all those shifts in the industry. When Ford died (in 1973), it wasn't really the glory years per se for directors; it was really a time when Hollywood was somewhat on the decline. After passing through those four eras I mentioned, Hollywood was going through a downturn. These days it's still a producer-centered system, you know, over there. Of course, it has changed in some ways. John Ford had to adapt to all those phases and changes in the industry, and still he managed to make a remarkable number of works.

Another thing that comes across about the lifestyle of John Ford and his crew is how they were all such workhorses. I was really struck by that. That's pretty typical of people who make movies on set. That includes Ford, a director through and through. He is on set at nine in the morning and gets moving, on his chair behind the camera, waiting for everybody to show up. Which is his way of saying he liked what he was doing. He was really a director through and through, a true movie person. Reading this book really calls up a lot of scenes; I can almost see John Ford appear right before my eyes.

Obviously, I'm a director myself, and I've had my fair share of experiences, but the way I saw eye to eye with the company side—or didn't—is a lot like John Ford's situation, the way he was always putting up a fight. In this respect, we were both held in check by the studio system, so this book was very interesting reading for me.

John Ford made so many movies in his time, and it's indeed true that not all of them were masterpieces. But still, in each of them there is a kind of "air of John Ford" about them, you know. A kind of aura. It's just John Ford's personality, maybe. He can be almost brutally direct, but he is also really caring. Everyone ends up being part of a "Ford family," cast and crew included. He takes them all under his wing. Of course, they're all working together, and it's from that that I think this atmosphere comes out. He really gets close with his staff, he treats them all like family, the actors too. That's where the strengths of John Ford's movies come from.

I tell my crew this all the time, but when you're shooting a movie, the crew's feelings get transmitted just as they are into the movie. It's hard to put it into words, but John Ford's works all kind of radiate with the warmth that must have been a part of the set. That's a testimony to the power of John Ford's social skills, how he brought people together to do their jobs like a big family. That's where I think that aura comes from.

EDITOR That image of "Pappy" must come from that feeling, then.

KUROSAWA Of course. In Japanese we would call him the same thing, "oyaji." In my team too we call the older actors *oyaji.*

EDITOR When I read the book and saw that John Ford had directed 136 movies, I was shocked. I had no idea it was that many.

KUROSAWA The thing is, it's 136 films, but many are short, not the length of a film today, because in the silent era they made a lot of shorts. Many of them were made without a script, when they would just start filming with the seed of a story; works like that are included in that total of 136. And on top of that, John Ford filmed his films really fast. Even after talkies became popular, he could have the whole thing finished in about forty days. In the silent era, I think he could produce them in a matter of a few days, right.

But it was quite a sea change when production moved from silent to talkies. When dialogue began to be spoken aloud, all of a sudden words started to carry more weight. The actors had too much dialogue. So John Ford adjusted to this new dynamic: he made dialogue short, and cut out the unnecessary parts. Maybe he just did this to make the movies more truly cinematic. After all, film was silent in the first place. Even if the actors don't speak that many words, you have the image, which is able to tell the story. I think Ford put a lot of weight on the silent image.

EDITOR I read in *Something Like an Autobiography* that you saw John Ford movies like *Iron Horse* (1924) and *Three Bad Men* (1926) when you were in middle school?

KUROSAWA Oh yes, I saw them when I was a child. I also watched a lot of pictures with the actor Harry Carey. I would guess that a good half of them were John Ford movies. Even in Japan, new movies with Harry Carey played almost every week, and everybody was just enthralled with them.

EDITOR Were these the silent Westerns?

KUROSAWA Yes, that's right. Oh, but they were entertaining. Harry Carey was such a renowned actor—not just because he played the hero parts. Even if he played, for example, a minor cowboy, he had the acting chops to flesh out the part as a full human being. It was much later that Westerns turned to focus on action—the same as *chambara* films in Japan, actually.[2]

EDITOR Oh, is that right? Kurosawa-san, around when did you first become aware of the name of John Ford as a director?

KUROSAWA It was *The Informer* (1935). Before that, before John Ford really broke out as a director, he focused on making commercial works. He was working hard behind the scenes and learning on the job, getting a

Kurosawa with director John Ford in 1957 on the set of *Gideon's Day*. Courtesy of Kurosawa Production Co., Ltd.

sense of the craft, what cinema itself was. It finally all fell into place for him as he was heading up *The Informer*. This made me rethink everything—it was clear I was seeing the work of a great director, and I had to backtrack and think about what I missed earlier.

John Ford had started laying the groundwork for *The Informer* years earlier, but the studio didn't let him go at it. Because *The Informer* was a success, gradually he was able to take charge of his own productions, and *Stagecoach* (1939) came out, *Grapes of Wrath* (1940) came out, *The Long Voyage Home* (1940), and then *How Green Was My Valley* (1941), and on and on, up through *My Darling Clementine* (1946).

The Diasporic Irish

EDITOR *The Quiet Man* (1952) is a story set in Ireland, and as someone with Irish roots, John Ford had a real attachment to Ireland, didn't he?

KUROSAWA Yes. I wonder if he hadn't long felt that Ireland was his real homeland. John Ford had kind of an Irish temperament, right, and sometimes it would show up quite forcefully in his films.

EDITOR Right when he got married, the Irish revolutionary movement had just broken out, and Ford left his wife behind to go to Ireland all by himself. That decisiveness, once he had something on his mind . . .

KUROSAWA He did have an incredible will to make things happen. For instance, Monument Valley, the location you often see in John Ford's Westerns—in those days it was way out in the middle of nowhere, wasn't it. The nights were cold, and the days were boiling hot. Just setting up camp and getting down to work in a place like that takes a lot of physical work, right. And on top of that, when the war started he joined with ordinary soldiers to work making films on the front. He was making movies in places where bullets were flying, you know. He was doing such a hard job and so he ruined his health in that way, right.

I imagine you drink like there's no tomorrow in order to forget such a lot of bad experiences and hard times. And then his eyes also got really bad . . . But even if he had a lot of terrible things happening to him, John Ford never talked about it to anyone else, so, well. He drank like a fish to forget things like that, but in the end I think it was pretty terrible for his body. And everyone around him was drinking like crazy too.

EDITOR Did you ever have a chance to drink with him yourself?

KUROSAWA No, by the time I first met him, I think it was around 1957, and by then John Ford wasn't allowed to drink anymore. Several years after that I met him at the Sanno Hotel, and John Ford ordered some scotch up to his room for me on the phone. But the room service waiter only brought a glass. John Ford flew off the handle, and he told the waiter to bring him a bottle, which he treated me to. But everyone around John Ford, all the crew who were attached, when they got together they all drank like fish, you know. John Ford himself couldn't touch a drop. They would scream out in Japanese things like "sake ga nomita~~~~i!" [*laughs*] They would all burst out saying things like "Sake!" or "Kirin beeeer!" but he couldn't really drink, you know.

EDITOR Going back to your earlier point about Monument Valley: getting there was quite an expedition, wasn't it?

KUROSAWA Absolutely. Even today there's a place called John Ford Point.

It's kind of a famous tourist spot now, but it's really hard to get there, and back in those days the transportation was really inconvenient; everything took work. Finding a landscape like Monument Valley. Or finding Ben Johnson, the stuntman whose riding form was like a poem, and guiding him till he become a star. That's the trait that allowed him to make Westerns of such quality.

EDITOR *Stagecoach* is now regarded as one of the classics of the Western genre, but at the time, the people on the production side opposed it, because they said that the Western was an obsolete genre.

KUROSAWA It never fails that people will get in your way if you want to do something really new. More often than not, the films that management flatly opposes turn out to be masterpieces, don't they? A good director, which is to say a film auteur, is always thinking one step ahead—at least the ones who are trying to do something new. In Ford's case, when the executives didn't follow his idea, they thought it was too risky and would refuse to fund a picture. But then you have someone like Darryl F. Zanuck, the producer at Twentieth Century–Fox, who practically ordered Ford to make *The Grapes of Wrath*. That's because Zanuck himself was a real moviemaker, someone who knew the business as a "movie person."

EDITOR But John Ford and Zanuck clashed on multiple occasions, didn't they?

KUROSAWA Zanuck was a true movie person. He wrote scripts, and his editing was quite skillful. But at the same time, he had a dictatorial side, and he would do things like arbitrarily edit down someone's film. So he would piss off John Ford. But in my eyes, anyway, Zanuck's cutting didn't ever really ruin a story.

First of all, Zanuck was responsible for Ford making the films we think of as his representative works, right. Films like *The Grapes of Wrath, How Green Was My Valley, My Darling Clementine*. He was, after all, a devotee of cinema, so he was able to do things like that, right. After Zanuck, the people who became studio heads didn't really know movies; he was really different from the later people who would do anything to make money. When times changed and people who treated the set like a factory took over, things got even rougher for John Ford...

EDITOR It seems that Zanuck was very skeptical about (among others) John Ford—he thought Ford might have lacked a real commitment to his films, because he hardly ever watched the daily rushes.

KUROSAWA That's because John Ford knew his staff really well, and he trusted them enough to let them do the work without his supervision, having the faith that it would work out. Whether he watched the rushes or didn't, John Ford had a sense of how things were going, because he had that kind of character. That's a big contrast to me. I feel uneasy unless I see the rushes for myself and it's hard for me to let go. But Ford had that kind of trust in his crew, right. He didn't worry and would leave everything to his crew while he'd get on his yacht and go off somewhere. He was able to do that because he trusted them, right. The John Ford style is to protest that the crew would ruin his work, but his grouchiness was all a schtick, and he meant the opposite—that they would do a fine job.

But indeed, John Ford was quite a boss. Just like Zanuck was a boss. When they both got drunk, they would clash mightily. Both of them had just too strong a personality.

EDITOR This book recounts conversations with actors, a lot of episodes that are very interesting, aren't they? John Wayne, Clark Gable, Henry Fonda...

KUROSAWA John Ford did so many things that only *he* could have gotten away with. When they were on the set of *The Informer,* he played a trick on Victor McLaglen, who was starring. He told McLaglen, "I've changed the schedule. You're not working tomorrow. Take the night off and go drinking." He had some friends take him out and get him really drunk so that he had a hangover. Then the next day, had him rousted to appear in the court-of-inquiry scene.[3] Victor McLaglen got an Academy Award for Best Male Actor for that role. John Ford certainly stirred up some interesting situations—situations someone like me never could have pulled off.

There was one time when Clark Gable asked Ford to let him redo a scene. Which he did, but without actually shooting it; John Ford would do things like that. Clark Gable got mad and protested that he had told Ford he wanted to redo it. John Ford agreed that indeed he had told Gable he could redo the scene, but he never promised he would actually *shoot* it. [*laughs*]

EDITOR That was on the shoot of *Mogambo,* right?

KUROSAWA Yes, exactly. Clark Gable was quite a star, but he couldn't really remember his lines. He was never too excited about the job and was always going off hunting. And that's what pissed off John Ford. What the hell is he doing, or something like that. John Ford got mad because he had already wrapped up the scene, but Gable decided he didn't like his performance and wanted everybody to do it all over again. So, of course, Ford is going to get mad; that's just too much. Anyway, I think that's the incident in question.

Beating Up Henry Fonda

EDITOR What about the incident where he punched Henry Fonda in the face?[4]

KUROSAWA Henry Fonda had played the lead in the Broadway version of *Mister Roberts* (1955) for seven years, and it had been a huge hit.[5] Then when Henry Fonda was playing the same role for the film adaptation, and they were on the shoot, he offered some opinion to John Ford, who just suddenly punched him. Whether Henry Fonda was right, or John Ford was right, I have no idea. From Henry Fonda's point of view, he had played the role for a long time and felt like it belonged to him, and John Ford being John Ford probably wanted to do things his way… Unless I hear both sides, I really have no way of knowing who was in the right and who was wrong.

EDITOR But to get up and punch someone in the middle of a conversation, that does seem rather outrageous, doesn't it?

KUROSAWA Well, that's John Ford for you. Henry Fonda and John Ford had that kind of relationship, and in fact it was John Ford who made Henry Fonda's career what it was. Didn't Henry Fonda say that during the shooting of *The Grapes of Wrath*? In the very last scene, in the farmworkers' camp when he leaves his mother and goes off as a wanted man, the camera movement is really complicated, but they do it all in one take. They did a lot of rehearsals over and over again, taking a lot of time, and even after all that work aligning everything for a perfect take, and the crew were pleased with the shot, John Ford would just say nothing, and would walk away somewhere. [*laughs*] When that kind of thing happened, he usually wouldn't say something like "Great job, everyone," John Ford. Even when the whole crew thought they pulled off an amazing shot, John Ford would just stay mum, look like it was just business as usual, say nothing, and head off somewhere.

When I met John Ford in London, it was during the shoot for *Gideon's Day* (1958), and I went to visit the set. He sat me in his own director's chair, while he made an actor redo his lines over and over again. Finally, he called "okay," and to the actor, "that was wonderful, thank you very much," in an exaggerated manner, and turned to me and winked. [*laughs*] He felt just the opposite. Sometimes he would do the perversely opposite thing. That was just the John Ford way.

EDITOR So, if an actor didn't know the ins and outs of "Pappy's" personality, they might be completely baffled.

KUROSAWA Well, Jack Lemmon must have been very pleased to make his début in a John Ford film in *Mister Roberts*. One day Jack Lemmon came to watch the shoot of an earlier film of John Ford's. An older guy who was wearing ratty work clothes walked up to him and said, "Say, you would make a good Ensign Pulver in *Mister Roberts*." Jack Lemmon replied, "Why don't you say that in front of John Ford!?!" It's a funny story but the other man replied, "I *am* John Ford. We start shooting in Honolulu in September."[6] He realized immediately who Jack Lemmon was and could see his potential, and cast him on the spot in a role that fit Jack Lemmon very, very well. Well, probably John Ford had seen Jack Lemmon's movies before, which might explain it. I've been told that such a brash way of dealing with people was very Irish.

EDITOR His dialogue with John Wayne on *Stagecoach* is also a masterpiece. Up to the point when John Ford cast him for the main role, he really needled him. He would provoke him, saying things like, "Isn't there anyone around who can play the Ringo Kid?" "I just wish to hell I could find some young actor in this town who can ride a horse and act. Goddammit Duke, you must know somebody."[7] John Wayne knew what he was up to the whole time.

KUROSAWA Right, right. He made a point of just spending time with John Ford on his yacht, eating and drinking with him, trying to catch some big fish like a swordfish. At the time, he was a regular in some pretty minor Westerns, and John Ford made no effort to use him any differently. But John Wayne was always around. And over time, bit by bit he learned from John Ford, and then all of a sudden Ford cast him as the lead in a picture. That sense of rhythm is John Ford in a nutshell.

EDITOR Quite masculine, right.

KUROSAWA Very masculine. And a real pro. It seems that in his later years John Wayne had some right-wing tendencies, but John Ford wasn't like that. Ford loved the military, he loved the navy, he even fought in the war. But he also liked Kennedy, and didn't he get really liberal late in life? What he liked about the military and the navy was all that rule following, the simplicity and transparency, the all-male environment, and the workplace sociality. Even if he was a nationalist, that's not the same as being a militarist.

I met him after the war, when I also met John Wayne and Henry Fonda; people say that John Ford changed after the war. They say he got a lot more mellow, not like the old "Pappy." The person I am familiar with is the postwar, calmed-down version of John Ford. But even so, there were times when he did things like punch Henry Fonda in the jaw during the making of *Mister Roberts.* [*laughs*]

Bullying as Method

EDITOR During the shooting of *Stagecoach,* John Wayne was constantly chewed out by John Ford, right, and called names like "dumb bastard" (idiot) and "big oaf." He even said, "Can't you walk instead of skipping like a goddamn fairy?"[8]

KUROSAWA That kind of thing happens a lot. Directors will say all kinds of things. In their minds, they are always calculating. They might think, "Well, if I say it like X, maybe I will get Y," or "How about I say it like that?"... They might lash out and swear at someone, or praise them, to try to stir things up. And that's regardless of the director, that's how everybody does it, you know. It's not that they're trying to intimidate people; they're doing what it takes to make a good picture, and that's part of it. So John Ford would probably say that he's not doing this personally, he's just trying to make the best film possible. Basically, he had to plow straight ahead, keeping other people in line while paying attention to them, focused on the movie.

Trash talk and insults were a kind of hobby for John Ford. In some ways it was kind of a joke. I think he said that because John Wayne's way of walking was moving his ass a bit when he walked. He walked that way his whole life. It became his kind of trademark. So, that's why Ford said to him, "Stop walking like a fairy." Probably he got a big laugh out of the crew. Is John Wayne really someone who would let that get to him? That's how it works on set. Directors toss off lines like that all the time. They know just how to hit you where it hurts. Then the crew will break out laughing and everybody relaxes. That's what makes things flow on a set... Afterward, if you take the words out of context, they really do seem quite awful.

EDITOR The writer—Dan Ford—seems to take this too much at face value.

KUROSAWA That's right. The staff all know that you shouldn't take the throwaway remarks of a director too literally. It's just a game, hitting someone's sensitive spot to get everybody to laugh, though the person it's directed at might get embarrassed. On my sets, every night people are all together, and everybody gets to drinking, and people really let it fly. If you don't know that atmosphere... Well, it is pretty likely that his grandson doesn't really understand how things work on a set.

EDITOR In the writer's interpretation, Ford treated John Wayne harshly in the beginning on purpose in order to rally the sympathies of the rest of the cast and crew, because he was something of John Wayne's patron.

KUROSAWA Those cast and crew are not the kind of people who are going to get jealous because he chose John Wayne. [*laughs*] When a new up-and-coming person like John Wayne arrives on the scene, they will throw all their effort into making him look good, so the film looks good. Say you're the lighting crew—when the actor has had it and wants to give up, you'll sweet-talk them along so you can make them look just a little better. The crew are like that, from the costume and makeup on down. On *Kagemusha,* when I suddenly cast Ryū Daisuke for the role of Nobunaga, the staff pulled out all the stops to make him look good. On top of that, John Wayne was like a member of John Ford's family. They were buddies; he would go onto Ford's yacht, drink with him every night, play cards with him. There was no bad blood between him and the rest of the cast and crew.

EDITOR So, it's more a case of "well, now it's his turn to get roasted"?

KUROSAWA That's right. The thing is, it was a really difficult role and could really give John Wayne a big break. Everyone else must have known that their own future was riding on that performance. So that's why John Ford would say things like "stop that faggy way of walking"—in order to break the tension. That's how I read it anyway.

Farewell to Katharine Hepburn

KUROSAWA One more thing that surprised me a bit in this book was that John Ford and Katharine Hepburn had been romantically involved. I had no idea. But it turns out that right before John Ford died, Hepburn came to see him in the hospital. They talked about old times for the entire day, until she finally left. That was their last goodbye... such a lovely story.

EDITOR He and Katharine Hepburn had worked together since *Mary of Scotland* in 1936, I think. When the shooting was over, they took off for a month together, but it's written that they split up after.

KUROSAWA I can only imagine that the two of them must have fought like crazy at the beginning, and on the set, too, given how stubborn both of them were. It's so interesting how somewhere in there they started to enjoy each other's company. There's a movie just like that with Spencer Tracy and Katharine Hepburn. They fight like crazy, but they fall in love, and then in the end they get married. The relationship with Hepburn sounds a lot like that situation in the movie.

There's an amazing thing written in the description of their last meeting together: "But the most important guest was Kate Hepburn, who came out from New York to spend a week with John," and for a week, she was able to be with him.[9] Then Ford writes, "They talked about old times for hours on end. My grandfather got so animated and tried to rise to Hepburn's banter, and shortly after, John turned on the blarney and tried to present a stiff upper lip, but in the end he had to say good-bye to her."[10] Hmm, I think this might have gone a little bit differently. I wonder if he wasn't exactly drawn into her banter; it's more like, as they were talking, bit by bit old things came to the surface. " 'But in the end he had to say good-bye to her.' " That part really devastated me.

John Ford was someone who only rarely did interviews. If someone really versed in film had been able to talk to him in depth, maybe a different book could have been written. I'm not really sure that this book captures the feeling of being on set. But it does have a lot of insight given that it was written by his grandson. For example, near the end, it tells a story about how after *Seven Women* (1966), John Ford fell into a depression, and one time he was convinced that everything was over for him—"I'm not all right"—and he fell over drunk. His grandson wanted to help John Ford, got him up onto a chaise longue, and made him comfortable. This kind of care happened because he was John Ford's grandson; his account of that incident left quite an impression on me.

The Artisans of *Maadadayo* (1993)

In this interview-essay, Kurosawa weighs in on his hopes for cinema crossing national borders and advocates for recognizing the work of film artisans through the lens of his last film, *Maadadayo.* He dwells on the perplexities of his own fame overseas and objects to getting shoehorned into being a "Japanese" director, as opposed to a "planetary" director.

Maadadayo, the film I just finished, is all about how education might actually happen for people. One kind of learning happens in the classroom, of course, where you're taught by the teacher, but that's not the only way. More often than not, you end up learning from the teacher as a human being. And that is exactly what's missing from teaching today. The kind of teacher–student relationship that now exists is a shadow of its former self—the teacher is more or less a kind of salaryman.

My grandchildren tell me about their teachers these days, and it sounds like the old-style teachers don't exist anymore. Back then the teacher–student relationship was the most important thing in the whole idea of education. When I heard this, I thought it's really a shame that those connections have dwindled. Back in the day, we would get together all the time and go hang out at the teacher's house. We were constantly going back and forth to his house. My generation *has* had that kind of experience, but young people these days don't have that same kind of access. So a lot of people get really envious when they see this movie. As for me, I had a teacher named Tachikawa-sensei when I was in elementary school. He was a regular elementary school teacher, but a progressive guy, and his teaching style was really new. In many ways, I feel like I was raised by Tachikawa-sensei. His teaching style coaxed out each person's personality and allowed their specialness to come out.

Films can't help being shaped by the era they're made in. Actually, instead of thinking they're made entirely by human "makers," we should say they appear in the world, are created through all these contexts. I have scripts sitting around from the old days that never got made into films. Sometimes people will ask for permission to make one of them into a new film today. But if I wanted to use one of them for a new film, it would be an utter failure. It's simply that too much time has passed. The scenario and all the production elements probably meshed well with that era back when it was written, but if you plunked it into the present, you would see that it's out of sync. The ambience of an era has such an effect on a director that it can't help infusing the film—so an old script can never be a good "fit" ever again. A director inevitably gets exposed to the goings-on of the world and ends up being influenced by them.

Japanese people have come so far since the war, and we've gotten to a point where we need to rethink a lot of things. I think I could make this movie because I was sincerely thinking—even in the background—about things like foreign aid, the way the bubble burst, what it really meant to be a "Japanese person" in the past, issues in education, people struggling to get by.

I wasn't really thinking of these things consciously. If you shoot a film with the intention of shoving a message down the audience's throat, the film won't turn out well. What I felt at that time just came out naturally in the course of the film. Hyakken-sensei never actually sang the song about "bribery and corruption right and left" that appears in *Maadadayo,* but somehow it just organically came out.[1]

No doubt, I highlighted the issues about postwar Japanese people's subjectivity in my early movies. Take, for example, *No Regrets for Our Youth.*[2] Then *Ikiru* picked up on the sixties' version, when I realized that people were throwing themselves into their work to an alarming extent and were going to lose themselves. Some people have seen the film as a wake-up call, but really, if you make a film just to shock people into some sort of enlightenment, it's bound to fail.

Overseas / Alongside

I like to say that film is a kind of forum (hiroba, 広場) of the world.[3] What I mean is that the moviegoer lives a certain life alongside the characters on the screen. This means you share those feelings—you suffer when they do or worry when they do, get pleased by something or laugh, get angry or cry—all those feelings. No matter what country you're in or what part of the world, everyone has these feelings. That's because even if the words for talking about it might be different, as a fellow human being you can feel with a character on-screen, coming to a kind of "understanding" with them. No matter where in the world you are from, that's how you watch a movie.

Kurosawa films are popular with people overseas, so people often ask me if I do anything to appeal especially to foreigners when I'm making a movie. That would be ridiculous—and also pandering. Of course, my everyday life is in Japan, and Japanese people will draw on Japanese things; I just express what is right in front of me. And since I'm Japanese, I tend to depict Japanese-related issues, and people abroad happen to think this is interesting. As you know, I see a lot of films from different places, and in that same way I get a sense of those countries. Film doesn't really care about national borders. It plays an important role by enabling people to understand each other, actually. So, for example, when a Japanese person saw John Wayne in one of those old Westerns, he didn't really feel like someone completely other. He would seem like a viewer's grandfather or something. That kind of proximity—the ability to observe without exactly identifying—is really quite amazing, isn't it?

Cinema is about to enter a genuinely "planetary" age, and we will need to come up with ways to know how we recognize each other on a global scale as mutually related human beings.[4] The importance of cinema is only growing over time. Film is unusual because of its history of crossing national boundaries to come into contact with different people and make it possible for them to empathize with each other. The role of cinema is getting even more urgent because it can help people all over this planet live together in peace.[5]

Even if I'm watching videos at home, I find myself wanting to turn out the lights and take in the movie. I want to immerse myself right into the film. Sitting in the dark, as time passes, mingling with the figures on the screen—that is a very important experience. I don't really want any part of movies that are chopped up by commercials, and I don't want to be watching in a place where you hear the phone ringing all the time. In the end movies are best seen with a good sound system, a big screen and a pitch-black room—which I guess means seeing them in a movie theater.

My father was in the military and he was very strict. When I was young, educated people tended to look down on going to the theater, but he was very forward thinking and would take the family to see movies. And not just movies: he used to take us to see popular theater and other things too.[6] Well into the twentieth century it was hard to change the public's thinking that the movies were out of bounds for educated people. It was really quite astounding that my father had such an open mind back in the Meiji period.

This kind of parenting was quite rare. At that time for most people, it was really considered deviant to go to the movies. Tachikawa-sensei was exceptional, actually; if you got found out going to the movie theater by some other teacher, you would get thrown in with the bad kids. Given the sentiment in those days, it was very unusual that my military-trained father was so open-minded about entertainment.

Artisans over Artists

There was a time when Japanese cinema ran with the best film industries in the world. We need to do something to get the industry back on its feet. Some of the main problems with Japanese cinema came of age along with the economic growth of the 1960s. Film directors looked less critically at the lives of Japanese people, and scenario writers seemed less skilled. One more thing is that directors with an experimental or independent sense started to insist they were "artists" and began to make difficult films. In reality, a really good film is a pleasure to watch—entertaining or fun. Directors who make films that are too showy and pretentious about their point are really the worst. A film should be easy to get absorbed in, a pleasure to watch; it should speak to you through the workings of the film itself. I recently had a chance to see Satyajit Ray's film *Agantuk* (1991).[7] I found it really affecting, and it was also a pleasure to watch. It talks about profound issues in a deceptively simple way. So, what I mean to say is that good filmmakers are all artisans.

The Japanese Communist Party had a lot of clout in Tokyo at one point, and there was a split between artists and artisans. There was one person who insisted that he was an artist, not an artisan, and I butted heads with him many times. In my view, the very idea that you could skip over the craft of being an artisan and declare yourself an artist is ridiculous. But my way of thinking is forgotten, on its way out these days.

On top of the pretension, if your films are full of nothing but depressing stories, they will just wear down the audience. In the past people used to talk about comic relief, where filmmakers would throw in entertaining parts here and there to make the film lighter. But that light touch from time to time isn't part of films anymore. Pretentious artist-type directors don't connect with audiences like they should. They should remember that viewers pay good money to come to theaters, and they come to have a good time. They misunderstand how to say something to an audience—which is from within the world of the film. That's why people have turned away from going to the movies. It really is possible to make entertaining films, even films that take on huge and difficult subjects. There are good ones out there . . . that are appreciated because they are interesting as films, and I feel like that has been forgotten. Satyajit Ray's films say a lot; they move me greatly, and they are superbly made as films. This is because first and foremost he is an artisan.

A lot of people devalue the work of artisans or look down on them, which makes me angry. I really prefer being called an artisan to being called an artist. My theory about cinema is that it is not a classroom where people come to be taught something: it's something people come to watch and enjoy. This means making people laugh out loud, or sometimes making them cry. It probably does have those didactic elements somewhere, but we are taking people's money in exchange for giving them a movie. And movie people with pretentions to art want to say something like, "How about thinking a little while you are at the movies." Above all, people should be entertained.

For instance, often you will see a banquet scene in a movie, right? These are the kind of scenes where each artisan is at the top of their game. A film can have multiple eating scenes, which if they finished in a day would be fine. But in some movies—take *Maadadayo*—shooting stretches across several days. You might end shooting for the day, and the prop master will have to remember how far a given character has drunk down his beer that day; they take a picture, and then take measurements, remember exactly where the character set down his glass, or remember how far someone bit into a given dish.

Or you go to the set one day and notice the ceiling. It's really high, but the workers might have to clear away the dirt and grime. You might wonder why on earth they are cleaning the ceiling, but the actors are actually going to be eating on set, and you want the actors to be able to eat without worrying about dust falling into their food. The work is really significant when the workers do things so conscientiously, and the production becomes quite a pleasure to work on. Without really thinking about it, you end up following their lead.

Kayama Yūzō and Tsuchiya Yoshio mix medicines in front of the *tansu* chest that stores the clinic's medicine in *Red Beard.*

Everybody is on pins and needles, working hard to get everything right down to the last detail. And somehow or other over time this becomes evident in the overall work itself. I mean, of course, it doesn't literally show on the screen, but somehow or other you can see it. And you can feel it, too, you know.

That's what makes the work of a first-rate director so hard. Theo Angelopoulos is one such director, completely focused on all the details. All those complexities and details reinforce each other and grant a real power to the image. If you start cutting even little corners, there's no end to the compromises you will make. How far would you let it slide? Once you start, it's a slippery slope. This is what I'm always telling people. You have to keep at it and refine your work until there's nothing possibly left to do. We're taking the viewers' money, so we have an obligation to them to make all that work visible. Working so intensely also makes the work much more interesting, you know. When it becomes interesting, you apply yourself even more, without thinking about it. And that's real work. Working just because you think you should out of principle isn't real work.

A good example of this is the *tansu* chest with the drawers in the middle of the house in *Rhapsody in August*, or the one in *Red Beard.*[8]

You may remember that in Red Beard's shop there is a *tansu* that stores the doctor's medicine. We don't have it around anymore, but at the time there was a magnificent lacquerist who came to paint it. Several of the drawers opened, and he carefully painted all the way to the corners of the drawers. When I told him it was fine not to be so obsessive, the lacquerist insisted it had to be that way. He told me, "Sensei, if the inside were to look new, you would feel uneasy. I would feel uneasy too. That's why I do it this way." You need that dedication at every level to pull off a real work of cinema.

If you start cutting corners, you know there is no end to it. Once you start cutting corners, you might as well give it up entirely. Though when I say that everybody laughs.

Everybody ends up working until you say, "It's okay! You can stop now!" Unless you say something, they will just keep refining things, so you have to say, "It's okay, stop!" but they will just say, "Okay, just a little bit more," and keep right on going. The whole thing won't come off right unless the whole crew is that committed. The camera captures everything.

I would just like to tell you how I dread going to screenings. The crew have no idea how to react to the film when they see it on the screen. There's absolutely no chance that the crew will ever laugh at a screening, for example. In the scenes when the audience is supposed to cry, they'll cry without any hesitation. I understand why, but they just won't laugh, and I worry I've done something wrong. The crew are worried about how their specific scenes appear on the screen, and the actors are all worried about their performances, so no one ever feels like they have the room to laugh, I'm sure. But when a regular person ends up joining us, they always end up genuinely laughing.

Apparently Tokoro Jōji was really worried when we were screening *Maadadayo*.[9] He didn't even laugh at the ridiculous parts. Then we tried inviting a regular viewer to the screening, and he finally relaxed.

At one point people talked about how cinema was in a downturn due to the influence of television; I would agree, and it's really no joke. The substance of television and cinema is completely different. When television first got off the ground, the film company executives were thrown, and they decided to make movies cheap and fast so they wouldn't lose to television—but they were mistaken. First off, you can watch television for free, so there's that. People said that if they were going to put down money and go to the theater, there was no way they would settle for movies that were just like TV. In that case it would be better just to stay home and watch TV.

We need to make movies that can only be made on film using the tools that only film has. Cinema is cinema. But despite that, moviemaking has come to imitate TV production in an appalling way.

Tokoro Jōji leads a celebration of teacher Uchida Hyakken in *Maadadayo*. Courtesy of Kurosawa Production Co., Ltd.

When the movies disconnected from daily life, a lot of things started to come apart with the film studios themselves. The studios really need to come up with some sort of vision. They need to tap into their actual affection for the cinema. The studios don't really spend a lot of effort thinking about what is really possible in the medium of film. So they end up making weird genre things, more or less betting in the dark on films they think will make a lot of money. But that's not really the way to go about it. If you take the process of making good movies seriously, viewers will pay you back by watching them seriously. But if you cut corners by thinking things like, "This ought to bring people in" or "If we tweak it a little there that should do the trick," you will never make a movie that appeals to people.

A Feeling and a Movie Called *The End*

I've always been fairly awful at foreign languages, but I have been able to travel the world without really feeling like I was missing out. I feel like anywhere on the earth is my home. But when I think about the actual natural environment it gives me a very uneasy feeling, and I wonder what will become of my home, the earth. Looking around at today's politicians, I wonder what the hell they are doing. If we keep going as is, in the blink of an eye the earth is going to be jeopardized. The first thing that should happen is that the world's politicians get together and do something to protect the planet.

As it is, they're doing nothing but things that will damage the earth. Even though humans are one part of nature, we forget the most important thing. Even in Japan many people say that people interested in the environment are just some kind of fringe. You see, there's a big problem. I almost want to ask, are there truly no politicians in this world who act on things? Someone has to come out and lead, or we are all screwed.

It maddens me enough that lately I think about making a movie called *The End.* It just worries me to no end, where we are. It's such nonsense, really. We really have to commit to thinking about this for real.

When *Dersu Uzala* played in the film festival in France, it set off a really strong reaction. At that time in France, awareness about the natural environment was quite high. Parties like the Green Party were very invested in protecting the environment. There were a lot of ripple effects after that, and when *Dreams* came out people were very worked up about protecting the natural environment, so again the response was really strong.

Along those same lines, we really ought to be able to live without building so many nuclear power plants, you know. Some critics have said that *Dreams* put forth this message, and I have to agree. In the part with the last dream, "The Village of the Waterwheels," Ryū Chishū puts his finger on it when he says, "We don't treat the most important thing in the world like it is important." Viewers who saw it overseas picked up on that idea a lot more than people did at home. Critics in Japan were all up in arms about why I had to include nuclear power plants. And what's worse, they said it was not even an issue, to which I responded, "Well, it certainly *is* a problem." They insisted that there were so many more "aesthetic" objects to put in and wondered why I wanted to include such a "distasteful" thing, and so on. But to my mind, you can't really call it distasteful per se. You have to be curious about what is happening to the natural world, and you have to look at reality directly without backing away.

About landscape, it's gotten difficult to look for locations these days. In Japan, there's nothing like "scenery" left anymore. For instance, with the river we used in *Dreams,* you wouldn't believe how long it took us to find that river in Azumino.[10] There was so much engineering work all around it; the water was dirty and it was a mess. These days I think it would be almost impossible to shoot a *jidai-geki* in Japan. The only solution would be to shoot in a foreign country. [*laughs*]

I went to Kyoto lately and was absolutely crushed. I've been coming to visit Kyoto for a long time, way before it got to the sorry state it is now. From time to time I take a little trip to relax someplace like an old inn in Kyoto, and when I go for a walk around the city, it just provokes me. No matter how I try, I always end up getting angry. I mean, they're out there selling souvenirs right in front of the relics!

I wonder why Japanese people don't have any confidence in their own country. Why they seem to put foreign objects on a pedestal over their own and look down on Japanese things. They will only start respecting Japanese things for the first time when they are reverse-imported in from foreign countries. I wonder where that lack of self-regard comes from. I think we have to chalk it up to a sad sense of national character.

A good example of this is ukiyo-e. These were sold on the street, right.[11] Nobody thought very much of them, but when foreigners began to treat them as important works of art, Japan perversely started to treat them like prized possessions. That's really a pitiful story. And that stance hasn't really changed even now.

One symptom is that many people take pride in never seeing Japanese movies. But Japanese films are incredibly well regarded in foreign countries. Whether you're talking about Mizoguchi or Naruse or Ozu, people really treat them like cinema gods, and they are always being screened somewhere overseas. But in Japan, they are rarely ever screened. This is what I am always trying to tell people. Young people today don't watch these older films, and I want to tell them to get into the theaters! I just don't understand why they don't.

I've said the same thing many times; I even said it the time I was awarded my Academy Award. It's great to have film festivals that screen new films, but wouldn't it also be fantastic to have festivals that screened films from the past? This is a project I hope to work on. When you watch the works from the past, their creators live on, on the screen, even though they may actually be gone.

There are always festivals showing my films in foreign countries, but not in Japan. This March, though, it seems they're having a festival at the Hibiya Chanté, but you know, they didn't program *The Bad Sleep Well*.[12] It drives me crazy when they leave out a film that says something on point about the world we live in. Absolutely no effort to screen it. [*laughs*]

Striking Out / On Your Own

Recent movies from Asia are just stunning, don't you think? They're really on point with their craft and serious in their themes; they are the real deal. You can see the difference when you compare them to Japanese films. We ought to pay attention to those differences. It's going to take the emergence of some real cineasts to get the Japanese film world back on its feet again. Young people complain that they have no money, or that there's no funding around. Sometimes I think they're waiting around for a perfect story to show up that basically forces them to film it. They say they have a good story to tell, but really there's no way to tell until you're in the middle of it. You have to start the script, do all your background work, and commit to making that your story. Then it's a question of getting down to work.

To tell you the truth, I wonder if young people today are putting in the work it takes to make a film. And if they have the drive to do all it takes to get it made. If they do, by all means, put in the work to see it come to life. I tell them that if they get that far, and it's really a good idea, somebody will put up the money to fund it. They're not going to just get passed over.

John Cassavetes's first work *Shadows* (1960) was shot on 16 mm, you know. That's one way you can get it done. The head of the Cinémathèque française told me that there was a fantastic 16 mm film I should see, so I watched it at the Cinémathèque. When I saw it I was really moved. When I asked what kind of a person the filmmaker was, I was told, "He's young, and he's right here." Cassavetes was right there in the screening room. So I went up to him, and just when I was on the verge of saying "Congratulations," he fled straight out into the hallway. Langlois then explained that "he's just shy."

Later I wrote to a number of people to dig up more of his films, but they all told me that *Shadows* was the only Cassavetes film out there. I was pretty sure that someone with such talent wouldn't just vanish. And then later he made the very interesting picture *Gloria* (1980) at Warner. I didn't make the connection to the filmmaker from before. After the movie, I was told it was the same filmmaker who had made *Shadows* and I was floored; I was thrilled to see more of his work. Asking around,

I found out that Cassavetes's works weren't really known in Japan. It seems that a retrospective of his works is playing in the near future.

Here's how Jim Jarmusch managed to make his *Stranger Than Paradise* (1984). He would borrow a camera on his day off and he pieced together little scraps of film that people gave him into a whole movie. That's amazing, isn't it? You can make a very smart film if you're that resourceful. He could, anyway, because he was really passionate about making the film and just stuck with it till it came together. It's not going to work out if you're just complaining about how hard everything is, right. I know you can pull it off if you have the faith in your own talent and the fire to make it.

One more thing I'd like to ask young Japanese directors is why they don't leave the country and travel. I myself don't speak a word of any foreign language. But there are people whose job it is to translate. You can learn so much more from meeting a director than you can from watching their films. You'll find lots of ways to exchange information if you just jump in, and that's how the world gets smaller. These kinds of relationships are possible, but Japanese directors still cling to an "island country roots" mentality.[13]

For instance, if you go to a film festival, you'll find that the participants from Japan usually end up clumping together. Why go all that way if you're going to just stay with the same people? There are so many people from other countries, and unless you try to strike up conversations with people, the whole trip is meaningless. But most Japanese people are hopeless. They need to make more of an effort to extend themselves. It probably does mean spending some money, but you really need to become friendly with people in different places. There are so many more things to learn if you can talk to really world-class directors. The people who make these world-class films are really accomplished people.

I often tell my crew that it's worth making an all-out effort in the preparation stage of a film, even where things can get tedious. I say this most often to people working in areas with a lot of little details like costume or props—even if it can be downright boring at times, try to make a genuine effort. As you work intensely, over time it will start to become more enjoyable. Because it's enjoyable you'll put in a lot of effort, which makes for a real commitment. The process of making gets to be enjoyable. Even as you're grinding through things that seem trivial, you will find yourself enjoying the work. You know the work has meaning behind it, so you can truly feel it is enjoyable. And when you do, you find yourself working hard, without even thinking about it. You might not be able to will yourself into working hard, but if you can find it enjoyable without thinking about it, that is real work. It's all about never treating anything like it actually *is* trivial.

Even today there are times I get so angry at a shoddy job I just about erupt in fireworks. Usually this happens because someone has done something really careless. For example, the reason I blew up during the shoot of *Maadadayo* is that when we were shooting the landscape, the ruins that you see after the air raids, I told the assistant director to hide part of the background that was getting in the way off in the distance.[14] What I meant by "hide" was to get rid of the objects off in the distance so that they didn't end up on-screen. One of my techniques as a director is to shoot with an extreme telephoto lens. And when we were editing, those things were right there on the screen! And then I blew up. "I didn't tell you to shoot the hidden stuff, I told you to blot out the stuff in the background! Use the angles to cover up the background with some burnt-out buildings or whatever so we can't see it!" So I really bit his head off, and asked what the hell he was doing.

The reason that happened is that as we were editing, right when I had just found the best angle and was about choose that shot, all that stuff suddenly appeared on the screen! When this happens I always get furious and start yelling. The assistant director and everybody got kind of quiet, and my daughter came over. She said, "Papa, did you yell at everybody today?" I said something like, "What? Oh, I yelled?" and had completely forgotten about it. The crew all knows that this kind of thing is bound to happen.

But lately I've gotten away from exploding in this way. I've finally learned that these explosions wear you out. [*laughs*] As you get older these things tend to happen less. But by this point everybody is pretty used to my thunder. In fact, I think that simmering in silence is actually more stressful for the crew. Naruse is a good example: if he got mad, he would just hold it in. I think that is actually more terrifying. And it also tires you out. Instead, if you just explode once, then it all calms down afterward. [*laughs*]

Kurosawa on the set of *Maadadayo*. Courtesy of Kurosawa Production Co., Ltd.

Actors and Soundscapes

This is only one example, but actors tend to have one big blind spot. They'll be really pleased with a performance and think they've done well. And that can be a real trap. But the thing is, they really can't tell objectively by looking whether they've done well or not. When people are satisfied with their performance, chances are it wasn't actually so good. The director can see things more objectively and have a sense of the overall picture, but it's hard. My take on performance is a bit technical. Many people think it's a good thing that an actor would be happy with their performance, but I disagree. Sometimes the actor's judgment is right on, but plenty of times it's off. Matsumura Tatsuo has a lot of screen time in *Maadadayo*. In the beginning, I flew off the handle at him. But once the banquet scene was over I didn't have to say anything more. He had some kind of breakthrough. I didn't really have to push it. Then at one point even *I* recognized I lit into him a little too hard. But in my defense, sometimes there *are* times when you have to get after someone like that. Matsumura-kun, he got mad right back at me and asked why he was the only one I was riding so hard.

Sometimes it works out that you push someone for a while, and then boom, they have a breakthrough. Once they get into their groove, they've found it. And you never have to say another word. The thing is that even if actors feel like they have done a good job, they actually have no objective idea if their performance in a scene was good.

Sometimes you just have to hound people like that. It can be rough on the actors. Take the banquet scene. At first we rehearsed it when there were a lot of reporters around. Then I was pretty rough in my directions to the actors. But then the next day, they were able to pull it off perfectly, exactly like I wanted. I was impressed at how good it was. That scene was a turning point, and I never had to say another word. That's how that process works. Matsumura-kun didn't understand the thinking behind my strategy, so he got upset and was swearing his head off about being singled out when I yelled at him.

All directors are like that. With the actors you really have to push them. You just can't get around the fact that you push them pretty far at times.

Actors these days are having a hard time of it. In order for them to grow, you have to give them challenging roles—now you've done this and figured it out, let's move on to something else a bit more challenging. So over time their repertoire is capable of more and more. But what ends up happening is that a director who knows an actor can play a certain kind of part well will ask them to do it exactly the same way. It becomes impossible for an actor to grow if they get into this kind of a rut.

This kind of situation happens a lot especially when actors appear on TV. Even if you are not happy with your performance and ask to redo it, the director will tell you, "No worries, it's totally fine." You're really not feeling good about the whole situation, but things have to keep moving. Sometimes it's so rushed that even if you mess up your lines, they still tell you, "No problem." Even if you point out where you messed up and ask to do that part over, they will still tell you, "No worries, it's totally fine." TV production is just too rushed.

I've said in the past that cinema is what you get when you multiply image and sound. The same thing goes for making a *jidai-geki*—like in *Seven Samurai,* there are scenes set in the village. We can imagine the kinds of sounds people in that era might have heard, people in the Sengoku era. But we really don't know. We *do* know there were blacksmiths, and we know that there were street peddlers who sold oil for lamps and things like that. So we put these things together and tried to make a sound for that era that seemed based in reality. We don't have the same kind of everyday ambient sound because these days the acoustic world has gotten quiet and gone indoors, but for the purposes of the film, we try to make a soundtrack that fits with the time and place.

People who've seen the film tell me they loved how the sound reminded them of the world from that time, as they knew it. On *Seven Samurai* we used optical recording, which tends to degrade, so the sound is actually hard to hear, compared to when it came out. Magnetic recording would've preserved that sound a lot more effectively.

Since we're talking about preservation, I'm really curious to know what the soundscape of the Heian period was like. Someplace like Shōsōin has a lot of instruments, don't they?[15] I would love to try out each of them. Just to be able to hear what sounds they make.

We had a hard time getting a handle on the sound in *Maadadayo* too—the movie that's about to come out. We can make a decent guess at some of the main sounds that should be there in the Meiji-era scenes, but the setting is really on the border between premodern and modern worlds. Some people's points of reference are clear enough that if we didn't get certain sounds right, they would clash with what people know. For example, street vendors that walk through the town selling their wares. There are people around who have that as a living memory.

We tried really hard to get the right effect for the neighborhood streets, with their background noise. The sensei's house was located right by Yotsuya mitsuke—which at that time was a stop on the Tōden streetcar line. So of course we would want to include the train sounds. Locomotives would also pass through, and every once in a while you'd hear a freight train go by. There were a lot of different sounds to work with, and it was quite a headache to get it right.

Our soundscape today is really kind of dull in comparison. Everything is electrified, so the sounds don't stand out from each other as much. I talked about this in *Something Like an Autobiography*, but earlier in the twentieth century, in the Taishō era when I was growing up, all the noise of voices in the town was connected to the human body. People could hear those sounds of peddling and sales all over the city. Moviegoers could get a really strong sense of that in films like *The Lower Depths* and *Red Beard*. To get the right sound for scenes that were set just a bit earlier, we visited a retired *rakugo* artist at his home, and asked him all sorts of questions about the sounds the street vendors made. We recorded his renditions and tinkered with them a bit and put them in. People like the *rakugo-ka* were really key to getting across the atmosphere of that era.

Maadadayo is set right in the middle, between the Edo-period *jidai-geki* films and right now, so if we used sound from a little bit later it would be off, and on the other hand, too-modern sounds like we hear today would also ruin it . . . It was really quite a headache for us.

The Art Lost on Politicians

Most filmgoers in Japan are pretty low-key, but people overseas are much more excitable. If they are into a film they might stand up and start clapping in the middle or get so carried away with cheering that they miss the next scene. That's not so unusual for audiences over there.

Inoue Hisashi told me the other day that when they showed one of my films—I think it was *Sanjūrō*—the audience went really crazy. Things got kind of rowdy, and people started banging on the projection booth. They demanded that the projectionist back up and show this one sequence over again! [*laughs*] I think it must be a lot more fun to watch my films overseas since people have such visceral reactions compared to Japanese audiences. They completely get into the imaginary world of the film. Maybe Japanese spectators are just more polite than they need to be. The American spectators are especially fun to be around. They really get into the world of the film, jump right in.

If people overseas like your film, they'll really show it. They consider film to be worth appreciating, and just love it. For example, when there is some sort of reception at a film festival, they will be keen to talk about cinema. They'll ask if you've seen this film or that one, and right off the bat people from such different places have something to talk about.

I really think Japan is the only place where the politicians are completely clueless about what's going on in the film world. Overseas, people really value cinema. Over the years I have traveled abroad a lot, and the biggest difference I found is that in many places it's just very common for people to go to the movies as an everyday thing. There are always politicians at these kinds of events, and when I find myself seated next to them, it often turns out that many politicians and their wives have seen my films. People are able to have actual conversations—they ask me what I thought of this scene, or they tell me they were really bowled over by some other scene. Japanese politicians just don't have anything to say.

Laurent Fabius is now secretary of the Socialist Party of France, but when he was prime minister he decorated me with the Order of Arts and

Letters. He could carry on a conversation about all my films, starting with *Sanshirō Sugata.* He told me he had been a fan of my work ever since he was a child.

Japanese politicians are just not like that. They're almost proud of not going to the movies, and even not knowing anything about them. That's just awful, and I find it so depressing.

Edited by Nagasaka Toshihisa

II
In Conversation

Seven Samurai, Redux (1991)

with Inoue Hisashi and Yamada Yōji

In this roundtable with fiction writer/playwright Inoue Hisashi and director Yamada Yōji, Kurosawa recalls the stunning debut of *Seven Samurai.* The three old friends delve into details of the production as well as backstories of the "samurai" actors, especially Mifune and the famous fishing scene, and lament why a true samurai movie can no longer be made in Japan.

INTERVIEWER *Seven Samurai* is showing in movie theaters all over the country right now. It's playing at its full three hours and twenty-seven minutes, with a completely original print and a newly cleaned-up audio track. Inoue-sensei, you once wrote that you've seen *Seven Samurai* thirty times, and you'll be ready to die once you've seen it twenty more…

INOUE This time will make it thirty-one. So I have nineteen times to go before my time is up. [*laughs*] I feel the same way about every really great movie: Every time I see it again, I realize all over again how good it is.

Even now I remember so clearly the first time I saw *Seven Samurai,* back in 1954. I was working in the middle of the mountains in Iwate, and I got a day off and went off to Morioka. I was just floored. It was so different from any *jidai-geki* (period dramas) that had been produced before. Stars at that time, like Hasegawa Kazuo and Ichikawa Utaemon, were always so beautifully decked out, and they were still connected to the old-school styles of *shinpa* and kabuki.[1] With *Seven Samurai,* you had almost none of that. The story also was completely different from the kind of bad-guy good-guy characterization we were used to, the *kanzen-chōaku* morality we knew from the theater. It was all about how these different groups ran up against each other—the samurai and the bandits and the farmers. As a huge movie fan just out of high school I was really stunned, or maybe "entranced" is a better way to put it. I was utterly transported, and the movie ended before I knew it.

YAMADA I saw *Seven Samurai* in a packed movie theater in Shibuya. There were so many people in front of me, I couldn't even really see the screen. I was peeking in between all those people's heads and getting only glimpses of those bunches of people running around on the screen. As I was watching I could feel myself melt into them as one of the crowd—it was all so exciting.

KUROSAWA One reason it was so different from all the earlier *jidai-geki* was the wigs. I asked Maeda Seison to help make sure the art direction looked really real, and he told me that the wigs on the earlier movies had been kind of strange.[2] In order to hide the *habutaé,* they had to make the ponytail part of the actors' hair hang way low into their faces.[3] Whereas with a real *chonmage* there is a lot less hair on top. Seison-san really put his foot down. He said that those *chonmage* are "like slabs of yōkan jelly from Toraya."[4] Yamada's father, Yamada Junjirō, was head of makeup. He did some research and came up with some kind of new material to cover up the scalp, different than the more traditional kind of *habutaé.*

YAMADA What about this story? The crew who worked on *Ikiru,* the picture that came right before *Seven Samurai,* really worked like crazy. Just when it seemed like the Kurosawa-gumi were getting completely fed up, Kurosawa-san surprised everybody by saying, "Let's try to make this one fun, it's one of these big blockbuster romps, like a Western... It'll be *easy.*"

KUROSAWA Hmm, I'm not so sure I said it would be easy.

YAMADA Well, at least the story wasn't totally depressing, like *Ikiru,* where the main character is dying of cancer. The crew was told that this time things would be upbeat and filming would be an easy ride. So they all thought, "Okay, here we go. If that's what he says, it will be fun." And that's how everybody got suckered in. [*laughs*]

KUROSAWA It is true—that's how things started out. But once we got underway, it turned out to be not so easy after all. [*laughs*] The thing is, what makes it hard—and different from a Western—is that there are so many details to look after. For instance, there are thirty-three bandits that attack the village, right? Every single one of them in the story has to be killed, and they all go down in their own subplots.

INOUE You're talking about the way that Kambei [Shimura Takashi] pulls in these episodes when he draws the thirty-three circles on his map of the village, and crosses one out each time they knock off a bandit?

KUROSAWA Right, each time a bandit falls it's so detailed, individuated... you can't just wipe out all the "enemy" at once, like you can with a Western.

YAMADA Wasn't the release date supposed to be in August or September?

KUROSAWA Well, I did suspect from the beginning that we might not make it on time. [*laughs*]

INOUE And that is exactly where your level of craft comes in—both you, Kurosawa-san, and Yamada-san. You take a story that could just be routine and make it complex.

YAMADA Wait a minute, you can't really put us in the same boat. Even with all the complexity, I would have made sure the shoot ended on time. [*laughs*]

From One Samurai to Seven

INOUE I've heard that your original plan for *Seven Samurai* involved tracing the day of a single samurai.[5] Getting up in the morning, washing his face, getting something to eat, going out to the castle, making a terrible mistake at his job. And the story was supposed to end with him committing *seppuku*...

KUROSAWA That's the part that was hard to figure out. Exactly how a samurai lives his day-to-day life. Did he really wash his face in the morning? Did he brush his teeth? If he ate his meals at the castle, did he bring his bento or was he served his meals? Hashimoto Shinobu-kun, who wrote the scenario with me, did a lot of research, but there were a lot of little things we just couldn't dig up.[6]

YAMADA Now that you mention it, most of the time the samurai in a *jidai-geki* don't have anything to do at home, since it's peacetime. So when they're there, they're mostly drinking. [*laughs*] But actually that lack of material probably worked out for the best, since in the end you were able to make the *Seven Samurai* that we all know.

KUROSAWA When we'd hit a dead end, Hashimoto-kun would come up with some kind of history backstory. One time we got stuck, he told us that there were nonstop raids by mercenary bandits in the Sengoku era, so farmers would end up hiring samurai to protect their villages.[7] Something about that clicked—that's how we ended up going in that direction.

INOUE Where did that number of exactly seven samurai come from? Not five and not nine. Was that just a sudden flash of inspiration?

KUROSAWA I told the producer Motoki Sōjirō that the story would basically run in such-and-such a way, and he said, "Kuro-san, what's your title?" I was kind of thrown, since I hadn't really thought about it, and I just jotted down *Seven Samurai,* which seem to really please him.

INOUE So it wasn't something you had come up with a lot earlier. Many films use numbers in their titles...

YAMADA It seems like it's always odd numbers. Three, five, seven... those are big. But there's also *Twenty-Four Eyes*... that number definitely leaves an impression.[8]

KUROSAWA I just went with a gut feeling, and it felt like we needed seven, minimum. To protect the village, that kind of thing.

INOUE You manage to give each samurai a distinctive personality, and the ensemble comes together really well, even though you have so many "main" characters. It's a marvel to me that you were able to write such a script. It's just so well put together. Take, for example, Kambei, the leader. He's not sure about joining up with the farmers at first, but changes his mind after spending the night in a cheap roadside inn. A laborer who is also staying in that inn takes a jab at him: "Hey, samurai, these poor slobs are all eating millet. They're stuck with millet so you samurai can get your white rice." Kambei shuts him up and decides he's going to throw his lot in with the peasants. My favorite part is where he says, "I won't let this rice go to waste." That line brings tears to my eyes every time I see it.

YAMADA It makes you cry, indeed.

INOUE You would expect someone who takes on a job like that so impulsively would be a complete failure. He does lose, in a way—but he doesn't die. The gods are surely on his side looking out for him. He doesn't end up any richer, and he also doesn't end up with all the glory. He doesn't benefit from his position in any way. But in this world we need people like him: people who feel compelled by the pathos of the farmers, who will say "I won't let this rice go to waste," and will fight to the death even when their side is quite possibly doomed. It's a real shot in the arm for the viewers to see someone like Kambei. He puts his life on the line over a bowl of rice, keeps on fighting, and manages to stay alive until the job is finally over.

KUROSAWA I can't quite remember when it was, but one day a high-ranking member of the SDF visited the set, and he asked me who gave us advice on military strategy for *Seven Samurai.*[9] When I told him we hadn't gotten advice from anybody, he was shocked. He said that Kambei's tactics were a lot like the ones from the U.S. military's operations manual.

YAMADA Wow.

KUROSAWA He said he wanted to use that scene in a textbook, and I told him sure. You should be able to tell a story about strategy without making mistakes even without advice from experts, if you have some basic sense. In this case, in order to protect a castle, you have to make sure it has a breach—but only one. You use it to draw in the enemy, and even if your side has fewer people you can put up a good fight, right.

YAMADA Kambei definitely has that kind of sense; he doesn't let anything lead him away from what he's committed to. He's the least likely of the bunch to go off and do something rash.

INOUE He's also the kind of person who will step up in a crisis. Like when a complete stranger tells him that there's a child being held hostage inside a house by a thief, and they need his help. He shaves his head, dresses up like a monk, and saves the day. He might do something totally heroic for that one bowl of rice, but he'll step right back into everyday life when the crisis is over. Kambei has both of those sides to him, and I think that's where his appeal lies.

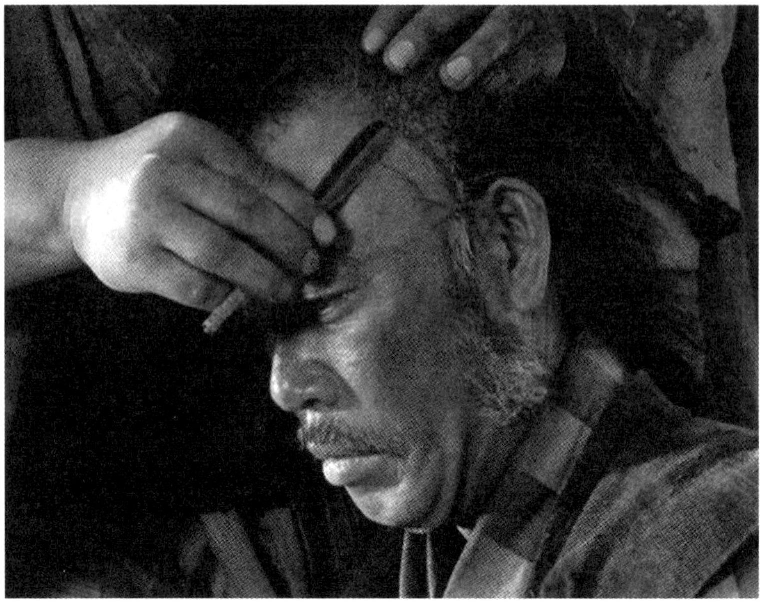

Kambei (Shimura Takeshi) has his head shaved in *Seven Samurai* to impersonate a monk.

KUROSAWA Actually, a couple of scenes in the film come from old books of *bugei-dan* (warrior stories): the one where Kambei gets his head shaved and the one where Heihachi splits wood. We rooted around and did a lot of research in collections like *A Brief Account of the Combat Arts in Our Land* (Honchō bugei shoden, 本朝武芸小伝).[10]

Scriptwriting as Mountain Climbing

INOUE It was very smart to give Kambei the backstory of an old friendship with his comrade in arms Shichirōji (Katō Daisuke).

They run into each other again by chance and pick up their old roles. Kambei is the world-weary elder, and Shichirōji is his former underling, and they meet again and face death together once more... Their reunion and the bond between them bring the whole story together.

Then there's Kyūzō, played by Miyaguchi Seiji. He plays the consummately professional samurai: someone who makes his way through the world with his sword. But he ends up getting shot to death. Such an ironic ending, almost elegiac.

Shichirōji, played by Katō Daisuke, reunites with his old comrade, Kambei (Shimura Takeshi), in *Seven Samurai*.

Kyūzō (Miyaguchi Seiji) vanquishes a would-be challenger, catching everyone's eye before he joins with the other samurai in *Seven Samurai*.

YAMADA Miyaguchi really did radiate a kind of cold-bloodedness. I wonder what made that quality come out? His face really had a quality of cold-bloodedness, almost like it was carved into him. [*laughs*]

KUROSAWA I only used Miyaguchi-kun for roles that required really strong characters. In *Sanshirō Sugata II,* he plays one of the Four Guardians of the Kōdōkan, and he was a yakuza boss in *Ikiru.*[11] His face was very convincingly cold-blooded. Of course, in real life he was quite mild-mannered. You could hardly find a person more mild-mannered than he.

YAMADA He really was an intellectual.

KUROSAWA He was really a gentle person, wasn't he? But if you look closely, you could see he has a sharp edge to him, like a razor.

INOUE His quickness was really amazing, like when he tears out of the mill in *Seven Samurai,* or when he dodges bullets.

KUROSAWA Chiaki-kun, who plays Heihachi, was an athlete who used to run track when he was younger. Everybody thought he would be the fastest in that scene. But it was no contest at all. Actually it was Miyaguchi who ended up being the fastest. I was really pleased that my gut feeling was right. He was also extremely even-keeled.

YAMADA His physique was a good fit for the part. Very trim, with a small frame, so agile.

KUROSAWA But I have to say, at the beginning everyone was kind of skeptical about him. They really wondered if he could pull off the samurai image, with his looks. They thought he was too small, like a sprite from a fairy tale. [*laughs*] I was kind of unsure... I was afraid I had miscast him, but as we were fixing his wig and costume, somehow it all started to work.

YAMADA Filmgoers must have thought, "Holy smokes, this guy is really strong." He actually had no clue about how to use a sword, though. [*laughs*] All the way through his career he played that kind of strong, steely role to perfection.

Chiaki Minoru, as Heihachi, courses across a field after the village alarm sounds, alerting everyone to the *nobushi* bandits in *Seven Samurai.*

INOUE Two of the samurai had a humorous aspect to them. One was Chiaki Minoru's Heihachi. He was killed off first, if you remember. Then next to die was Inaba Yoshio-san (Gorobei), Kambei's very capable second-in-command.

The samurai who added humor to the story were killed before the real battle started, and only the ones with military skill were left. When the scenario is solid like that it makes everything else fall into place: which characters are going to get killed and how, or how their lives are going to be spared... how you were able to write such an exquisite script is a mystery I will never figure out. Kimura Isao-san's Katsushirō and Mifune Toshiro-san's Kikuchiyo also balance each other out terrifically. The seven samurai come together, commit to the cause, fight... some of them die, some live on.

KUROSAWA Tolstoy's *War and Peace* is really at the core of that script. I don't know how many tens of times I've read it. I remember it almost to the last detail and I've picked up all kinds of things from that book. *The Rout* is in there, too, that translation of Alexander Fadeyev by Kurahara Korehito.[12]

Inaba Yoshio as Gorobei, cheerfully heckling Heihachi, who splits wood to pay his keep in *Seven Samurai.*

YAMADA The script was a collaboration with Hashimoto-san and Oguni Hideo, wasn't it?

KUROSAWA Right. We holed up in a ryōkan in Atami called Minakuchi-en and managed to write it in forty-five days.

INOUE Is forty-five days fast, for a script?

YAMADA It's fairly quick for an entertainment film. How did you decide who was going to die and where?

KUROSAWA Well, it all just kind of worked out naturally. I basically followed my gut feeling. Like, the story will get messy if we don't let this character live in this scene. Or the other way around: if we let this one live afterward it might get messy. I think we broke it into parts and took on chunks of material each day. That's basically the way we do it. It's step by step, day by day, just like when you're climbing a mountain. People say you shouldn't look at the top, you should keep looking at your feet while you plod along.

And sooner or later, before you know it, you're at the top. If you look at the summit as you're going along it gets harder.

YAMADA And if you look behind you it's scary too.

KUROSAWA Keep looking at your feet while you're walking, and before you know it you get to the peak. As you keep trudging, the wind will start to change and become refreshing. As the wind passes through, you start to sense that you're nearing the top. That's how it goes with walking in the mountains. It's just like that. You're writing the script, and at a certain point something happens: suddenly there's a mysterious momentum. It occurs to you that if you rewrite an earlier part, it will get more interesting, so you go forward at the same time you're moving backward, in a way. You don't really think about what's beyond the road right in front of you.

INOUE I know that situation well. I suspect it doesn't work if you just write with your conscious brain. Somewhere in your unconscious mind something important is lurking, and you have to pull it out. Overthinking things has led to so much bland writing. I've made that mistake myself, but fortunately there are also times when ideas come out of nowhere. When that happens the writing goes really well.

Trouble at *The Hidden Fortress*

KUROSAWA The three of us checked into a ryōkan to write, but Oguni never wrote a single word. He usually clams up for a while and reads what we give him. Then at some point he has a breakthrough.

Hashimoto and I would encourage each other: "Maybe we can't finish it in two days, and maybe we can't finish it in three days; we'll just keep pushing through and we're bound to figure it out." The other one would say something like, "Hey, you say that, but..." and we'd keep thinking and thinking. Finally, Oguni will say, "Okay, let's look at that part one more time," since "it feels like something is off somewhere in there." And voilà, we'd start the whole thing over again, and he'd go, "Ah, right there it's not really written quite right. If we straighten out this part, that part ought to flow better too."

YAMADA It's good to have one of those people around.

KUROSAWA When we were working on *The Hidden Fortress* there's a scene where they cross a checkpoint on the river. Mifune is escorting the princess, Yuki-hime. They've been traveling with the hidden gold for seven hundred kilometers, and they have to pass through the enemy checkpoint. We had a lot of back-and-forth about that part: "Shouldn't he lead her like this?" "No, that's no good," Oguni argued out loud. "How about this?" "An enemy is going to be able to figure that out, there's a sentry standing there." "That's no good, there's no way they'd get through there." "They can pass through there, which is more fun, what should we do?"... Oguni thought and thought, and suddenly he slapped the table and announced, "Got it."

INOUE Ha, ha, ha, ha.

KUROSAWA When they cross over the checkpoint, do you remember when Rokurōta pulls the piece of wood from the cart and shows it to the sentry?

YAMADA "I found something strange. You might want to look into it." [*laughs*]

KUROSAWA When he pulls out the stick and gold pokes out from the piece of wood, all hell breaks loose. The official demands to know where he found it, and Rokurōta tells him such-and-such. Rokurōta tells the official that it's his gold, and the official better give it back or he wants a reward. The official tells him to shut up and go away, and tries to kick him out (laughs). Mifune playing Rokurōta probably should have gotten out of there as fast as he could, but he keeps insisting "give it back, give it back!" all the while the official keeps yelling at him to go away.

INOUE Yes, that's right, even as the official is kicking him out, Mifune-san keeps saying, "Give it back, give it back." [*laughs*]

YAMADA It's the same thing as bringing a machine gun into an airfield. Telling them you have a pistol, then... [*laughs*]

KUROSAWA That's just what it is. An ordinary person would never come up with something like that. Oguni was magnificent, being able to come up

Mifune Toshirō as Rokurōta escorts the princess Yuki-hime (Uehara Misa) to town and through a crucial checkpoint in *The Hidden Fortress.*

with such ridiculous plot twists. These days people have lost the knack of writing scripts, but he had read all the classics, and his knack with storytelling was just unparalleled.

The biggest problem with scenario writers these days is that they don't read anything that's even a tiny bit old. When I want to give an example of a model we can use, and want to refer to a novel, they haven't read any of them. Oguni was very well read in many different areas, so he always had that kind of knowledge right at the tip of his fingers.

Kikuchiyo / Mifune

YAMADA Kikuchiyo plays a really important role in *Seven Samurai,* doesn't he? I've heard that you added his character after you'd already started writing the scenario.

KUROSAWA That's right. Initially we had imagined Mifune-kun as the Kyūzō character, but as we were writing, we decided that if the whole story were serious the movie would be boring. So we thought we'd try adding in a character who was kind of a wild card. That's how Kikuchiyo got into the picture. We thought it might be more interesting to have Mifune play that role.

YAMADA I've heard that Oguni originally wanted to have an imposter student, a "tempura" student like the ones they used to have at that time.[13] But he ended up with a "tempura" samurai. [*laughs*]

KUROSAWA Well, right, the imposter part stayed, though it ended up being a peasant posing as a samurai.

INOUE When I think about it, Kikuchiyo could have turned out to be anyone. Think about that scene where the bandits attack the mill and burn it down. Kikuchiyo rescues the baby and bursts out crying. He clutches the baby and sobs, "That's me, I was like that." His people were farmers, and he's a man who understands the farmers' feelings so much it hurts. But he can't stand the thought of being a farmer and decides to become a samurai. Though he can't quite manage to become a samurai. He's an imposter samurai, right. He also could have become one of the bandits, if things had gone differently. So, Kikuchiyo covers all three groups—peasants, samurai, and bandits. And at the end he's the one who manages to kill the head of the bandits. The imposter samurai ends up killing the bandit... when the script is that good, that kind of twist almost writes itself.

KUROSAWA There's a scene where Kikuchiyo and Kyūzō and Katsushirō go off into the mountains behind the village and ambush the bandits, right. That scene was really powerful because of how Miyaguchi-kun (Kyūzō) cuts the enemy down with his sword. But then there's Mifune. He's been hiding in a tree, and he jumps down. You wonder what he's about to do, and he starts beating up the bandit. That move also impressed me.

YAMADA That wasn't something you had planned in the scenario?

KUROSAWA Not really. In the beginning we decided that Mifune would hit him, and that's what we rehearsed. So I was kind of surprised when it changed. I thought his improvisation was really inspired. A regular samurai would never be able to beat the crap out of someone like that with his bare hands.

INOUE Mifune-san really pulled off the *fundoshi* physique quite well.[14]

YAMADA I've heard stories about women overseas getting excited at the sight of Mifune's bare bum. You're talking about the scene where he plunges into the river to catch some fish?

KUROSAWA Right. We had to rehearse that part over and over, and eventually the fish got tired and didn't flop anymore. People would have to keep catching more fish to bring him. That was really annoying for Mifune too. Lots of the cast were watching from above, but he had to dive underwater and stash the fish in his *fundoshi*. He pulled it out and let out this crazy yell, like "Look, I got it, I got it!"

YAMADA Oh, so that's what happened.

INOUE It's good that's all he pulled out of his *fundoshi*. [*laughs*]

KUROSAWA He was actually pretty stunned that the fish seemed like they'd lost consciousness. [*laughs*]

INOUE When the film came out, there were some reviews that claimed the movie made fun of the farmers. But if you look at the scene where Kikuchiyo harangues the other samurai, that interpretation is completely silly. First he goes, "Farmers are misers, weasels, and crybabies! They're mean, stupid, murderers!" and then he lets loose: "But tell me this: who turned them into such monsters? You did! You samurai did!"[15] In that one outburst he really painted a clear picture of the farmers, wouldn't you say?

KUROSAWA Their argument was that because Kurosawa comes from a samurai family, he is making fun of the peasants. I really wonder if these people watched the film all the way through. After all, at the end, doesn't Kambei even say, "The victory belongs to those peasants. Not to us"? Everybody seems to have an opinion about that last scene.

YAMADA Mifune-san's speech about the farmers leaves quite an impression.

INOUE The farmers have a stash of armor helmets that they have plundered from fallen warriors. Mifune wears one of those helmets and rages at the samurai: "But tell me this: who turned them into such monsters? You did! You samurai did!" That's such a great scene.

YAMADA That's a long stretch of dialogue. When Mifune-san played in a Tora-san movie for me, when there were four lines, he would say to me, "How am I supposed to remember four lines?" and would look really pained.

KUROSAWA The helmet that Mifune-kun is wearing in that scene was actually a National Treasure.[16] At that time, there was a man named Myochin who made helmets, and he made a lot of the helmets for the bandits. In fact, among those were two National Treasures. Afterward Maeda Seison-san got furious at me. "Kuro-san, those are National Treasures. Wearing those on a movie set is outrageous." [*laughs*]

INOUE He was completely naked, except for that National Treasure helmet on his head. [*laughs*]

KUROSAWA In that scene, Mifune said he was a peasant, too, so he asked if it was all right if snot ran out of his nose. I was flabbergasted and asked if he could really do such a thing on demand. He said he could, and then he really did it.

YAMADA Really? Snot came out of his nose?

KUROSAWA It did. Okay, give it a try anyway we decided we'll shoot it, and as Mifune was yelling in that scene, the snot came out, dripping… I was so shocked. And it was really nasty-looking.

INOUE He became an actual peasant. [*laughs*]

KUROSAWA It was really quite something, but in fact I told him I couldn't use it, and I had to cut it.

YAMADA When Misora Hibari sings "Sad Saké," doesn't she actually cry?[17] At the end of the song, tears are always trickling down her face.

INOUE She must have amazing powers of suggestion.

YAMADA But I wonder about making her nose run.

INOUE I imagine you can actually feel yourself into crying.

YAMADA Tears get in your nose… when that happens, water ends up running out of your nose. I wonder how it works with snot.

INOUE Maybe he had that stashed away in his *fundoshi* too. [*laughs*]

KUROSAWA I was really stunned. I wondered, "Who *is* this person?" From time to time he would sniffle, then while he was yelling, more of it would come out. And the whole time, he was saying his lines without a hitch. It was an amazing performance, but I couldn't use that part.

INOUE Was it gross?

KUROSAWA Nasty.

The Twilight of Samurai Actors

KUROSAWA With the rerelease this time, Tōhō threw all their weight behind it and made a new print. I feel it's really important to share with young people how many really great Japanese films exist from back in the day. Ozu-san, Naruse-san, Mizoguchi-san, Yama-san—all those pictures feel really fresh and entertaining even if you watch them today. People overseas watch them pretty regularly, but they're hard to see in Japan and that's a big problem.

YAMADA That's exactly the problem. So often I think that if they're going to make such lousy movies, they might as well just screen the old ones. In *Seven Samurai,* you can find everything that makes people enjoy going to the movies—the very essence of entertainment.

KUROSAWA When people ask me why Japanese movies have gotten so terrible, I always tell them that in the past directors could shoot the things they wanted to shoot. Recently it's gotten so you never hear that coming out of the mouths of management. The people who really understand movies are those who *make* the movies. When a director is ordered to make a certain kind of film, it's really hard to work up the energy.

INOUE When it was made, *Seven Samurai* cost 210 million yen. That's about the cost of seven regular movies…

KUROSAWA Well, it did make about a hundred times that at the box office. Management would probably say it would have made more if it had been shot on budget, but that's not true. That movie is entertaining to the exact degree that it went over budget.

INOUE In the movie, there was a village elder. At one point he says to the farmers, "If I had told you to bring ten samurai, you would have brought fifteen, so I told you to bring four. It ended up being seven, which was just right." [*laughs*]

KUROSAWA That's exactly right! But now that it's all shot and I'm looking at it now, even *I* think making it was quite an ordeal. At that time I didn't really have that impression. That's how it goes with making movies.

YAMADA There are a lot of parts of making *Seven Samurai* that you couldn't duplicate today. For one, Japanese people's physique has changed quite a lot, hasn't it? All of the actors have longer hands and feet.

KUROSAWA Yes, that is true, isn't it.

YAMADA Young people today don't really seem like the Japanese people of the past. The species has moved on.

KUROSAWA The one with the oldest-seeming Japanese physique was Katō Daisuke. [*laughs*]

YAMADA Indeed, you can't be in a *jidai-geki* unless you have a wide face.

INOUE I really love Katō Daisuke in this movie. When Shimura Takashi's Kambei says to him, "You know, we could very well die this time around," and he just grins.

YAMADA Mifune-san really had a physique that looks good with a katana, didn't he?

KUROSAWA That's because Mifune-kun really isn't that tall.

YAMADA One of these days people may have to look abroad to find the right actors to play in samurai films. [*laughs*]

KUROSAWA Well, if you get into the habit of holding your sword out properly and walking, gradually your body will get into shape. If you think about how you stand in golf, you bend your bum down just a bit and you kind of look like you're addressing the ball. Back in the day when people used to stand, they didn't completely straighten out their legs.

YAMADA No kidding. So you could tell at a glance if someone was a townsperson or a samurai, couldn't you?

INOUE Now that you mention it, everyone in *Seven Samurai* had their own particular way of running. There were a lot of scenes with people bending over and running kind of hunched-over. When they're running away, or when they're falling over after being cut down with a sword that means they also fall forward. I don't know why, but that really made an impression.

KUROSAWA Well, indeed the training that peasants and samurai received was quite different. Peasants mostly fall forward. And then sometimes they slip and fall. I'm guessing that when push came to shove, the only ones who could run properly were those who had martial arts training.

YAMADA Indeed, the form of the samurai running is quite beautiful. Especially that moment when the bandits finally arrive, when the camera captures Shimura in motion, running. That was really stunning.

INOUE There's the scene where the bandits keep coming, rampaging toward the village. I think it's when Mifune-san climbs up on the roof. And then the bandits who are riding their horses down the hill behind the village flood down, coming in for the attack. The villagers and the samurai all assemble in the town square. It's just one camera that captures all of this. It's just unbelievable.

YAMADA And the bandits were all so terrifying.

INOUE Terrifying. At that time, the conditions for making sync sound on film were not great, so there were a lot of effects used. You really couldn't tell what the bandits were saying. [*laughs*] You might have imagined they came to shake down the town for something completely different, if you misunderstood the words.

YAMADA Tani Akira was one of the bandits, wasn't he? I didn't catch that at the time.[18]

INOUE The person who held the rifle was Takahara Toshio, wasn't it?[19]

YAMADA The guy that was whacked by Mifune-san, yes. There were really so many incredible actors. People like Tōno Eijirō-san, Yamagata Isao-san, and Kamiyama Sōjin-san had small parts and made their cameos.[20]

INOUE What was really interesting was Kyūemon's grandmother, right. She comes out with a *kuwa* [garden hoe] and kills one of the bandits who had been captured. When I skimmed over the cast list, I didn't even notice her name. It turns out she's a resident of an assisted living home in Suginami, in Tokyo. I heard that when she got cast, she insisted that because she was going to be on film, she didn't want to wear just any old clothes, she wanted to look nice onscreen. [*laughs*]

KUROSAWA The elderly people in the movie were all excellent. When I'd block out their parts and tell them how it would go, they would just roll with it. Also, they knew how to socialize and have a good time; they seemed to like the bentos; they knew how to enjoy themselves.

INOUE That older woman wasn't really able to say her lines, so the assistant director, Hirosawa Ei'ichirō, talked to her a little bit about her life and found out that her close relatives had been killed in an air raid by a B-29. That made me realize, oh, that's what she must have been feeling like. So when the time came to go after the bandits during the shoot, what she actually said when she attacked them was, "My house was demolished by a B-29."

YAMADA She just couldn't bring herself to say, "My house was demolished by bandits," could she? [*laughs*] So in the end the dialogue got dubbed in.

KUROSAWA Right, that was a little impossible. To use *rakugo* language, that woman was like a *chōchin* baba, a *karakasa* baba.[21] Her wrinkles were quite amazing. I think she passed away shortly after. She was so good, I was so surprised. The extras were just as good as the professional actors. They could do things so naturally.

YAMADA To find the older person who appears in the illusion scene in my film *My Sons* (1991) we also looked for someone in a care home, just like *Seven Samurai*. We tested someone, but in the end it didn't work out. He was actually a former actor who had a distinguished career. We should do our recruiting there all the time; the actors are always still working.

The Danger Level of Katsushirō and Kimura Isao

INOUE I always really loathed Kimura Isao's Katsushirō character. I don't know... it's something about his face.

YAMADA Ha, ha, ha, ha.

INOUE There's a scene in part 2, where Miyaguchi Seiji goes off by himself to the bandits' hideout and steals a musket. And then when he's lying down, taking a nap, Kimura Isao stands next to him. Tears well up in his eyes and he says, "You are... a magnificent person." It's the beauty and reverence on his face that does it to me. It's a kind of beauty that eclipses even feminine beauty. It's the dangerous beauty of a man who loves another man. [*laughs*]

KUROSAWA That was a great expression on his face. I was really overbearing with that scene. I kept telling him how to do it till he got it right.

YAMADA Just as he says, Miyaguchi-san makes a wonderful samurai.

KUROSAWA There's a scene very much like that in Fadeyev.[22] The young, very green samurai is quite clearly infatuated with the older leader. That's when he says, "Magnificent." I wrote that younger guy's adoration for the older guy into the story from the very beginning.

INOUE While everyone else is obsessed with getting ready for battle, Kimura Isao-san is off doing other things, like picking flowers for the girl Shino from the village. I was like, what are you doing?!? Is this the time for picking flowers? Get moving! [*laughs*] But as I watched it over and over, I gradually started to like Kimura Isao-san.

YAMADA I get it. At the beginning you feel a kind of resistance to him, to Kimura.

KUROSAWA One night, the crew were all drinking together. I had somebody bring Isao's wig over, and everybody tried it on. Nakai-san, the

Katsushichirō (Kimura Isao) stumbles on his eventual lover Shino, disguised as a boy, as he strays from the group in *Seven Samurai.*

cinematographer, put it on and started dancing like the monkey in a *saru-mawashi* act.[23] Non-chan (Nogami Teruyo) looked like a little kid from an Edo-period temple school. I tried putting it on, too, and everyone fell over laughing. No matter who put on that wig, it was not flattering. The only one it flattered was Isao, and I told him he had a lot of nerve. At that time, he was already heading toward middle age, but it made him pass for much younger.

INOUE By then he was already over thirty, wasn't he.

KUROSAWA Right. He could skip through the woods like a teenager, on his way back from meeting Shino in the forest—and be totally convincing. It's a mysterious thing, that face of his. The wig of the young samurai fits him strangely well.

INOUE In that part, the music that dramatizes him is also interesting, isn't it. The music as Shino [Tsushima Keiko] works up her courage to seduce Kimura Isao on the eve of the big battle is a tango. It's tango-ing along, when the camera focuses more on him, and a flute comes in… [*laughs*]

YAMADA You're absolutely right: that hair doesn't look good on anyone else. The topknot looks best on someone with a long face like a kabuki actor. I wonder how that all went in the old days. Round-faced people must have always thought they got dealt a bad hand. [*laughs*]

INOUE Katsushirō apprentices himself to the leader he admires, Kambei, has his first experiences with a lover, and even kills an enemy. He becomes a full-blown adult. So in a way this movie is maybe also a coming-of-age story for Kimura Isao.

YAMADA What about the way that out of seven samurai, four of them die, all shot with a rifle. Didn't you think of having them killed by sword, at some point?

KUROSAWA I didn't want them killed in a swordfight with the bandits. I definitely did not want that to happen. I thought it would be cleaner to kill them off quickly.

INOUE That choice would be satisfying to the viewers too. These days it's common knowledge but when we were making the film, it came as a surprise to us to hear a *bang* sound after someone fell over. Which is to say the bullet was faster than the speed of sound.

KUROSAWA At the Venice Film Festival people told me it was weird that there was a sound delay with the shooting, but actually I did that on purpose, it wasn't a mistake. Shooting from that distance the sound actually *is* delayed a little bit.

YAMADA Especially the scene where Miyaguchi-san gets shot, when his body kind of staggers forward and falls in slow motion. It feels like you hear the sound as it follows his fall.

INOUE What you're talking about is the truth of the story, really. Meaning—not the truth of how physics works.

Even a Horse Knows Who's Boss

YAMADA The last scene—the battle where it is raining—leaves a really strong impression, so it *seems* especially long, but actually it's not, is it?

KUROSAWA Right. We shot it in roughly a week, but it was a nightmare to film. You go out in the morning, right. As soon as you get out there it's raining. You're sopping wet from morning till night. I was buried up to my chest in the mud, and as soon as I would yell "Cut," everybody would run over and pull me out of the mud. All of my toenails died because I got soaked in the mud every day. They all turned black and fell off.

INOUE That's an action scene that stands up to the Western, the Hollywood ones. Was that on your mind as you were shooting this one?

KUROSAWA People in Hollywood don't really have experience shooting in the rain. It rains so rarely in California you can count the days on your fingers. I *did* think that shooting in the rain might be a style that would be hard to imitate.

YAMADA Yes, I see. In American movies, you see the sun shining even when it's raining. [*laughs*]

KUROSAWA Getting back to the mud—in those days there was nothing like synchronized sound. During the battle scene all that sound was done in real time and dubbed in later. In the dubbing room, we would all crowd around a big tin plate that made for good sound, getting it all dirty, and the effects guys would be working like crazy. People would be running around, and the guys who were doing the horse sounds would be on horses galloping around. When the dubbing was all over, I was wiped out, and I fell asleep in the mixing room. At some point the studio people from Tōhō came in, and they yelled at the sound guys. They told them the set was a disaster and demanded to know what was going on. What happened was there was dirt splashed all over the screen; it was completely covered in mud. They had no idea I was there, right. I stuck my head out to say good morning, and they were all embarrassed, falling all over themselves to praise the work.

YAMADA The sound effects guys had a really hard time, didn't they? Day after day, they were totally covered in mud.

KUROSAWA Mud, and nothing but mud. It was quite a scene.

INOUE Your production went further with the effects than any other movie before—not just the effects, but especially that.

Kurosawa directs on the muddy, sodden set of *Seven Samurai*. Courtesy of Kurosawa Production Co., Ltd.

YAMADA The level of the typical movie didn't really get more sophisticated than the sound of high heels clicking on the cement. [*laughs*] We ran into a famous effects guy when we entered Shōchiku. He would play a flute to get the bird sounds, and if you said, "Hey Roku-san, I need a horse," he would do a horse whinny.

KUROSAWA I got quite a surprise when I went out to Shōchiku. It was in the mountains, and I could hear birds singing. I thought it was tape-recorded, but a funny old man came out, making little bird sounds.

YAMADA That must have been Roku-san. [*laughs*] People would tell me that his "dog barking off in the distance" was better than the real thing. At that time, Shōchiku was mostly making *sewa-mono* with *wagoto*-style acting.[24] The kinds of stories we see in *Seven Samurai* would be unimaginable, with all their rawness and period details. Hirasawa-san, the assistant director, said they worked so hard on the production they had nothing left to give, and everyone was deeply moved. Each different studio has its own kind of traditions, don't they?

KUROSAWA Yes, right. Shōchiku doesn't really use *aragoto*-type characters. But on the other hand, if you want to shoot in a *yashiki* estate or something, they are totally set up. They are real pros in their own domain, and that's where they can make your job easier.

YAMADA We were told to stay away from horses and boats. [*laughs*] Sometimes the horses don't listen to what you tell them, so they can be a pain.

INOUE Shōchiku wants you to avoid all the annoying things. [*laughs*]

KUROSAWA With horses, you can only use them a certain number of hours each day. If you try to push them beyond that, they get stubborn and refuse to move.

YAMADA Really.

KUROSAWA If people try to push them beyond their limits, they just balk. A horse can get up the most speed when it's going uphill on a gentle slope. It's easy to fly along, and not scary for them. If they can see the descent in front of them—then they get spooked.

Out in the fields there is grass growing, but there also might be lots of stumps around. If that's the case, the horses will refuse to run.

INOUE Hirosawa, the assistant director, had some good stories about horses. As the shoot got longer and longer, the horses learned which humans they should pay attention to. So after half a year, when Kurosawa-san would say "Start!" the horses would be all ready to work. [*laughs*]

KUROSAWA When I would say, "Yo—I," the horses would start walking in place.

INOUE The horses, they understand.

KUROSAWA They're quick to pick things up. And then when the shoot was over, after the battle, everyone gathered and left the set together, right. The horses lined up behind each other in a row. And when it came time to pass by me, they gave me the side-eye and left the long way around. [*laughs*]

Postwar Democracy and the *Jidai-geki*

INOUE When I first saw *Seven Samurai,* I couldn't really put it into words why, but I was really moved. Those of us in our generation came of age under militarism. The war ended, democracy came in, there was a new Constitution, and suddenly the world was full of peace. It was the heyday of democracy, and though we were children, we felt the loss of a world. At that time, we clearly understood that the village elder who owned that mill—Gisaku, his name was—was the kind of person who would be the future of the Japanese nation. Which is to say—he was someone who was usually a bit set off from the world, just doing his thing, but when there's an emergency, people in the village depend on him. He's got no money, and he's got no real power, but in time of crisis all the knowledge he's picked up through life experience is suddenly relevant. When the whole world around him is in crisis, there is Japan, way off in the East with this amazing Constitution, to act as a compass. *Seven Samurai* clearly conveyed that we ought to listen to the opinions of those people who had those ideals and were protecting the Constitution—living their basic, honest lives. I felt like that elder millowner Gisaku embodied the way we ought to live in postwar Japan.

YAMADA Yes. After I saw the movie, I distinctly remember feeling that something complicated and new was in the works.

KUROSAWA One time I heard from a moviegoer who made me furious. A letter came from a woman who said she was upset I had released such a cruel movie. She said that she was on her way to study in America, and if this film were released it would damage her reputation as a Japanese person. Oh, I was mad! Look at the Westerns, don't they mow down the Indians?!? The bandits are just a bunch of gangsters. What could possibly be wrong with battling against them? I asked her. I was so mad I was shaking, and I wrote back a letter that was about two centimeters thick.

Then there was the time the general secretary of the Socialist Party, Wada Hiroo, came to the set. His assistant said to me that the bandits are people too.

INOUE You mean human rights? [*laughs*]

KUROSAWA That was the implication. I just yelled out, "What are you talking about?!? Do you really think I am saying that these bandits are good people?!?" I said most people think thieving and raiding are bad things. I told them it's a *jidai-geki,* so it's pretty much a given that there is going to be fighting. When I asked what they wanted me to leave out, this Secretary Wada told his assistant to shut up. This kind of thinking is really dangerous. These people in the film are killed for a reason. I guess that kind of thinking was popular at that time.

YAMADA That seems pretty typical of that time, for someone to have that kind of opinion.

INOUE But I suspect Japanese people worked through a lot of the arguments about killing people by having conversations like that. People who thought that way, versus people who thought it was wrong. *Seven Samurai* made people able to have that kind of debate about violence. Wasn't that one of the reasons it had such an impact in Japanese popular life?

KUROSAWA In some of the reviews in America, people said I was "greedy" as a director, because I throw all kinds of things into a movie. That was fair since that film was really crammed with all sorts of plot points. Until that film came along, the kind of film that was in favor had more of an *ochazuke* style—spare and clean, without a lot of fussy ingredients.[25] I'm not like that at all. I make works that are like broiled unagi, with a nice piece of cutlet on top, and on top of that, a mound of curry, so that just looking at it you're full and you can't absorb any more. There is a generous variety of ingredients thrown in, but despite that, it doesn't feel too heavy.

INOUE Which is to say that the basic frame of the film is quite simple. But the details are quite rich in substance. I think that's an important point. If the main story is complicated, but the details are not fleshed out, what you end up with is just a message movie, and it alienates people. I think those of us who saw *Seven Samurai* shared the experience of seeing something very rich on the screen, set within a basically simple story.

KUROSAWA First you plan out the overall structure in a quick-and-dirty way, and get it set up. Without those first broad strokes, you won't be able to fully sketch in the fine details, right. If you put all your energy into the details, the whole thing will be too loaded up to hold its shape.

YAMADA If the trunk is nice and sturdy the branches can spread out quite far without throwing things off balance.

INOUE In my case, I often have so many branches that the whole tree falls over. You try pruning a little here, and then if it doesn't stabilize, pruning a little over there. Sometimes you end up pruning so much that you chop away the whole tree. [*laughs*]

YAMADA If the crew pays too much attention to detail it can get frustrating. I'm paying more attention to the big picture, and you would think I wouldn't care about the details. That's not actually the case. But it's my job to make a sturdy trunk, so to speak, and since they are in charge of the branches and leaves, I prefer to leave the details to the crew, including all the little things that are invisible on screen.

KUROSAWA You're right. There's nothing left for your crew to do if you don't delegate the work. When everyone understands the rhythm of the work, the job is really satisfying, actually interesting. When your crew looks at a picture, they have eyes only for those kinds of details. They get really attached to seeing their work—"Oh, we did such a good job there!" [*laughs*]. Unless you have that kind of satisfaction with what you've made, you can't do your job, and then when you remember what that satisfaction feels like, you want to do it even better. So at some point someone always asks me how I managed to keep my energy up for so long. I tell them I can't just will myself to keep it up. The work itself has to be interesting, and if it's interesting, I said, then I can work on it forever.

Superfans

INOUE Have you finished writing your next script?

KUROSAWA Yes. It's a secret, though.

INOUE Now that you say that, I'm very curious to know what it's about.

KUROSAWA Oh—listen to what happened when we were in preproduction for *Seven Samurai*. An actor mentioned to me that someone from Tōhō seemed to be very enthused about the movie, and the studio exec told him there was a good part coming up. So he called me directly to thank me, and he said his wife was also very excited about this prospect. I was really in a bind. I had zero intention of using that guy in the role, but I also didn't want to embarrass him. The relationship between an actor and director is really delicate.

I have a lot of wild stories about strangers who have… interesting expectations. Once I got a letter from a guy I'd never met. He insisted I act as the matchmaker to an actress he was infatuated with and wanted to marry, things like that. When you brush them off, you get a lot of blowback—"What are you doing you asshole!" "You aren't listening to what I'm saying!"—things like that.

INOUE That sounds wild.

KUROSAWA It's a mess. One time I was really surprised when a guy introduced himself to me as Andrei Bolkonsky. He had a proper name card and everything.

INOUE Isn't that the main character in *War and Peace*? [*laughs*]

KUROSAWA I was doing a Q-and-A at a theater in San Francisco or somewhere, and a Japanese guy suddenly came up to me. That was Andrei Bolkonsky.[26] He told me that it was impossible that I didn't use a gifted actor such as himself in my films—and insisted that I put him in a film. He made sure to tell me that it was for my own good.

INOUE He sounds like he must have been very taken with you. Clearly, he adored you. His wording is a little hard to take, though. [*laughs*]

YAMADA I completely understand those people who get really stuck on you and hover around obsessively, if that's what you're talking about. I have to admit I did this as a student, mooning around in front of the house of someone I looked up to.

INOUE Yes, I was the same way. [*laughs*]

KUROSAWA There's another one who actually left a good impression afterward. Long ago, when we lived in a tiny house in Chitose-funabashi, one day someone came to the door and asked, "Is Kurosawa-sensei there?" "No, today he's at the office." "Oh really?" He looked so happy, and then turned around and left. Most people are disappointed when they find out you're not there, but this guy just looked happy and left. Then one day, I ran smack into him in the entryway of our house. My wife whispered in my ear that it was that guy, and I asked him to come in and asked what he was here for. He started off, "Actually, it's a really dumb story, but..."

He said he had made a bet with a friend. About whether you could walk naked from Kyōbashi to Shinbashi without anyone stopping you. They did rock-paper-scissors and this guy won, so his friend had to follow through. And his friend actually *did* walk naked all the way up the main street of Ginza, all the way to Shinbashi. Nobody got in his way as he was walking down the street, and he said his friend got all the way to Shinbashi. Of course, there's probably no connection, but after a while that friend got tuberculosis and died.

INOUE Ohh.

KUROSAWA Before he died, the guy's friend told the guy that he had done such an embarrassing stunt that he wouldn't be able to die in peace unless his friend—my visitor—did something really embarrassing, something a lot of people saw. Something intensely embarrassing. So, he ordered the guy to appear in a movie, and not just any old movie, something by Mizoguchi or Kurosawa. The guy thought about it for a bit, and Mizoguchi is older than me, and I guess he must be more intimidating, so that's why he picked me. His friend wrote it up in his will and then he died, so this guy thought he had to follow through on the promise and that's how he got to my house. So when he was told I wasn't here, that's why he looked so happy. Then when I did accidentally run into him, he said he was really flustered. So when he asked if he could appear in one of my films, and I said no, it doesn't work that way, that's why he looked so happy and walked away. [*laughs*]

YAMADA That's a wild story.

KUROSAWA He looked totally upbeat; he was smiling, and he said thanks and went on his way. He had done what he came to do.

INOUE That story could make a pretty good movie.

KUROSAWA He was a good guy, that guy. He put his heart into it. There are so many weird stories, and out of all of those, his is the most interesting.

Pure Films of Broken Nature (1990)

Dialogue with Inoue Hisashi

In a second conversation with fiction-writer/playwright Inoue Hisashi, Kurosawa reflects on his recognition at the Academy Awards. The conversation also features Inoue's reading of Kurosawa's *Dreams* in terms of the elements it shares with Noh theater. It includes real dreams, cutout episodes of *Dreams* that were never made, and a shaggy-dog story from Kurosawa about why film is like a dog.

INOUE At some point—I don't know whether to call it the middle of the night or dawn this morning—I watched the ceremony for the sixty-second Academy Awards (1990) and I felt very proud. You received a Lifetime Achievement Award, which I think is only given out to one person about once every ten years. I had the same feeling you have when you see your country's flag on display for the Olympics, but for me it was like a hundred or a thousand times that, the feeling of "finally a Japanese winner!!!" I think people who came up in our generation who have watched your works in real-time felt a particular thrill from this bit of good fortune. I was so delirious with happiness that I couldn't get to sleep until almost seven in the morning. Honestly, I am so grateful to you.

KUROSAWA Oh no, it was all my pleasure to do. That was after all a gift of friendship. As they see it from the Academy, I'm over eighty years old, and over the years I've had a chance to meet many people in the industry. It was those people I owe for all this celebration, I think.

INOUE Of course, I'm sure that plays a part in it, but in any case, your works themselves are really something to be reckoned with. It's kind of tacky to put it this way, but there aren't that many Japanese people overseas who are called "sama," with the honorific, instead of the same "san" that normal people get. Kurosawa-san, you are physically bigger than the guys who introduced you, Steven Spielberg and George Lucas. Their attitude was super reverential, and the atmosphere felt like a break from all the competition of the awards. It was almost like the two of them were greeting their former teacher, wasn't it?

KUROSAWA Young people like Lucas and Spielberg have a kind of awe for people who in Japanese we would call "sensei." Our ages are quite far apart, and that generation feels like they could be my children; those two as well. When I appeared like that in front of John Ford, I was really formal and on my best behavior, way back then. As we age and younger people step in, that's how it goes, right.

INOUE Around when you got that award, wasn't there a lot of popular sentiment against Japan? In America Japanese people were especially unpopular. Given that the pillars of American popular culture are baseball and the movies, I'm imagining the effect of one unassuming Japanese man getting such an honor at a once-a-year event in Hollywood, capital of the movies. That's the effect it had on me anyway. Good grief, I must sound like a pure Japanese nativist! At the same time, I hoped you wouldn't be the only Japanese person up there. You and your work are a treasure for the whole world. I also hoped that one of these days there would be more than one Japanese person on stage; for the first time in a long time, I had a really satisfying evening.

KUROSAWA But wait a minute—in my opinion, we'd be a lot better off if young directors would be more active about getting into the international arena. If they did, they'd make more friends in the industry, and even if financing didn't come from Japan, they could find a lot of support with allies from elsewhere. There are networks of film people all over the world.

INOUE Elia Kazan once said famously that film is a lingua franca, and through your appearance on that show we could see it's actually true. The audience all got up and gave you a furious standing ovation. They didn't hold back because of your race or nationality. It came across very vividly how a shared love for cinema translates into a love for humanity. And the vehicle for that strong sense of passion was you, Kurosawa-san.

KUROSAWA People have called Audie Bock, the woman who was doing interpretation for me, "Kurosawa's Foreign Minister." When it was all over, she congratulated me. She said she had never seen such an enthusiastic audience at the awards.

The Real Meaning of "Only in the Movies"

INOUE Spielberg and Lucas must have been so nervous on that day.

KUROSAWA We had a rehearsal the day before the main event. At the end of the introduction Steven was supposed to introduce me by my name, "Akira Kurosawa," but he forgot to. I was sitting there in the audience watching, and my son, Hisao, had to nudge me and say, "Get up!" So I got up and went to the stage, and I really just wanted to reassure him, to not be nervous.

Spielberg always wears a baseball cap and tennis shoes, right. Lucas is—in a word—shy. He doesn't generally make appearances at big events like that, and the papers the next day were making fun of them because for once they appeared in black tie: their formal dress was out of character, given their usual casualness.

INOUE I learned a lot about the format of the show, too, which was interesting. It was really lively and had a style, and—I mean this in a good way—it was kind of in-your-face about its authority, in a very polished way. It started off with the head of the Academy introducing Spielberg and Lucas. Then the two of them introduced you. It was enjoyable to watch, and their expression of the gravitas of the honorary Oscar was so elegant.

KUROSAWA Also, in the middle of the live broadcast commercials are cut in, right. During the commercials, we would go out front, for a smoke or something. While we went out for a break the network cut in a series of shots of people sitting in the audience. And those wouldn't all be the same people: they would have on deck different shots of lots of different types of people dressed up in different ways—older people, young women, Black people. When people would leave their seats, there would be a signal. Someone would call out a number, and people would come to fill the empty seats. It doesn't give a good impression to show empty seats on TV, right.

INOUE I imagine if viewers see empty seats, they check out and get bored, too, so the network wants to avoid that. The presenters throw in a lot of jokes, as well. As Billy Crystal was presenting one award, just as he was about to announce the winner and you could feel the tension, instead he launched into a monologue: when he was a child, he was never allowed to stay up late and watch TV. What?!? you think, and then he tells you that the only time he was allowed to stay up late was to watch the Academy Awards, till four in the morning. So he thought it would be a good idea to have the Academy Awards every night. This would never go over if *I* were to tell it. These sorts of jokes were scattered here and there throughout the ceremony; the direction was really very good.

Lucas and Spielberg did a really deep introduction of your works, touching on almost all of them. They said that when they were gearing up to start a new film, they would watch most of your films. They would gather their own thoughts about their current project while watching yours. This shows how they both believe your films contain something fundamental to cinema itself. Not novels, not theater: a cinema sensibility, a cinema beauty, a cinematic sensory world that jumps out at you from the screen. I've heard people say that being able to immerse yourself in that kind of essentially filmic experience can make you rethink all your ideas about what cinema really is.

KUROSAWA That's exactly the question that's most on my mind, all the time—how to get to that place of pure cinematic possibility. The reason why it absolutely has to be a film, right. It's really a crapshoot whether a work you've poured so much effort into will actually become a "film" or not.

Here's an interesting story for you. Shiga Naoya has a short story called "Bear," and there is a passage where the narrator's son appears. That part is an essay the son writes about a dog called Bear. The son writes, "My dog looks like a bear, but this part looks like a tanuki, and this part looks like a *kitsune*," and he keeps saying how many things his dog looks like, on and on.

And then at the very end he says, "Well, actually he's a dog, so he looks most of all like a dog." [*laughs*] And that's also how I think about film. Sometimes in films there are elements like literature, like theater, parts that are like painting, musical elements—there are all sorts of elements. But, well, actually it's a movie.[1]

I don't actually even know yet what film really is. I'm not really a theoretical person, so it's hard to give a theoretical explanation. I just know that when I shoot a film, sometimes it just comes to me that: "Now that, *that* is film." When it all comes together, I get so excited. And sadly, in each film, maybe I will have that feeling two or three times, and I will mostly end up feeling: well, not quite. Here and there I might think, "Oh yes, that is cinema," and that is the feeling that I am always going for, even if the times it comes through are really few and far between.

Noh into Film

INOUE I saw your new film, *Dreams,* and I was really moved. I don't really know where to start, but in your movies, I think there's almost nothing accidental in them—your input as a director can be felt in every little corner. You said that if you're going to make a film in color, you want to raise color to an expressive level, not make the scenery a copy of a realistic landscape. The arrangement of color on the screen is highly calculated and lush, almost painfully so. In *Dreams,* I was especially taken by the way you treated the water and the soil. For example, the way you shoot the soil. *Dreams* is made up of eight different episodes. In the first one, "Sunshine Through the Rain," the character—we'll call him "you"—is about five. He goes out into the forest and wends his way between the immense cedar trees in the forest. There's a road where you can see the soil, which is moist, and full of organic material, and looks like it would grow anything you planted in it. And then you go back home, and then next time you go out into an open field. The road opens into a field covered in flowers. And there again, the soil is rich, fertile.

Soil comes up twice in the second episode, "The Peach Orchard." The first time is when you are a little older, and you run after a young girl on a path into a bamboo forest, and that soil is just magnificent. Soil made up of bamboo leaves that have fallen and decomposed for who knows how many years. These days you can buy compost for your garden at any nursery, but if you wanted to get your hands on something like bamboo forest soil, you would really have to pay a fortune. It's really high-quality soil, the kind you'd grow prize crops in. In contrast, the soil behind the boy you see as you look down from the terraced steps in the peach orchard is really a barren, sickly kind of color. When you see the contrast between these two soils, you can almost physically feel that the relation between the soil and the trees is broken—even though it's a beneficial relationship that should be good for humans too.

In the third episode, "The Blizzard," the snow is the main character. There's that moment when the mountains suddenly break through, and you start to feel some hope for the characters.

The fourth episode is a story about you as you return from the war. The soldiers who served under you appear to you as ghosts—Private Noguchi and soldiers from the third platoon, who in "real" life have all died. I was stunned by the sound of the soldiers' boots, their rhythm and pounding that echo out from that big tunnel. Kurosawa films are known for their stunning use of sound effects, but in this scene the echo of the military boots transcended just being sound and took on its own momentum as basically the symbolic sound of war.

KUROSAWA I think that scene might be some sort of new world record; it's a long shot of about sixteen minutes. The magazine of the camera will only hold a thousand feet (ten minutes), right. As you're watching that scene, as you hear that thumping, bit by bit you can feel your chest tightening up, you know. We needed duration to do what that scene should do. And if we didn't shoot it in just one long shot, that kind of power wouldn't come out. About eight minutes into it, I had to yell "stop," and scurry around to change the magazine, yell "start" again, and pick up where we left off shooting. All in all, it came out to sixteen minutes and ten seconds. We needed the heaviness of that duration to ground the story.

On top of that we were shooting around dusk. Which means that there's no way you can get two days alike with the same shooting conditions. The reflections on the clouds, whatever—there are so many things that can vary, right. So I just decided to get it out of the way in one day, in one shot, and that's how it all happened.

INOUE Kurosawa-san, you've been watching Noh for—I don't know how many decades. I had the feeling that all that experience came to fruition all at once in that dream in the "Tunnel" episode. Terao Akira played "you" in that one. He's a traveler, rather like the *waki* character from a Noh play. Private Noguchi and the Third Platoon are the vengeful ghosts, the spirits of the dead, which is to say the *shite*. The tunnel is the *hashigakari,* and that ground underfoot, with all that pooled stagnant water like you used to see right after the war, is the stage. That telephone pole is the pine trees. The concrete in the back, the steep bank looks like the *matsubame*.[2]

KUROSAWA [*smiles*]

INOUE If you will indulge me a bit more, that episode is like *mugen* Noh. It folds in *mugen* Noh into the midst of a dream. This is your cleverness, like a vast and wonderful joke. On top of that is the sense of tension you can feel throughout the whole episode. Honestly, I think that is the standout scene out of all of your movies. Many accomplished people have challenged themselves to make contemporary Noh, and each and every one of them has failed. This episode alone is the only exception. I wracked my brains to think about how that scene could have stirred up such a tension, but hearing your remarks just now, the puzzle is solved. That unprecedented long take has got to be one reason for it.

I just got all excited riffing on this... so as the episodes continue, the earth gradually gets worse. In the episode with van Gogh (the fifth, "Crows"), the earth appears fertile and alive, but in the sixth and seventh ("Mount Fuji in Red" and "The Weeping Demon"), the earth that appears is completely awful, more like dirt. Then in the last episode ("Village of the Watermills"), once again the earth—the soil, underfoot and in the landscape—that appears is wonderful. It's very appealing. Though the film is made in an omnibus style that allows for a lot of variation, your stamp as the director can be seen throughout the whole film. It seems my comment has also become something of a "long take"—my apologies!

KUROSAWA "The Weeping Demon," the seventh episode, was set on Miyakejima, in the lava. It's really rough terrain; you can hardly even walk. It's so bad that it can take several hours just to go a little way. That road we shot, we made it from soil we mixed with the ashes of Mount Fuji.

Earth, Water, Death

INOUE I also wanted to bring out how there's some element of death mixed into all the episodes. In the first episode, the mother tells "you" that you can't come back in the house because you have seen the *kitsune* wedding, and she tells you to go beg the forgiveness of the *kitsune,* then slams the gate.[3] As she closes the gate, she casts you, and us, out into the world. The first episode makes this moment into a symbol, a challenge. It suggests that people are always perpetrators with respect to nature; they're only a minus and never a plus. I felt like she was trying to get the message into the boy's head so that he can respond to it later in life: telling him, you have to live by facing up to those forces like the *kitsune,* or nature, while you're constantly repairing the damage to them, basically for your entire life.

KUROSAWA Well, when you're a child sometimes it's raining even when the sun shines. When that happens, you want to go outside and play. It's fun, so you don't even care if your kimono gets all wet. And then your mother scolds you, right. You're looking forward to the *kitsune* wedding, while knowing that if you see it something awful is going to happen. They actually told us that at the time. So you end up having a dream where you see the *kitsune* wedding. It was so scary like that. You always wondered what you would do if you happened on it by accident.

INOUE In the last shot, you see a rainbow on the other side of the field of flowers. Underneath the rainbow is the *kitsune* village. The boy who is "you" has to run to reach it, but he's so young he's not able to run that far. From the boy's point of view, that gap is the distance and the depth he will cover over the course of his life. It's a really bewitching opening, kind of an invitation, isn't it? A wonderful way to start.

KUROSAWA The rainbow was thanks to ILM's special effects. But the mountain in the background didn't end up looking like a real Japanese mountain. Fuji-san is a strange kind of mountain, isn't it—with its flat top. But if you look closely at that shot, the summit is actually kind of jagged. When you think about it, there's really no other mountain with a shape like Fuji-san anywhere in the world. When an American special effects artist designs the silhouette of a mountain, it just doesn't look like Fuji-san. To my eye, the mountain on the other side of the rainbow ended up looking like an American mountain, and it looked out of place. In the end after talking back and forth we sorted it out.

INOUE That procession of *kitsune* winding through the tall cedar trees was quite delightful, wasn't it? The choreography, the makeup were both superb.

KUROSAWA The makeup design for the *kitsune* took forever to figure out. Maybe half a year. At first we tried out a vinyl-like mask, so that the actors' faces looked transparent, but in reality you could subtly see the human face through the mask. And on the face itself we used a kind of exaggerated makeup, which made for a really interesting effect. But the masks ended up looking shiny when we used lighting. So that version ended up not working, and in the end we had to give up the mask and allow the human realities to show through—things like facial hair poking out here and there—and we made it work.

INOUE The second episode uses the setting of the peach orchard to call out how humans are constantly doing damage to nature, even killing it. It suggests that behind the seeming joy of the peach festival pageantry lies a mysterious force. Something completely apart from the doings of the child himself, more like the power humans possess, like some kind of karma, to move things toward death.

And in tension with that, in the third episode we see the power the natural world itself holds over death.

We soon forget the toll war has taken, and we casually consign the dead to an existence of numbers and statistics. But the fourth episode is the terrifying and sad story of those statistical soldiers who wander the world in real form. The fifth is the story of when "you" meet Vincent van Gogh. Van Gogh is going mad grappling with his impending death, but the scene is shot in the bright sunlight.

The sixth and seventh episodes are kinds of *jigoku-e,* Buddhist hell pictures, that suggest that if we keep annihilating nature at the rate we are, there is really no alternative for humans but to die this horrible kind of death.[4] The story in the last, eighth, episode is basically the philosophy of an ideal, the most human kind of death. There's one line of dialogue that goes, "Humans are really just one part of nature," which means that since they are, after all, one part of nature, they should have a kind of dignified death that is its own kind of joy, satisfaction. Kurosawa-san, before you made *Dersu Uzala,* you said, "I want people everywhere to know the story of Dersu, who managed to live in tune with nature. In my view, people have got to be more deferential to nature. Humans themselves are one part of nature, and they need to come around to living in tune with nature. If we destroy nature, we too are destroyed. So there is a wealth of things we can learn from Dersu." The village we see here is, in fact, a Dersu village, no?[5]

Kurosawa-san, I think you have been thinking about death all along in your own way. In the dream where the old man talks about a good death

Ryū Chishū leads a funeral procession, celebrating a long life well lived in the last episode of *Dreams.*

being "living to a ripe old age," I think we hear your own view of life and death. The joy we see in the funeral that is in the eighth episode, is that not the ideal kind of death for a human being?

KUROSAWA Well, in fact during production I asked one of the staff who was working away behind the scenes which part of the film he liked best. He said that the part he liked best was the part in the "Village of the Watermills" sequence, the eighth episode, where the old man in the village says, "Some say life is hard. That's just talk. In fact, it's good to be alive. It's exciting." He very much agreed with the philosophy of living intensely while you can. I thought it was just great that a person who did his incredibly important behind-the-scenes job would see the film in that way.

INOUE That eighth episode seems like the dream you said *you* experienced, while it also seems like a dream *all* of us actually experience. A personal dream extends out to be a dream everyone has. And that's why that funeral is such a moving scene.

KUROSAWA In that scene, you might remember that there are a lot of elderly women. Those same actresses played in *Seven Samurai* when they were young. [*laughs*] When I saw them again after such a long time, we all gave each other a big hug, and I realized that we've all grown old.

INOUE The part in the first episode where the mother scolds the boy and tells him to "apologize for all you are worth" to the *kitsune* brings all the episodes together into one story. If you interpret that to mean "be as close as you can to nature, for if you don't you will suffer a most horrible death." It's an unsettling but wonderful story. I've never seen a story like that on the screen before.

In earlier works of yours, I've noticed a pattern: a character or characters will have very strong personalities, and because of that they will clash with some kind of force or other, and a struggle will unfold. This time the story is a little different, isn't it? Earth, water, and then death. A set of things that shouldn't be a story actually resolves into a story. That's really brilliant; I take my hat off to you.

The Interface Between

KUROSAWA Dostoevsky has an interesting saying about dreams. He says dreams are the ideas that slumber at the bottom of people's hearts, and when you are sleeping they turn into realities and float out into the world—a very mysterious process, according to Dostoevsky. He says dreams can be an incredible expressive device. A radical, bold, and audacious device. Dostoevsky marvels at where this expression might even come from.

I was thinking about this when I was taking a bit of a break in Gotemba. I spent some time thinking about dreams from the past that I still had strong memories of. And then I realized, Oh that's how it goes. Whether it's dreams I had in my youth or ones from much later, these thoughts and ideas came out expressively in a different, somehow changed form. It seemed kind of interesting to me. When people have dreams, a strange kind of genius emerges, I thought, and I wrote down the first dream, or episode. And that process was quite a lot of fun.

Then the next day I wrote down one more dream. I kept repeating this sort of dream diary, and after a while I managed to write eleven. Then I compiled them and showed them to the crew. The crew said it was interesting and had the makings of a film. And that's how it all got off the ground.

We had to omit three of the episodes I initially thought of, though. They would have been technically very difficult and would have ended up costing a whole lot of money. My son was working as the producer, and he said,

"Oh, please, Dad, give me a break!" [*laughs*]

INOUE What were the episodes that you had to omit?

KUROSAWA You may remember the ashura statue at the Kōfuku-ji temple in Nara.[6] It's a pretty popular statue, and it has a lot of admirers among creators too. Recently, monks in Kyoto were ordered to pay the taxes for their temples.[7] And even though the buildings didn't belong to them personally, they shut down the temples so nobody could access the buildings, which just made me furious. So in my film the ashura gets mad too—and that ashura has three faces, and each of them starts to talk. It also has six arms, right. Its hands make all kinds of mudras, which make these famous heritage spots in Kyoto like Kiyomizu temple and Kinkakuji temple lift off—as if a tornado makes them fly away. Then after a while, the statue brings them back and the monks feel a little embarrassed. That was the basic story. Then there was one called "Flying," which also used special effects, and imagined world peace actually coming about. That one would have had many, *many* people in it, obviously, since it concerned people all over the world. There was no way to estimate how much that one would cost either. That was the episode where my son told me to cut it out.

INOUE That's a shame you had to leave them out, but the eight episodes you have ended up relating in a pretty wonderful way, didn't they?

KUROSAWA Yes. In the end "Village of the Waterwheels" brought them all together. And it ended up being just the right length.

INOUE Watching those stories of earth, water, and death, I feel like the movie was asking me to question where our focus on "development"—building, economic growth, technological "progress"—has led. It's saying the choice of "development" is not everything and asks if there might be other ways to live in the future. Of course, this film doesn't have an overt message like that.

KUROSAWA Well, but that *is* what the world's politicians should be doing today. At this point the planet is all connected, and we have to think about it that way.

Kurosawa and the cast on the set of "The Tunnel," episode 7 of *Dreams*. Courtesy of Kurosawa Production Co., Ltd.

Sublimity Ruins You for Real Life

INOUE Kurosawa-san, your movies have a depth to them, but they don't hit you on the head with a heavy message. They're movies that ordinary people can enjoy. Critics in Japan don't tend to give high marks to films that are entertaining, like yours.

KUROSAWA Yes, I agree with you. If people find a film *really* entertaining, then in my opinion it's a good movie. If it's only *kind of* entertaining, that's a different story. These days I can't think of any comedy that makes you laugh like crazy. Comedies are what's most missing from film these days. I think they're the most difficult, really, comedy. In the past people never tried to get away with stupid things like just making goofy faces or dressing up in weird getups, to try to make you laugh.

INOUE With characters like Private Noguchi in "The Tunnel," the situation is heartbreaking, but it is also quite absurd, isn't it? The "you" character tells him he is dead, so he should go back to where his body is. But he looks back so longingly toward his old house. That is a really *deep* kind of absurdity—you're not just writing him off as wacky or irrational.

KUROSAWA Yes! that's right. Private Noguchi comes back to life just before he dies and has a dream where he eats his mother's *bota-mochi* (sweets).[8] That's a story that I heard from Honda Ishirō [who assisted on the film]. Honda was a soldier for a long time, and he told me the story actually happened. The soldier passed out and dreamed that he returned home to eat *bota-mochi.* And after he described the dream, he died. It's a strange detail to be so vivid—why *bota-mochi*? Strange, but also strangely full of pathos.

INOUE Terao-san, as he plays "you," gives orders to the dead soldiers of the Third Platoon. "Attention! About face! Forward march!" They respond by retreating, obediently, grudgingly, with the sound of their boots the only thing with any energy… it's so sad and so strange. Just so deeply absurd.

KUROSAWA During the war, Nagaoka Teruko directed Chekhov's play *The Marriage Proposal,* which I saw at Tsukiji, a real masterpiece.[9] You could really sense the protagonists' feelings. The Ivan character goes next door to ask the hand of his neighbor Natalia, but his proposal gets thrown off by a bunch of misunderstandings, and they end up fighting. It's really funny: the whole proposal almost ends up falling apart after all these disasters. The second play was Kubota Mantarō's production of *At the Fishing Hole* [1937].[10] Some parts of the play were so entertaining I kept bursting out in laughter. People kept giving me funny looks, so I had to get up and go outside.

INOUE That was a double bill, wasn't it.

KUROSAWA Right. And it was just so funny that afterward, I was walking through Ginza toward Yurakuchō, and every so often I would just start laughing. That production was what I would call a real comedy, to be honest.

INOUE Your movies really have a lot of humor in them, so people who are inclined to comedies will really enjoy them. Take the scene in *Yōjimbo* where Katō Daisuke, with his chubby legs, runs away from the graveyard. It's shot in long shot, so even though you see him running furiously, he hardly seems to be moving at all. He's trying to get out of there but getting absolutely nowhere.

KUROSAWA We shot that shot with about a 500 mm telephoto lens. I'm the filmmaker responsible for really establishing a repertoire for telephoto lenses. Even on set I would be able to work in 500 mm lenses for the regular shots. Mostly I shot using 40 mm or 50 mm. Even if I did a shot that was technically a close-up, my thing was that I never brought the camera in close. I'd gradually bring it farther out. If an actor sees the camera right next to him and thinks that only his face will be on camera, he will act only with his face. And that's not really good acting. You should be acting with the full body, which will in turn come out in through the facial expression.

For the sea that appears in the second half of "Mount Fuji in Red"—we shot in Miyakejima—we shot with an 800 mm lens. The camera is placed very far away, so the actors don't actually know where the camera is set. They have no way of knowing, and thus responding. That's because if you were to shoot this with a typical lens, the waves would be so far away you would hardly be able to see the white at the top of the crests. The coastline ends in an overhanging cliff, and we had to make sure to get in the waves.

INOUE The movement from there to the surface of the land is really a terrifying color.

KUROSAWA We used a bit of dye to get that color on the surface of the land. We scattered some red stuff around. That's where there is a nuclear explosion, and Mount Fuji itself melts down. And then we had a thousand and some people fleeing. The extras that were on set were holding things—bright yellow, or red, or blue, right. We didn't really get the feeling we were hoping for, so we bleached out some of the color. We gradually took away some of the color from the crowds of people who were in that scene. It got kind of dark and faint, as they got covered in waves of dust. Tinkering with those kind of things was really a pain.

INOUE Did you shoot only the crowd scenes in advance?

KUROSAWA That's right. It took the assistant director and the crew about a day to prepare, and it took me about two hours to shoot. *Boom,* quick like that. With crowd scenes, if people get bored, it ruins everything. At first people are really into it and totally focused. But after a while, they start to drag, and ask me, "What, again?" [*laughs*] So getting the crowd scenes done really quickly is a real art.

Terao Akira's soldier is confronted by a hostile dog in "The Tunnel."

Screenplay as Seedling

INOUE The role of Private Noguchi in "The Tunnel" is played by Zushi Yoshitaka, who also played the role of Roku-chan in *Dodes'ka-den* when he was a kid. I felt a funny kind of nostalgia watching him, as if we had grown up together. His Private Noguchi was really excellent. And Terao-san also was really good in that role.

KUROSAWA At the end, you might remember the dog that comes out. Training that mad dog was really something. I was trying to use the dog as a metaphor for something like the terror of militarism or imperialism, but Terao actually adores dogs. His affection for dogs must have come across, because the dog just kept wagging its tail at him.

INOUE He's wagging his tail while he's barking his head off. [*laughs*]

KUROSAWA Even when he was supposed to be going in for a bite, the dog would keep wagging its tail. He probably would have barked more if Terao had been someone who obviously hated dogs. There was a trainer who stood in back. He kept screaming at the dog to be more fierce. Oh, that was a mess.

INOUE In that role Terao-san stood in for all the Japanese people who had survived the war, right. He has lost something important and was totally defeated, exhausted; that feeling comes across strongly.

KUROSAWA Right. He is—for instance, say that before there had been a field full of flowers, but it isn't there anymore. At that point, it's as if he is really looking out over that field, though it's not there anymore. It turns out that some actors aren't really able to do that. They just pretend to be looking at it, and that's all. And they cut corners with the dialogue too. There are some people you have to tell, "Look, you have your lines, I know, but you're not listening to the other people's lines. You need to say your own lines *after* you listen to the person before you." The bad actors don't listen to the other actors' lines. They just wait for their own turn to come up. Whereas the script says that they should listen actively to the lines before them; listening is really the most important part.

INOUE It's the same thing in theater, isn't it? If there is a play with seven characters, the entire dialogue of the other six people is also *your* dialogue. A good script will always make this the case. The dialogue should develop cumulatively out of the situation and personality of each respective role. That's why there is nothing more important to either a play or a film than the script. Kurosawa-san, you yourself have said that "the screenplay is the seedling of the film." You can grow a good movie from a good screenplay.

KUROSAWA Yes, exactly. If the screenplay is excellent, even a second- or third-rate director can make a good film. But if the screenplay is third-rate, even a first-rate director has a really uphill climb.

But I think a play and a screenplay are a little different. Sometimes if you're working in a large theater, you will turn to the audience and speak the dialogue in their direction. That's not the case with film. If an actor is talking to you, Inoue-san, I'm going to tell them to really talk to you. Then the camera will move to the best position and can shoot from there.

INOUE Some productions involve a big star acting all alone on a large stage. A lighting room in the middle shines a spotlight on the stars. When the star's lines are over, the spotlight turns off and then shifts to the next person who is speaking, while the first actor is completely still. Some stars act as if only their lines exist, and they don't react at all to the other actors' lines. Like you said, Kurosawa-san, they just don't listen to dialogue apart from their own lines. And the effect is that the world of the theater, with its special space and time, doesn't get built. It's a mess, right. Kurosawa-san, I hear that part of your method is shooting your sequences in order, from the first scene to the last. I'm guessing you did that for *Red Beard* because the process of shooting over time lets us follow the story while it traces the growth of the character. And if you skipped over parts, that sense of character would be lost.

KUROSAWA Mizoguchi-san would stop the camera. He would get everybody lined up ready to shoot, then take a really long shot. In my case, I might have two or three cameras going, each of them shooting at slightly different times. So that means we try a lot of different camera movements and rehearse a lot in order to make it match up with the actors. My crew are all used to working in this way, so the cinematographer and the lighting guy can get things up and running fairly quickly, but unless the crew is really experienced it's hard to pull off three cameras operating independently.

The Cinematographer Is the Director's Eyes

INOUE Tell me if my intuition is right here. Film is such a powerful medium because the director lets us see the story through their eyes, I think. In theater, the point of view can be different because of the position of the audience's seats, or because an audience member might be focusing on a star actor that they're a special fan of. Each audience member is their own director and cinematographer in their heads, and they have the freedom to play around with the way they watch. But with cinema, the director can force you to listen to some particular dialogue by using a close-up shot or look at a particular scene through a long shot. The director controls everything from the size of the lens, to the amount of light that gets in, to the kind of lens. You are utterly dependent on the director's point of view. If there is a good script, and the director has a really perceptive way of expressing it, it affects us. Kurosawa-san, your process is to use three cameras, and then choose from the three shots the one that best fits what *you* want to see. So editing is a constant flow of the shots you most want to put on screen. And then you make it fit with what the moviegoer most wants to see…

KUROSAWA That's right. The camera should really be picking up what the viewer most wants to see on screen. So the cinematographer has to shoot in the way the director wants to see things on screen.

INOUE So if you shoot at this angle, with that lens, and this kind of lighting, you can get across your own aesthetic at the same time you get the audience to go "aha" in appreciation. Someone who can make these two streams match is a good director.

KUROSAWA If two people are talking to each other, at some point you want to see a person's face, and you want to see their expression, right. And you want to make a connection between what the camera sees and what the viewer anticipates. Over the course of a long take, the actor has to be able to own that space. If it's only the camera that responds, the viewer is going to end up being aware of the camera. So if the camera keeps moving while the actor is stopped, that's when I shout, "Cut!" If I don't get the exact right moment, it's ruined. Finding that exact moment is really difficult.

INOUE So a lot depends on whether the cinematographer can understand your process, right.

KUROSAWA Right. The cinematographer I'm working with now, Saitō Takao, is so good he surprised even Spielberg.[11] He's over sixty years old, but to this day I still call him "Taka-bō," as if he were a child. We've been working together since we were more or less children. So he can tell at a glance what I want to do, and say, "Yeah, I got it." That's what it means to really be a crew member. If I have to be explaining every little thing all of the time it really gets in the way.

John Ford's shoots are the same. John Ford looks around silently, and he might say something like, "Cavalry, ride here from over there" or "Indian, to the middle of the river." He's looking at and taking into account the landscape or the quality of the light. Everybody is used to John Ford's style, so he can say things in shorthand like, "Just stop there" or "Cavalry, to that hill!" So he's able to make a picture of the caliber he does. On his crew are people like Ben Johnson, who people say makes riding a horse look like a poem. Bolting into a full gallop, or just walking the horse across the screen. It's quite amazing, that sensibility.

INOUE Every element is full of life. In principle, a director wants to cover each and every angle of the film, doesn't he? But in reality, one person can't do it all, so other people become their right-hand person, taking charge of the light, the camera, and all that.

KUROSAWA Sano Takeji was an excellent lighting designer.[12] He spoke in a really low voice and would sort of mumble things, and I would always ask if people could hear him, and they couldn't. But despite that, the lighting crew that worked underneath him could hear everything and would always answer, "Got it, boss, right on it." It was funny, they were only able to hear what their own boss was saying.

INOUE Donald Richie quoted you in *The Films of Akira Kurosawa* (published in Japanese translation in 1979). In the last chapter, you ask, "Why can't people be happier together?" The question is one you have continued to ask through all your works. You played with this theme consistently throughout your works. But, in fact, as you were making a film with the small community that a crew is, you were able to realize something like this happiness. That level of satisfaction is palpable when you see the movies themselves.

KUROSAWA Starting with the staff, I tell everyone connected to the film that "if you work as intensely as you can, it's going to get fun and exciting." And everybody does find it fun and exciting. Sometimes I try to call it a day, and they'll push me to go a bit longer, because they are enjoying their work. If you don't make the film in that way, it just won't attract viewers. As soon as *Dreams* was finished, I started right away writing another script. I started to take a bit of time off... maybe next year, I was thinking. But the crew said, "Are we going to have to wait another five years? That doesn't work for us." So that sunk in, and I kept on writing. Everybody seemed so down about taking time off. As of now we have plans to start shooting this summer.

INOUE For Kurosawa fans such as myself, five years is a long wait.

KUROSAWA In my head, there are so many films I would like to make. But at some point, you have to pick one to focus on. I think, "Hmm, maybe I'd like to give this one a try," and like you sprinkle water on a plant with a watering can, you start to look after it little by little, and it quickly grows up. And just like that, it reaches a point where we just have to do it.

With scripts I wrote in the past, if we initially failed to make them, they faded away; it's no use going back to try to pick them up again. They were made for a specific place and time, and that time has passed. Once that moment has gone by, it's really hard to pick it up again.

INOUE Yes, I understand that feeling well. There are so many variables that are so delicate: the way you feel in the world at that place and time, and the way your brain cells are lined up, your physical condition, your connections with the immediate world. Living in the world, living under its influence, as a writer you continue to live. There is also the feeling that the era itself shapes your creative work as a writer. If that shifts even a little, everything has to find a different footing.

Lives and Afterlives of Film

KUROSAWA The production of *Dreams* came about more or less organically. I think it had something to do with turning eighty, you know. When he turned eighty, Tomioka Tessai's painting suddenly changed in style, right. With this film all of a sudden I could relax and I was able to make it. It's not that it wasn't overwhelming to make. In other fields, like Noh, it's the same: by the time you're eighty, you've made a lot of commitments, but most people will let you off the hook for breaking them and will let you do what you want. When I told that to the producers and everyone I thought they'd be surprised, but they just laughed, and I came around to thinking it was all right to cut loose a little bit. The thing is, we have no choice about making movies until we die. That's the only thing we know, really.

INOUE You once said something that has since become well known, as you know: the moment you stop thinking about movies is the moment you die. I think it's true that all creative people have the same kind of sentiment.

KUROSAWA When I think about it, over the years I've been so lucky to meet so many interesting people through this work. At some point my work here will end. And then I think about how when that happens, I won't be able to see these people anymore, people I've gotten so close to.

One time we finished the day's shoot for *Dodes'ka-den*. It was in Horie-chō, in the city of Urayasu, in an area where people used to dump their old junk. People went off and I was all alone on the set. There was a car there waiting for me as I just stood there. All of a sudden it occurred to me we'd all been together so intensely while we were making the film, but from then on I wouldn't be seeing them anymore. And that made me tremendously sad. My chest started to tighten up. We'd all been thrown together in that location totally by chance, and then we went our separate ways and I was left alone. It occurred to me I would never see those people again, and I felt that loss of camaraderie intensely.

Come to think of it, with *Sanshirō* we also went our separate ways. I spent time with so many different kinds of people. But with *Dodes'ka-den,* it was such a sad feeling it's hard to put into words.

INOUE Kurosawa-san, that makes me think: the very reason I was able to meet so many new people—through the film—is because of those partings. When I see Minami Shunsuke from *Dodes'ka-den* I feel nostalgic for his presence; everybody was so young. Mifune Toshirō and Miyaguchi Seiji from *Seven Samurai,* they were young too; but to tell you the truth, they've remained the same age to me all these years. When Miyaguchi-san asked you what you had in mind for your next picture, you told him, "I want you to put on a hat." He was supposed to play the admiral in *Tora! Tora! Tora!* [*laughs*] Our mysterious relationship with film is made up of such things.

People get older year by year, but film keeps its feeling of "now" from the time it was made. It gives such a poignant sense of time, that film should be suspended like that while we keep moving. Our twentieth century has seen its share of problems. But there's no mistaking that film has made people aware of human interiority and all of its complexities in an entertaining and fruitful way. Film is the best medium for representing time in its movements from moment to moment. Film can freeze time, capture a sense of "here and now" so that it can be realized again later. To my mind, film is the quintessential experience of the twentieth century.

KUROSAWA The screen is something like the *hiroba* (forum, 広場) of the world, and viewers can experience all the emotions, from suffering to celebrating, along with the action on the screen. There is no other space that allows such a direct contact with the world, in my view.

For example, there is no Japanese person who thinks of somebody like John Wayne as an "other." That's the kind of medium film is. That is the most profound power that film has. Politicians should also realize this power. In order for outsiders to understand Japan, directors should film for real what people are thinking for real and lay it out for people all over the world to see—that would be the best course, I think.

III
Remembering Kurosawa

Kurosawa's One Hundred Films

Kurosawa Kazuko

Kurosawa Kazuko ventriloquizes her father's voice to give an overview of the list of one hundred films and imagines how they form Kurosawa's ideal cinema viewing experience. The meditation is punctuated with the pull she feels toward remembering how she and her father experienced film together. The essay touches on popular Japanese media figures like *benshi* Tokugawa Musei and television presenter Yodogawa Nagaharu, and describes encounters with many other directors including Satyajit Ray, Andrei Tarkovsky, Martin Scorsese, and John Cassavetes.

At some point in the past, my father made a list of a hundred films that he especially liked. This chapter is a re-creation of that list.

These films all surfaced from memories of time I spent with my father. Some are from times when we would stop at a café on the way home from the movie theater. Others are films I heard my father bring up when I tagged along on his TV interviews. I remembered some more titles from times we'd watch TV or videos together and talk about them. And other memories came from conversations we had around the dinner table when everybody would talk about the different movies they had seen . . . I tried to put all these memories into writing as precisely as I could, to get his "voice" down just as it was.

If my father had named all the movies he liked, they would be countless, he said. Needless to say, it would be impossible to rank them all in order. And some movies he thought were absolutely stellar didn't even make the list. I limited myself to one film from each director, and I included works I had vivid memories of watching and discussing with my father, along with some ideas about films my father adored but never talked about in public. That's how the list of a hundred came together.

As I was working, the memories would well up. I would suddenly want to see my father again and tears would come to my eyes. I regretted not asking him all the things I should have, but I kept writing and remembering, remembering and writing.

As I wrote down all these memories, I could hear my father urging me to never stop being curious about movies. At times I had the feeling he was praising me for a job well done. Thanks to his encouragement, it was a pleasure to put this all together.

My father would be overjoyed if readers of this list ended up seeing even one new film, as he loved movies with all of his heart.

Right now, in 1999, former Kurosawa-gumi members, headed up by the director Koizumi Takashi, are working intensely to turn my father's script for *After the Rain* into a film.[1]

The space left by Akira Kurosawa is a big one, but everyone is trying to work through the sadness by throwing themselves into a production that would make him proud. They are pouring all their effort into this tribute.

I put together the remarks that follow—alongside the list of films—from many sources, including interviews on television and in print, some of which have never been seen before.

Well, it's been a while now that I've wanted my own movie theater. Someplace I might call Kurosawa Theater. And I would screen for everyone the films that really meant something to me. There are fantastic films that don't really stand a chance in a proper theater, since—as you know—most of them pop up in small theaters and vanish after only a short run. At theaters abroad, though, you can have your pick of films from all over the world. In Paris there's even a movie theater that plays nothing but Japanese movies. This theater in Paris sees the value in Japanese films, but you're hard pressed to find that in Japan. This is an awful situation. Most young people don't know anything about either Japanese films or foreign ones, but there are so many good ones, and it seemed to me it would be great to have my own theater where I could introduce these wonderful works to new audiences anytime I want.

I tried my hand at selecting the films for this imaginary movie theater. There are so many I would be thrilled to show people. Even if you only deal with works from the talkie era, it's still a massive number, and then, of course, there are all the silents. After all, that's where the origins of cinema are, so I really want people to see some of the silents. That world of black-and-white silent films really represents a kind of peak of what cinema can be, working on all its cylinders.

For example, take *The Fall of the House of Usher*—it's silent, but the arrangement and the editing make you almost hear the sound. There's a main character who visits a decrepit old mansion; after a while, he picks up a classical guitar and starts strumming. The little waves outside the mansion go up and down . . . their speed and choppiness get translated into the guitar, making the sound of the wind.

Of the French avant-garde works, Luis Buñuel's *Un chien andalou* was amazing. Salvador Dalí worked on the script, and they drew on a number of Surrealist techniques. The lighthouse flickers off and on strangely, conjuring an atmosphere of madness.[2]

From Silents to Talkies

There's such a range of techniques you can draw on when you make a film, and I'm always saying that we should rethink everything from the beginning. When I make a film, I start off by challenging myself to think how I would shoot it if it were a silent production. I used a lot of avant-garde techniques in the filming of *Rashomon.*

The fiction writer Uchida Hyakken was quite used to watching silent films, and when talkies came around, he just stopped watching.[3] He said that watching silent movies was fun because you could let them roam in your imagination. But once you have to express things in actual words, all the fun is gone. That is, in fact, true. When sound film becomes possible and color becomes standard it's just too easy to let "realism" take over and become far too literal. A film can tend to overexplain things and then the expressive possibilities get lost.

When talkies came around, the early ones were pretty much all over the place, but once people got the hang of working with sound, some wonderful works started to come out.

Unfinished Symphony is one of those works.[4] It's a very charming little film. The main story is why Schubert was never able to finish his *Unfinished Symphony,* and the movie weaves the actual music in very cleverly. When the Schubert character plays the piano, it cues the sound of an orchestra; the music and the image tracks meld together brilliantly.[5] *Congress Dances* was the first film to use recorded playback technology. Filmmakers in Japan must have wondered how in the world the film could have been made like that, as no technology like that existed in Japan at the time. This was the work that made them realize that when you have, say, a scene with an orchestra, you don't actually have to *bring* the orchestra on to the set. You can record it first and film so that the image of the orchestra matches up with the recording. It's a lot of fun to watch and also why this film has such an important place in film history.

The beginning of the talkie era fell a bit flat because people were so on edge about the possibilities of sound that they neglected the rest. But eventually they hit their stride and used sound quite effectively. The same happened with color—in the beginning it seemed like they just wanted to flaunt the color itself . . . so the lighting would shine into dark places that earlier pictures didn't reach, which threw off the composition of the image with all the suddenly visible things. But eventually they got the knack of using color and lighting in clever ways, as well.

One time, Henri Langlois, the head of the Cinémathèque in Paris, was giving me a hard time for never having made a color picture. I told him that the color film available at the time didn't really suit me, and he replied that Eisenstein had already shot a color film more than twenty years earlier. He showed me the banquet scene from *Ivan the Terrible* and I have to admit, I was completely stunned, and then I finally came around to making a color film.

I first tried out color with *Dodes'ka-den* (1970), and then I jumped in all the way with *Dersu Uzala* (1975) and *Kagemusha* (1980). Around that time Langlois died, and I'm sorry I was never able to show him those works. When William Wyler and his wife came to the premiere of *Kagemusha* at Cannes and I mentioned this, his wife blurted out that surely Langlois is looking down from heaven—he must be on his way down to see my color film.

Until then I was never inclined to go to film festivals, but at that point I started to go to Cannes.

When the newspapers overseas announced that I was in town for the festival, Mary Meerson, who had been Langlois's longtime companion and collaborator, came to see me immediately; this broke my heart.[6]

John Ford, Larger Than Life

There are many essential directors in this world, but the one who really influenced me was John Ford. Do you remember that scene where John Wayne lights his cigarette off an oil lamp in *The Man Who Shot Liberty Valance*? I thought to myself, Can you really do that?—and I had to give it a try. These days people in the film world don't really talk about movies they have seen, but back in the day when you saw a good picture, people would be just over the moon about it, and for a while no one could talk about anything else.

Ford made social realist works like *How Green Was My Valley* and *Tobacco Road,* but the Westerns are the ones that are really meaningful to me. The classic is probably *Stagecoach,* but for me the standout is *My Darling Clementine.*

John Ford always treated me kindly. When I received an award from the British royal family for *Throne of Blood,* I was sitting in an aisle seat of the theater, waiting for the screening of the film, and someone off to the right stood up.[7] The man said, "Oh excuse me," and when he turned to face me, a dashing blue tuxedo and the Presidential Medal of Freedom on his chest caught my eye . . . I was shocked to see it was John Ford. It was! I was so surprised.

I heard that John Ford had visited my set right after the war when I was shooting *The Men Who Tread on the Tiger's Tail.* When I put two and two together, I remembered one time we were doing an overhead shot and I was looking on from above. A group of officers from SCAP came to observe. They watched for a while, then quietly left.[8] It seems that John Ford was one of those officers. He asked if I had gotten the message he left, to "give my regards to the director." Afterward he took a great liking to me and looked after me. He would call me "Akeera" in his American accent. [*laughs*]

John Ford stopped by Tokyo on his way back from the Korean War. At that time I really hated to be bothered and didn't have a telephone at the house. John Ford put the word out that he wanted to talk to me and had someone ask around. I got the word and went to meet him at the Sanno Hotel.[9] He came to the door in a dressing gown, fresh out of the bath, and told me we should have a whiskey together. When he saw that the "boy" came with just a glass, he got mad and barked at the boy to bring him a whole bottle.[10] He himself was losing his sight and didn't drink anymore, but the crew was more than happy to swig it down.

We talked for a while and when it came time to go home, he told me to hang on a minute. He came back dressed in his officer's uniform. He dragged along two aides and escorted me as far as the elevator. When I got on to the elevator he snapped to attention, and all three of them lined up and saluted, and just then the door slid shut. That rhythm—it felt just like a John Ford movie. Just like *The Horse Soldiers* (1959).[11]

John Ford died while I was making *Dersu Uzala,* but my staff kept the news from me until we were finished shooting. He had a mischievous side, and I suspected he had some sort of trick for shooting horses. When I asked him, he put his finger against his lips as if sealing in a secret and lowered his voice to say "time-lapse photography." Things like that were a lot of fun. When we would meet, he would give me a huge bear hug, saying "Akeera" and slapping me on the back—which really hurt! He really was a monumental figure.

That's how it is, you know; good film directors are almost all like that. Jean Renoir is the same way—warm and gregarious.

Earthly Poetics

When I went to visit Paris, Jean Renoir stopped by to visit. When I got to my hotel room, there was a message telling me that Renoir had arrived. Flustered, I went down to the lobby, and he was just casually standing there. It was so humbling to me to hear from the mouth of such a renowned director that it was an honor for him to meet *me.* That evening he took me to dinner at a little French restaurant where we were the only guests, and the meal was not to be believed.

I think very few people have been lucky enough to meet Jean Renoir. I've had a chance to meet so many kinds of people from all over the world during my career. Of these, I've gotten to be close with John Ford. Also Sidney Lumet, Andrei Tarkovsky, Theo Angelopoulos, Nikita Mikhalkov; I've been lucky to meet so many.

Shall I continue talking about these directors? I met Sidney Lumet at the home of William Friedkin with some other movie people from New York, and we had a rapport right off the bat.[12] The two of us got caught up in conversation, and everyone around us wanted to join in. We've been friends ever since. That night I told him I was having a hard time with the budget for my next film. He said that he would try to get something going in New York, and everybody put their heads together. Unfortunately, it didn't end up happening, but critics and all kinds of people made a real effort.

Lumet is a very entertaining guy. Once the conversation gets rolling, you get caught up in it, and you feel like you could go on talking forever. In New York, the space of a square block is pretty big, right? When they shot a certain film on location, he realized that moving around would be a huge hassle. So he picked up a pair of roller skates at a toy store, and he used them to zip around from block to block! That right there is Sidney Lumet. The chief assistant director would have to race around behind him to try to catch up. [*laughs*]

And Tarkovsky too—I was really close to him. Before, when I used to have an office in the old wing of the Akasaka Prince Hotel, he came to visit, and that was the first time I met him. That evening he just stood looking out at the night view of Asakusa. That setting ended up being woven into one of the scenes in *Solaris.* They reflected it through a series of mirrors and made a whole future city out of the red taillights as they were coming and going on the expressway.

When *Solaris* was finished and I saw the highway scene at a preview in Moscow, I thought, "That's the road that leads to my office! I feel like I'm on the way to my office." I remember the feeling of being in Moscow at the same time I was on the way to my office.

All of Tarkovsky's films are superb, but his depiction of water is especially stunning, as you see in *Solaris* (1972) or *Sacrifice* (1986). He shoots ponds or puddles so that you seem to be looking all the way to the bottom. Typically when you do a shot like that, the sky ends up getting reflected in the surface of the water.

When I was making *Dreams,* we filmed a scene on the river in the "Village of the Watermills" segment and wanted the same effect. We had to use a very large crane and hoist up a dark cloth to block out the sky. That's how we managed to give that impression of depth all the way to the bottom.

The cosmonauts in *Solaris* have an intense attachment to the earth. The shots of nature on earth go on and on, like when you see the sea greens undulating in the pond at the beginning. As you watch the film you start to feel like you also long to go back down to earth, along with the cosmonauts. The distributor thought that the footage of nature went on for too long and asked Tarkovsky to edit it down. But he refused; he said the whole film would be ruined if those sequences were cut. In the end they came around and left it as it was.

There's a part of Tarkovsky's works that's a bit esoteric. This is what makes it stand out, of course. It's different from the predictable films we have come to expect at the movies. His father was apparently a famous poet, and his visual works are also poetic.

Tarkovsky once told me that he makes sure to watch *Seven Samurai* before he starts shooting a film. Well, actually, before I start a shoot I always watch *Andrei Rublev* (1967) . . . he was really warm, a wonderful man. When I was in Europe I happened to hear that he had been hospitalized. I wanted to pay him a visit and tried to find out the hospital, but I couldn't find it, and my flight home had already been booked . . . shortly after, he died. It's so sad, losing him like this; I thought of him as a younger brother.

Angelopoulos and Ray

A funny accident brought me together with Theo Angelopoulos. I first met him at a press screening of *Alexander the Great* (1980). He brought up the name of a certain famous director and asked, "Do you know him?" I was kind of stumped about how I should answer, and when I answered honestly, "I'm not really that fond of him," he also said, "Yes, me neither!" [*laughs*] And from that point on it was clear we would get along.

I was really astonished when I saw *The Travelling Players*. There's a scene where the family of actors leaves the boardinghouse and heads out somewhere. They come back and start to put on the play, *Aeschylus* . . . the whole thing is done in one shot. The village scene from *Alexander the Great* is amazing in a similar way. The camera is set right in the middle of the action, and it spins around in a full 360-degree circle. Probably the crew had to run away so they didn't get in the way of the frame. When you look at that scene closely, the people who appear later look nervous. Imagine waiting for the camera as it turns and turns—and you think to yourself, "So far, so good." But if you make a mistake when it comes around in your direction, the whole thing has to start over for everyone and it's a huge pain. So it's no wonder everybody ends up getting kind of nervous. [*laughs*]

Anyway, that kind of intensity is amazing. Mizoguchi Kenji was the same way. When I was first starting out, I was making shots of around four minutes. I thought this was quite something and was very proud. But now that kind of shot seems completely normal. I often shoot shots that are even up to sixteen minutes and it feels totally normal. I told Angelopoulos that I had a sixteen-minute shot, but then he replied that he had a film that was a single take from beginning to end, *The Travelling Players*. A reel of film is only a thousand feet, but here's how it went, he said: he would be shooting someone's back or something, and the screen would go dark, right. But then the next reel got spliced in and the film kept going as if it were all one shot. I can't compete with that! [*laughs*]

Talking about film directors, Satyajit Ray is someone who often comes to mind. My wife actually said, "I've never seen such a magnificent person." He's so tall you have to look up to him. He has dark sparkling eyes, and he always seems completely comfortable, whatever the situation. I just find it really hard to feel so at ease. His films themselves have, what should I say, the turns and meanders of the Ganges River.

All of his films are masterpieces, but *Pather Panchali* is no doubt one of the most stunning works in the history of world cinema. I saw that film with Honda Ishirō, and he told me that that once you see that film, it ruins you for other movies.[13] For us he stood in for how we imagined India must be.

One time there was a party at the home of Satyajit Ray. Although it was summer, it was an unseasonably chilly day. My wife tends to get cold easily, and Satyajit Ray noticed right off. He came up to her and asked her if she was all right. He wondered if she might want to go home early, and so we did leave early. Like I said earlier, I have never run into anyone like him, anyone who had such a sense of warmth and caring. I've heard that Bernardo Bertolucci is shooting a movie based on the life of the Buddha, and I thought, "Wait a minute." I thought that if anyone is going to shoot a film about Buddha, it ought to be Satyajit Ray, and if someone is going to play Buddha, I can't imagine anyone other than Satyajit Ray in that role.

In India I had a chance to see the banyan tree. It has aerial roots, roots that drop down from the branches toward the ground where they form new trunks. The effect is that the many trunks of the tree don't get all bunched up, and they say that the canopy can spread for up to a mile. One time I was asked by Satyajit Ray to write something, and I wrote that there was no one like him: like that tree with a canopy that spreads for a mile around . . . he's really a magnificent person.

Some Strangers I Have Known

For work I often have a chance to go abroad. On those occasions, I often get a lot of strangers coming my way—some of them very strange. One day, a man came to my hotel in New York and told me he had some kind of illustrated book he really wanted to give me. "But I went to look for it and couldn't find it, and unfortunately today I have to fly out of town," he said. Then the next day, he came yet again. He had found the book.

[*laughs*] I asked him, "Weren't you supposed to be on a plane leaving today?" and he told me he canceled his flight and looked around till he found the book. He didn't say anything by way of introduction, so I just thought at first, well, there's another odd one, but later, someone told me that my visitor was Werner Herzog.

Later on when I saw one of Herzog's films for the first time, I was just floored. I think not many people have seen it, but it's just incredible—*Fitzcarraldo.*

I met Martin Scorsese in the same chaotic kind of way as Herzog. A strange man came tearing toward me, gesturing wildly with his hands. He seemed to be worked up about something. He insisted that films made in color are in danger of disappearing because the film stock degrades over time, and he was adamant that film needs to be preserved properly. I was baffled about who this frantic person was, and why he cared so much about color film, but someone told me it was Scorsese, and afterward we became friends.

When I was making *Dreams,* I asked Scorsese to play the role of Van Gogh, and he agreed. He sent me a tape of himself reading the lines and asked me if that was what I wanted . . . he was reading at such an incredible clip I really couldn't tell if it was good or bad; I couldn't even make the words out. He always seems so busy and is always in motion. He's always running around because he is so involved, leading the movement to preserve color film or spearheading the effort to get an Academy Honorary Award for Satyajit Ray when he was having health problems. Satyajit Ray was so ill he couldn't attend the ceremony for the Honorary Award, so Scorsese had a clip made of Ray in his hospital room, which he screened for the audience. Ray passed away soon after that.

Something about my encounter with John Huston left a strong impression, though I only met him toward the end of his life and I didn't know Huston well. One day I got a letter in the mail from another American I had never met. The letter said, "You should really write a thank-you letter to John Huston." Apparently, John Huston had appeared as a guest on a TV show, and he showed up late because, he said, he had just come from seeing a really great movie, and all he could talk about for the rest of the show was *Kagemusha.*[14]

Then some years later John Huston and I were chosen to present an award together at the Oscars. When I got to the venue for the rehearsal, there was some guy who yelled out "Kurosawa" in a loud voice, and when I got closer I saw it was John Huston. He said he had felt like he had known me for years. [*laughs*] I wish we had been able to meet earlier. At that point his health had really gone downhill. He was using a wheelchair and had a nurse attending him. He shot *The Dead* in that condition too. They had to release it posthumously; it's a real masterpiece.

Too Much Limelight for a Director

It seems many people think directors are a temperamental breed, but that's not always the case. Michelangelo Antonioni has a reputation among journalists for being intimidating, but I get along with him quite well. We went sightseeing in India together, and we ended up riding elephants because his wife said she wanted to ride an elephant, so we all went together. The journalists said they couldn't imagine how that even happened. In reality, he's actually not that gruff a person. It's just that when Antonioni gets the lens turned on him, he suddenly hides or runs away. For some reason people think of him as difficult, but really he just hates having his picture taken. He's actually a very entertaining guy; he cracks jokes and everything. But people fall for this image, and journalists keep fanning the flames. I bet that's what everybody says about me too. [*laughs*] Difficult . . . temperamental. Could I really be so temperamental like that year in and year out? That sounds exhausting. [*laughs*]

Mizoguchi-san was the silent type, no doubt. Naruse-san was quiet, too, and I found him so imposing.[15] When I worked as an assistant director, I slowly started to understand that if I told him to cut out the bullying and just teach me, he would just chuckle and wasn't actually very scary. But everybody puts him on a pedestal, that's why. And that can make you really lonely. If that happens, well . . . I can't stand that kind of thing, so on my set, everybody eats together and we all have a good time getting rowdy. As you might think, if you peeked into a set run by Ozu-san or Mizoguchi-san or Naruse-san, it would be silent. My set is really lively. That's because the set run by Yama-san, the director I learned from, was the same way.[16]

You know, many directors are actually quite shy. I had a chance to meet François Truffaut and talk with him, and he was so utterly shy he seemed almost embarrassed to be speaking at all. But he also appeared in films like *Close Encounters,* and a few others . . . I always wondered how such a shy person was able to do that. I was also quite friendly with Federico Fellini and met him a number of times, but when I talked about his films he would get quite shy, and his voice would almost drop to a whisper.

John Cassavetes was also quite shy, you know. Langlois, the head of the Cinémathèque française, told me that there was a movie called *Shadows* that I really ought to see. It was shot in 16 mm. It's a really wonderful film. Cassavetes came to the screening room and at that time, he was quite youthful, maybe around thirty. I thought it was a great film, and wanted to talk to him about it, but he got really shy and ran away into the corridor.

He was obviously so talented, and I was sure he would be making exciting new films. I kept expecting his next work, but he never seemed to put out any new films. Then about twenty years later, I heard good things about a film called *Gloria*, and when I got to the screening room, I realized it was a film by that same person. I was blown away, just as I had hoped I would be. During the time I didn't see anything from him it seems Cassavetes had shot quite a few pictures, but none of them had made their way to Japan. I saw him from time to time as an actor in other films, so I kept up with him in a sense, but I never made the connection with that youthful-seeming guy from years ago. I never imagined that shy person would be a working actor.

My meeting with George Lucas was quite funny. He invited me out to lunch when I visited Los Angeles. During lunch he told me that the robots in *Star Wars* were inspired by characters in *The Hidden Fortress*. As context—there are always people around who want to stir up trouble, and America is no exception. One guy actually asked me if I had come to America because I wanted to file a lawsuit. [*laughs*] Lucas was totally shocked by that idea, and of course I was thinking nothing of the kind.[17] I mean, once he brought it up it made sense, but the likeness had never crossed my mind. People in the U.S. are really upfront about letting you know they were inspired by your work.

Along those lines, the director William Friedkin told me that the subway scene in *The French Connection* owed something to *High and Low*, though you could argue that both of them are just trains doing what trains do . . . he told me straight out that *High and Low* had an impact on his own work and it made me feel so great.

You know, I think that people who do creative work have to build on each other's work. In Japan there are a lot of remakes, but even if you shoot a complete replica, it never ends up being exactly the same. For example, *Red Beard* was remade as a TV drama, right?[18] Someone asked the lead actor—who would play the role Mifune played in the original—"Won't it be hard to follow in Mifune's footsteps?" But he said, "I've never seen *Red Beard*, so I wouldn't know." What a way to answer! That's completely absurd. The costumes and everything were virtually alike, but they made zero reference to our work. My team and I worked our asses off to make all these things . . . I'm not complaining, but I will mention that all they had to say was, "Thank you for the idea." They didn't even make that basic gesture, so they had to tie themselves up in knots saying things like, "Oh, do they look the same?" Or, "But we never saw *Red Beard*!", which is maddening.

In any case, I am going to guess that no one else has met as many directors as I have. These days even if Japanese directors *do* make it to film festivals, they stick with the other Japanese people. It's kind of pointless to go all that way if you're just going to cling to the people you already know. They might just as well have stayed in Tokyo. If you can't speak another language, there is an interpreter there you can always use to talk to different kinds of people. Other directors complain that it's easy for me to say because people come seek me out, but not them. So I have to tell them *they* might have to be the one to reach out to other people. This dynamic really has to change. Directors are a pretty sociable crowd. If you really are that averse to people, I think you won't last long as a director. Of course, there are exceptions, and some people just really dread socializing.

Oh, right, speaking of socially awkward people, let me tell you a story. When I was making *Dodes'ka-den*, I heard from the chief assistant director that Matsumura Tatsuo told him, "Sensei really seems to dislike me. He looks at me like he really can't stand me."[19] I had to tell him, "Matsumura-san, the role you are playing is a really awful person. And you're doing a really good job of playing this horrible person. If I'm looking at you like I can't stand you, in fact it's the opposite: it means you're doing a great performance." And that seemed to reassure him. [*laughs*] I mean normally I can't really stand to be around such awful people. What's funny is that in reality, Matsumura is a really good person, so he's able to play an excellent bad person. It's like when a person who doesn't drink is able to play a drunk, like Shimura Takashi.[20] Hidari Bokuzen's drunk scenes were absolute masterpieces, and he doesn't drink a drop.[21]

The Splendor of Japanese Films

Once I start musing over all the films I want to show in "my" movie theater, there's no end to it. They are literally countless, and paring them down would be excruciating. Even if I counted *just* those that I can't bear to leave off the list, there are definitely more than a hundred. Cinema is barely a hundred years old, but there have already been so many really creative people. Japanese cinema is said to be on the decline, but it's hardly been any time at all since films have been made in Japan. So I'm quite certain that the future will bring us a lot of wonderful films. That said, the films that win at the box office are not necessarily of that caliber. Actually, it's the opposite—whether they are Japanese films or foreign films, the support goes to the mediocrities. That is the direction the film world is headed, and that is what I want to change.

What I mean is that really good movies are really enjoyable to watch—entertaining. They're not that demanding, they're interesting, and they're not predictable, right. When we break down the masterpieces, we can put them into different categories—just plain good films, masterpieces, *real* masterpieces, and so on. There are elegant little films, as well as huge, big-budget pictures. I want to include as many of these types as possible in "my" theater.

One issue is that a lot of Japanese film fans will only go to see foreign films. They have a kind of knee-jerk intellectual reaction that Japanese films are lowbrow and hopeless. And that is exactly why I want to include the masterpieces we have in Japanese cinema. If you look at the films on my list, you can see there's no superficially flashy films, and people should be able to see the beauty that really belongs to Japanese cinema.

There's a well-known film critic and programmer named John Gillett who made a speech at a screening at the British National Film Theater.[22] He said that if you look back at Japanese film history, you see it has produced so many great directors, and there was a time when the stars aligned to produce a rush of great works all at once—and this was unprecedented anywhere else in the world. And then he asked me what in the world made this happen? I told him that there was no special magic that explained it all. In that period directors were able to shoot the films they wanted, in the way they wanted. No one really meddled and told them what to do. But at a certain point, the film studios brought a half-baked version of the producer system, and the executives started telling people to do this or that harebrained thing . . . which is no way to make a good film.

This is the question I would pose to today's Japanese film world: If you're going to be throwing money at these terrible movies, why are you making any new films at all? There are so many great films from the past, why don't you just screen those? If you would just take care of them using the science we have these days, the image quality will get a lot better too. You should definitely start production on a new film if the project looks solid and it has a good script, but there's no reason to go to such effort making these lousy films just to make them.

Darryl Zanuck took over Twentieth Century–Fox when it was on the edge of bankruptcy. He held off making movies for a while. He picked a bunch of good films out of the vault of Twentieth Century–Fox and had prints restruck to show in theaters. There was no production cost, so in six months he had recouped his costs and the company was back on its feet! Someone should really do something like that in Japan.

Both Yamanaka Sadao and Naruse were quite popular overseas.[23] Those audiences are surprised that a director can take what they consider to be a tiny little incident and make it into a whole film. So that's why everybody pays such attention to the realist details of the mise-en-scène, or how to express tiny emotional cues. In France many people have seen all the Japanese classics screened at the Cinémathèque. They sometimes ask if there are more where those came from. Because the Cinémathèque's programming is so good, viewers outside of Japan are able to discover amazing Japanese directors who have been almost entirely forgotten in their own country.

In Japan, film comes in a notch below any other art, in prestige terms. In most other countries there are funders, investment funds for films who invest in film projects they think have potential. It makes a huge difference that directors have a high social standing, much higher than in Japan. They also have a lot more financial security. If a director can manage to get a certain amount of work, they can have [a] very decent quality of life. Though directors overseas tend to retire early, which is a little bit unfortunate. Take Frank Capra. I wish he had continued working for a while longer, but he had financial security, so he naturally just faded out.

Compared to that, in Japan you have to keep working pretty much until you're dead, right. [*laughs*] And on top of that, you're still a renter. Honda-san, for example, should have been able to buy a castle with the profits from *Godzilla* alone. Overseas, things are completely different. When René Clément retired, he owned a yacht, and Francis Ford Coppola was really well off. I had a chance to stay at Coppola's house around the time he was editing *Apocalypse Now*, and you had to take an elevator to get to the bedrooms that were upstairs from the dining room.

The Wondrous Tokugawa Musei

My father had a career in the military, and even though he was typically very strict, he was very supportive of moviegoing. He would take me to the theater from about the time I was in kindergarten because he was so keen on the movies. My first memory is probably seeing *Cuore.*[24] My memory is pretty spotty, so I didn't remember the title, but when I described a scene I remembered to Yodogawa Nagaharu, he said, "Oh, that sounds like it must be *Cuore.*"[25]

Then another time I remember being bored and pestering my older sister because we had gone all the way to the theater, and Charlie Chaplin never came on. To stop my complaining she told me that the neighborhood police officer was coming to get me.

But my real encounter with the movies would not actually come until later, you know. My older brother Heigo was a huge influence on me, as he was so well versed both in literature and cinema.

I was really schooled in the movies by my older brother. When I was in elementary school, I started to voraciously watch the films he recommended. This means that I've seen almost all of the really classic films that are hard to see these days, and the works that were so important in the history of film. When I think about it now, this was all thanks to my brother.

My brother worked closely with Tokugawa Musei. My brother chose to follow the path of the *benshi,* and he became fairly famous under the stage name Suda Teimei.[26] He worked in Tokyo until right before the talkie era, and he chose to specialize in foreign films in the theaters that focused on booking really good foreign films. The theater where my brother worked as a *benshi,* the Kanda Cinema Palace, was one such theater, and Tokugawa Musei's Tōyō Palace was especially well regarded. The modern *benshi* of that time were different than traditional *benshi* because they were expected to cover all the different roles of presentation—from skillful explanations of foreign film content and performing, to program selection, to advertisement. Their posters, too, were great, very inventive. For example, when they did *Doctor Mabuse,* the title characters read from bottom to top. And with *Blood and Sand* (Fred Niblo, 1922), at first glance the poster seemed to be a sheet of pure red, but if you looked closely, you could make out the small characters "blood" and "sand."

Tokugawa Musei in his heyday of 1932, on the cover of the new year's issue of a magazine highlighting *benshi*. Wikipedia.

Musei-san, like other *benshi*, was in charge of coordinating the accompaniment as well as the narration of the film. For instance, this is how one film went. A drunken guy approaches the sumptuous house of a wealthy man, carrying another man, and asks if the rich man will let the man on his back spend the night, and dumps him there. Musei doesn't say a peep during that part, no accompaniment at all. Time goes by and the man still doesn't wake up, and just as the rich man waves his hands to revive the man he thinks is sleeping, Musei suddenly lets out a scream—"Kyaaa!": the tragic cry of the man who discovers that the body lying underfoot belongs to his own son. Then the accompaniment suddenly begins, and the scene switches over to a lively carnival. Musei's direction was incredible. I learned a lot from these productions, and spectators were really trained to watch films by Musei-san's way of looking at things. For movie fans, Musei-san played the role of a guide. That's the kind of ideal movie theater I want to create.

One time Tokugawa Musei-san told me that I was exactly like my brother. It's true that I was sometimes mistaken for my brother when I was alone, but when we were together, it seemed that no one made that mistake. Musei-san said, "You are the spitting image, but it's like different exposures: where your brother is the negative, you are the positive." His metaphor probably hit the nail on the head. My personality was very upbeat, but my brother somehow always cast a shadow. My brother always used to say, "When a person gets to be thirty, things only get

Yodogawa Nagaharu introduces *Merry Christmas, Mr. Lawrence,* film number 84 on Kurosawa's list.

horrible. I will die before that" . . . and this is exactly what happened. It was about three years after he died that I entered the film world.

I Want You to Watch like Yodogawa Nagaharu

I've been asked if I watched movies differently once I started making them. That's interesting . . . but I don't think it worked out that way. Actually, I watch movies just like any other fan. That's where I learn the most. I think it's a mistake to analyze a movie just to shoehorn it into some theory and explain everything away.

By and large films aren't things that have to be explained. Sometimes people will ask what the "must see" points of a film are, but that's the worst approach you could come up with. That's because each person has elements that they like, and people should be free to watch as they like. Films are like polyhedrons; they have a dimensionality. You can look at them from many angles. So if you like a work, you can turn it over in your mind like a 3D object and look at it from many different angles. And by doing that, you can see new aspects.

I say this a lot—that film is a kind of public space, a place where people from all over can gather. If the people on screen appear to be having a good time, viewers can enjoy; when they are suffering, viewers suffer along with them. In that way people understand each other's experiences, and people naturally come to understand cultures that are not their own, right. I always say that film is an effective system for ensuring that people of the world get along. For instance, if you have seen John Wayne, there's no way you can see him as a stranger. People watch him as someone who is close to them. That kind of closeness is something to be valued. The most wonderful thing film has to offer you is the ability to coexist alongside a character as they go through a range of emotions, and to live alongside them.

You know, the thing I want to most get across is that I want you to watch a movie completely openly, without any filters. Just like Yodogawa-kun does: immersing in the film, with the attitude of "amazing, how amazing!" Yodogawa didn't care whether it was a sad scene, a beautiful composition, or something that just amused him: it was all "amazing" to him. That is the way someone who truly loves movies watches them, I think.

The List

1 ***Broken Blossoms,* D. W. Griffith, 1919, USA**
Lillian Gish plays a girl who's very proper—wide-eyed and neatly dressed. Her sister was Dorothy Gish, who was a bit more sensual, while Lillian was a little naive. It was excruciating to watch her character suffering at the hands of her father. I saw her again in *The Whales of August,* and you can tell she hasn't changed a bit. She's now the age of a grandmother, and I was surprised that she's aged so gracefully.

2 ***The Cabinet of Dr. Caligari,* Robert Wiene, 1920, Germany**
This is a signature work of German Expressionism, but it still holds up today. You know the look of Expressionist drawings? The whole set is constructed in that aesthetic. There are so many things to learn from those earlier works, you know.

3 ***Dr. Mabuse the Gambler,* Fritz Lang, 1922, Germany**
I saw this one as a child, back when Tokugawa Musei was the *benshi.* My brother dragged me along because he was a *benshi* too; it was really fun. With that sinister Mabuse as the master of disguises. I saw Abel Gance's *La roue* (The Wheel, 1922) around that time. I remember so vividly the flashback scene with the runaway train; that was really something.

4 ***The Gold Rush,* Charles Chaplin, 1925, USA**
Chaplin really had talent as an actor, and comedy is the hardest of all. Making people cry is easy. He also had talent as a director and was really well versed in music; he had so many talents he hardly knew what to do with them all. I think Beat Takeshi is a lot like that.

5 ***The Fall of the House of Usher*, Jean Epstein, 1928, France**

Even though it's a silent and is composed purely of images, you have the illusion of hearing the sound. That use of the image has some amazing expressive powers. Every time I start shooting a film, I make a point of asking myself what it would be like if I shot it as a silent.

6 ***Un chien andalou*, Luis Buñuel, 1928, France**

It's shocking—that scene near the beginning where the woman's eyeball suddenly appears on the screen and the razor slashes across it. Dalí's scenario is transposed to the screen so vividly, with the shots connected in that random-seeming way you have in a dream. When I was shooting *Rashomon* it helped me a lot to think back to those techniques of Surrealism.

7 ***Morocco*, Josef von Sternberg, 1930, USA**

Truly a moving picture worth the name. It was made on a very low budget, but it's really well done—especially the shifts in camera position and the textures of light and shadow that work so atmospherically. I was really impressed by this film.

8 ***Congress Dances*, Erik Charell, 1931, Germany**

This is the first movie that used the technique of playback, matching the songs to prerecorded sound. This is a real masterpiece, an operetta. Its songs move in and out of the story, working to develop the characters, and the flow of the camera is just fantastic. I watched it again, and as you'd expect, I thought about the many, many things we should learn from these old films.

9 ***Threepenny Opera*, G. W. Pabst, 1931, Germany**

I've often thought I'd like to do a remake of *Threepenny Opera*. Many people have taken a turn at their own versions, but I think Pabst's is by far the best of the bunch. It's really a great piece of work.

10 ***Unfinished Symphony*, Anthony Asquith, 1934, Austria/England**

This is such an elegant work; I really like it a lot. It uses Schubert's music very well and folds it beautifully into the overall drama of how the symphony was left "unfinished," with only two movements.

11 ***The Thin Man,* W. S. Van Dyke, 1934, USA**

Van Dyke was renowned for his action films, so the tempo is really good. It's based on a Dashiell Hammett novel, and the detective couple and their pet dog were really popular. It turned into a series, but the first one was really the most entertaining.

12 ***Our Neighbor Miss Yae,* Shimazu Yasujirō, 1934, Japan**

He was nicknamed Old Man Shimazu, since he had risen through the ranks to make it to director.[1] He paid his dues as an assistant director, and like John Ford or William Wyler, who made their way through the studio system, his works were really in a class by themselves. He was—how can I put it?—a true old-school movie person.

13 ***Tange Sazen—The Million-Ryō Pot,* Yamanaka Sadao, 1935, Japan**

Even back when he was an assistant director, Yamanaka was really mild-mannered; he always seemed to be a little in his own world, very subdued. But when he got to be a director, all of a sudden he became quite eloquent; he had a lot of talent. It was such a blow to Japanese cinema when he died much too young. On top of that, the studios haven't preserved any of his films, which really makes me mad. What the hell are they thinking?

14 ***Capricious Young Man,* Itami Mansaku, 1936, Japan**

This work of Itami's feels especially fresh. He experimented with a lot of different things in this film; it's a lot of fun to watch. Itami-san always spoke really well of my work, [and] he gave me a lot of good advice; I feel really lucky.

15 ***The Grand Illusion,* Jean Renoir, 1937, France**

This film stars Eric von Stroheim, who directed and starred in *Foolish Wives*; the film overall is amazing, and so is Stroheim. I was lucky enough to meet Renoir when I visited Paris. He's by far senior to me, so I was surprised when he spoke to me in such honorifics when we met. When we pulled away in the car, I was touched that he watched and waved until we turned the corner.

16 ***Stella Dallas,* King Vidor, 1937, USA**
Barbara Stanwyck is famous for this role, which dramatizes that a woman is strong, and a mother will do anything for the sake of her child. I got all choked up at the last scene. The singer Bette Midler played the same role in a remake, and it was also quite a good performance; quite a fine film.

17 ***Composition Class,* Yamamoto Kajirō, 1938, Japan**
Yamakaji-san was such a good teacher to me. It was really busy on the set, and Yama-san had me doing all kinds of things, and it was work, work, work all the time. Later his wife told me, "He was really happy" because he said "now Kurosawa is capable of anything." It's true, I realized: Yama-san taught me each of these things, from editing to script writing, costumes, and props on up. Now I realize all that running around has paid off, and I'm so grateful.

18 ***Earth,* Uchida Tomu, 1939, Japan**
Uchida Tomu had quite an incredible career. I think he was even homeless for a while. He was also an actor, and kind of an eccentric; I think he worked as assistant director for someone who had worked in Hollywood. His big-budget films are good, but I really like his early ones like *Unending Advance.* Unfortunately, a lot of his films are gone. I really wish they would think of some kind of film preservation law in Japan.

19 ***Ninotchka,* Ernst Lubitsch, 1939, USA**
This is quite a sophisticated work. Garbo stars in a part that's different from her usual role. I was surprised she was so good at comedy. Then again, it was Billy Wilder who did the screenplay, so it's no wonder the dialogue is so good. Lubitsch has been working since the silent era and made a lot of musicals, cine-operetta films; he is an amazingly talented man.

20 ***Ivan the Terrible, Parts I and II,* Sergei Eisenstein, 1944–46, Soviet Union**
Henri Langlois submitted my *Rashomon* to the Venice Film Festival, so I'm forever in his debt.[2] He told me I better take a look at how Eisenstein used color in the banquet scene of *Ivan the Terrible.*

He also told *me* I better start working in color, and it's true, when I saw it, I was bowled over. I started playing with color in *Dodes'ka-den,* and from *Kagemusha* on I used it for real. By that time, Langlois had died, and when I said I would have loved to have shown *Kagemusha* to him, William Wyler's wife said, "Surely he's arrived at Cannes (from heaven), and he's watching alongside us." Until that moment I'd always hated film festivals, but from then on, I made a habit of going to Cannes.

21 ***My Darling Clementine,* John Ford, 1946, USA**
The name of John Ford is, of course, synonymous with the Western. *My Darling Clementine* is basically a blueprint for how the movies should be. At just the right moment someone passes by on a horse; just like a poem as it glides against the landscape. It's just magnificent.

22 ***It's a Wonderful Life,* Frank Capra, 1946, USA**
In the end, the best thing a movie can do for you is make you glad just to be alive. It's got to make you feel good. That's what a Capra film does so well: it makes you glad to have lived a full life and leaves you full of goodwill that keeps your heart warm.

23 ***The Big Sleep,* Howard Hawks, 1946, USA**
To my eye, this is the most interesting of the Chandler adaptations. Hard-boiled is hard to get right, but Hawks's skill is remarkable—as an artisan who has worked his way up the ladder, from props on up.

24 ***Bicycle Thieves,* Vittorio De Sica, 1946, Italy**
This is a painful story. The style of the film really brings home to us the way the characters go through injury after injury, injustice after injustice. It's the best of neorealism—just a remarkable work, inventing a whole new cinematic style.

25 ***Blue Mountain Range,* Imai Tadashi, 1949, Japan**
Blue Mountain Range and *The Izu Dancer* have been remade so many times, but the first one is the best, as it usually is. Imai-san's version of *Blue Mountain Range* really gets the energy of that moment. Kama-san (Fujiwara Katamari) plays his cameo role as a teacher really well. Imai's adaptation of *Troubled Waters* was also superb.

26 ***The Third Man*, Carol Reed, 1949, England**

Reed turns an incredibly complex story into a riveting film. Robert Clasker's camerawork is terrific. It holds up as a film even today, and I've learned a lot from that camerawork—it's magnificent. *Odd Man Out* is also good, with its documentary style; he's quite a director.

27 ***Late Spring*, Ozu Yasujirō, 1949, Japan**

So many directors have learned from Ozu's camerawork—including people from overseas. Thanks to programmers abroad, even foreign audiences can get a proper introduction to Ozu's films. There are so many things to learn from those films. I wish filmmakers who want to make their mark in Japanese film would watch them with just as much curiosity. It was such a glorious age of filmmaking when Ozu, Naruse, Mizoguchi were all working.

28 ***Orpheus*, Jean Cocteau, 1950, France**

In the beginning Jean Cocteau was a poet, so it's no surprise that his films have that poetic tone. Having the henchmen of Death ride motorcycles was quite an inspired touch. Cocteau's unmistakable aesthetic is highly entertaining.

29 ***Carmen Comes Home*, Kinoshita Keisuke, 1951, Japan**

This was the first-ever color film in Japan, and it is very entertaining to watch. Two boisterous Carmens—both strippers—come back to the hometown of one of them and cause a big fuss. A lot of mix-ups happen and it's very funny. I really like this film a *lot*.

30 ***A Streetcar Named Desire*, Elia Kazan, 1951, USA**

I met Elia Kazan at the Tokyo International Film Festival. He was easy for me to get along with, but the organizers thought he was a real handful. We had a lot of things to talk about; maybe we got along because we both find tuxedos too fussy. His works are often called Social Realism, and he did a lot of pictures that take on big social themes.

31 ***Thérèse Raquin*, Marcel Carné, 1953, France**

Carné is most known for *Les enfants du paradis*; this film is more of a minor work, but I really like it. Its black-and-white look is quite cool and detached. This film shows you how a good script can make a film totally stand out from the pack.

32 ***The Life of Oharu,* Mizoguchi Kenji, 1952, Japan**
People used to tease Mizoguchi-san—saying he must have been put through the wringer by women. But his way of depicting women was unprecedented. It's something I could never do; it's hair-raising! At every level it's quite amazing. The art direction and long takes—everything. I've learned so many things from Mizo-san over the years.

33 ***Journey to Italy,* Roberto Rossellini, 1954, Italy**
Rossellini really put neorealism on the map; he paved the way for Nouvelle Vague directors like Godard and Truffaut. His take on realism felt very raw, very new. I've picked up a lot from his style as well.

34 ***Godzilla,* Honda Ishirō, 1954, Japan**
Honda is very sincere; he's a good guy. Imagine, if Godzilla really came along, most people would drop what they were doing at work and run for their lives. But the fact that the people in his film just stay calm and lead everybody else through the chaos out to safety... that's Honda through and through, really admirable. Honda was my closest friend, and given how stubborn I am, the fact that we got along as well as we did for as long as we did is truly a tribute to him.[3]

35 ***La Strada,* Federico Fellini, 1954, Italy**
Fellini's aesthetic in this film is wonderful. It's like a fine art all of its own. That kind of flair just doesn't exist anymore. The image has a very compelling presence, with the power to surprise and move you. I have met him a number of times, but he was rather shy, and we never got around to talking movies.

36 ***Floating Clouds,* Naruse Mikio, 1955, Japan**
Naruse was quite terrifying actually. If the acting didn't satisfy him, he would just say "that's wrong" and keep sitting there silently. That was really hard on the actors; they need to figure things out for themselves. I'm not so aloof; I can't help blurting out what needs to be said. People who came up through Ozu or Naruse or Mizoguchi are so well trained you hardly need to say anything for them to do their job.

37 ***Pather Panchali*, Satyajit Ray, 1955, India**
Once I met Satyajit Ray, I got a better grasp of his works. Such a sparkle in his eye; he was really a magnificent person. It was completely understandable that *The Hidden Fortress* lost to his *Pather Panchali* at Venice.

38 ***Daddy Longlegs*, Jean Negulesco, 1955, USA**
I'm very fond of this work. People might be surprised that I like this film, but it's so well put together. I'm not very light on my feet myself, which probably explains why I admire Astaire so much. I think Leslie Caron is great too.

39 ***The Proud Ones*, Robert D. Webb, 1956, USA**
The theme song was a big hit for Lionel Newman back in the day, wasn't it? That was a wonderful movie. Webb used Robert Ryan so well in his role, and the camerawork is amazing. As always, Lucien Ballard is just a model cinematographer.

40 ***Sun in the Last Days of the Shogunate*, Kawashima Yūzō, 1957, Japan**
The tempo is really great—so brash; it's a lot of fun to watch. It draws on a number of *rakugo* sketches like "Saheiji Who Overstays," and it's very well made.[4] Kawashima Yūzō has a real gift with comedies, and his style is absolutely unique.

41 ***The Young Lions*, Edward Dmytryk, 1957, USA**
This film is mostly shot in Cinemascope; the cinematography plays off the contrast of black and white to make the battlefield scenes dramatic. It seems like the work of an experienced studio director who's seen it all.

42 ***Les cousins*, Claude Chabrol, 1959, France**
It's an odd kind of film; a bit misanthropic, but he's such a good director. Out of all the adaptations of Ed McBain's novels, his *Blood Relatives* (*Les liens de sang*, 1978) is one of the best.

43 ***The 400 Blows*, François Truffaut, 1959, France**
Truffaut's films are so good, aren't they? His use of the child in this film is very sharp. I talked it up a lot at the time, but it closed almost as

soon as it opened. It didn't help that the Japanese translation of the title, *The Adults Just Don't Understand,* basically misses the spirit of the film.

44 ***Breathless,* Jean-Luc Godard, 1960, France**
Godard has made many works over the course of his career, and the fact that he's managed to keep up the quality shows how talented he really is. When I saw *Breathless,* I knew I was really seeing something new. Even now people imitate it. If people don't start doing something different, though, cinema is never going to go anywhere new.

45 ***Ben Hur,* William Wyler, 1959, USA**
The climax scene of *Ben Hur* would never have had the same impact if it hadn't been shot in 70 mm. The soundtrack was recorded in six-channel stereo sound, so you really feel immersed, like you are right in it; it's really well shot.

46 ***The Younger Brother,* Ichikawa Kon, 1960, Japan**
Miyagawa Kazuo's camerawork is outstanding in this one. The film got a special award in Cannes for the image. Ichikawa made so many films over the course of his career. I think Natto-san—his screen-writer wife, Natto Wada—supported it strongly from behind the scenes. Some people had harsh things to say about *Tokyo Olympiad,* but I thought Kon-chan was just being himself, and it was quite a fine work.[5]

47 ***The Long Absence,* Henri Colpi, 1961, France**
Colpi is one of the masters of editing, isn't he? I think this is his first work; it's a hell of a story. The protagonist sees a man passing in front of a café who looks exactly like her husband, who died in the war. That scene has always stuck with me. A good editor like Colpi understands that there is an entire movie in the spaces between the shots.

48 ***Stowaway in the Sky,* Albert Lamorisse, 1960, France**
You could never pull off this movie unless you were a master of stunts and tricks. The ending is really the best, where the boy just follows and follows the balloon. Lamorisse used his own child in the role, which was really quite dangerous. Apparently afterward Lamorisse was kicking himself for doing such a reckless thing.

49 ***Purple Noon,* René Clément, 1960, France/Italy**
It's a very simple film: truly cinematic, easy to enter its world just as soon as it starts. You completely understand the feelings of the main character, right. It moves along at just the right tempo, and the ending is also so good.

50 ***Zazie dans le Métro,* Louis Malle, 1960, France**
I thought this was quite a sophisticated work. It draws you in with the train whistle, then the real whistling, and you see everything through the eyes of the child, Zazie. Louis Malle also made *Au revoir les enfants,* and he's really good with children. *May Fools* is also quite distinctive, really a pleasure to watch.

51 ***Last Year at Marienbad,* Alain Resnais, 1961, France/Italy**
Resnais is certainly one of the main players in the Nouvelle Vague. Of course, this work is adapted from Robbe-Grillet's novel, and he stirred up so many critical debates. The movie can be hard to follow because it mixes things up: past and present, reality and irreality. Its techniques really put a lot of new things in motion.

52 ***Whatever Happened to Baby Jane?,* Robert Aldrich, 1962, USA**
Bette Davis always had such an interesting face, ever since she was young. So charming, quite stunning in *Jezebel,* and so good in *All About Eve*. I loved those films; she was terrific. She wasn't as old as the character she played, right; she was altogether fabulous. By the time of *The Whales of August* she had aged quite a bit, and she was still so good.

53 ***Lawrence of Arabia,* David Lean, 1962, USA**
This is the crème de la crème of 70 mm productions. I heard that after the scene when the camel ran wild and injured Peter O'Toole, Lean asked if he could keep going. O'Toole put his foot down—"Are you kidding!?!" I can understand how a director can get caught up in shooting. But I'm a little bit nicer on the set, you know.

54 ***Any Number Can Win,* Henri Verneuil, 1963, France/Italy**
Verneuil's suspense films are absolutely the best, great fun to watch. His use of music is also quite stylish and very modern. Verneuil plays Gabin and Delon off each other so well; both of them really own their

roles. The look of the black-and-white images is very sharp, and the overall film is great.

55 ***The Birds,* Alfred Hitchcock, 1963, USA**
There can be places in a Hitchcock film that are a little incoherent. But you don't really worry about it because one of the pleasures of a film is to be carried away, entertained—and his films certainly do that. That huge flock of birds is terrifying, and I'm actually baffled about how he managed to shoot it.

56 ***Red Desert,* Michelangelo Antonioni, 1964, Italy/France**
I had the chance to ride an elephant with Antonioni during a film festival in India. The reporters got all excited seeing us two "scary" directors perched on top of the elephant. But we're not scary at all! The journalists only get interested when they think we are angry, but it's so not true, we both agree. It would be so exhausting to always be so bent out of shape! The film uses the all-red interior of the seaside shack to deepen the drama, and you really get a sense of Antonioni's talent as a director.

57 ***Who's Afraid of Virginia Woolf?,* Mike Nichols, 1966, USA**
Elizabeth Taylor is just magnificent in this role. Such a stunning actress doesn't normally play the role of such a toxic person. If only Japanese actresses could stop being praised just for their good looks. No matter how major a star you become, you can still learn from Elizabeth Taylor's poise and risk-taking.

58 ***Bonnie and Clyde,* Arthur Penn, 1967, USA**
People treated me so kindly when I visited America. *Bonnie and Clyde* isn't very well known in Japan, but it's a great little film. When Penn was making *Mickey One,* he asked me to introduce him to someone good for the artist role, and I recommended Fujiwara Katamari.[6] When Kama-san asked me why I recommended him, I told him it's because there isn't a single line of dialogue, and we burst out laughing.

59 ***In the Heat of the Night,* Norman Jewison, 1967, USA**
The original novel is also really great, and the film adaptation is very well done. I really love Sidney Poitier, the cleverness you can see in his

eyes. It was very satisfying to see the resolution to the crime in that Mississippi town, where the racism ran so thick.

60 ***The Charge of the Light Brigade,* Tony Richardson, 1968, UK**
This film didn't get much of a critical reception, but I was really taken with it. It gets down to a really granular level of detail—like in the last shot when you can actually hear the flies buzz around the corpses on the battlefield.

61 ***Midnight Cowboy,* John Schlesinger, 1969, USA**
It was directed by an Englishman, but he gets the grotty late sixties feeling of New York perfectly, doesn't he? Of course, the acting is also superb. You get a real feel for how people struggle to connect and just to get some kind of a break in that city. It just seems like too much.

62 ***M*A*S*H,* Robert Altman, 1970, USA**
This film was a blast. The story seems all over the place, but the script is really tight. It's black humor, and very well done. After I saw the film I heard that the author of the original novel was a surgeon, which explains why the situations seem so spot-on. It also goes to show that you can also make a real antiwar film with humor.

63 ***Johnny Got His Gun,* Dalton Trumbo, 1971, USA**
There's no shortage of antiwar films, but most of them have battle scenes that ruin the message. It's easy to glorify war when you put the bangs and booms of combat on the screen. That's why this one is a true antiwar film.

64 ***The French Connection,* William Friedkin, 1971, USA**
I think the car chase in *French Connection* was one of the first on film—the action of it was amazing, with the car whipping around; so exciting. I was surprised at how many American films from that time have car scenes—opening the car door, getting in the car, pulling out of the parking lot. I'm always joking that if you cut out the car scenes, you'd lose about a third of most American movies.

65 ***The Spirit of the Beehive,* Víctor Erice, 1973, Spain**
The film starts out like a sweet fairy tale, but it turns out to be deeply

mysterious and terrifying. The film is very aware of the special cruelty children can have, and the children's performance overall is wonderful. Erice's crew has a real touch with the lighting and the camerawork; it's a great movie.

66 ***Solaris*, Andrei Tarkovsky, 1972, Soviet Union**
I was really close to Tarkovsky. He felt like a younger brother to me. One time we met up and got drunk and ended up belting out the theme to *Seven Samurai* together. His depiction of water, the way he captured it, was totally unparalleled. Honestly, when you see this film, you long to come back to earth just like the cosmonauts.

67 ***The Day of the Jackal*, Fred Zinnemann, 1973, UK/France**
The technique coolly traces each step of the protagonist, a contract killer, on his way to assassinate President de Gaulle. There is absolutely no filler in the story; it's so tightly wound its suspense puts you on edge; it's superbly told.

68 ***Conversation Piece*, Luchino Visconti, 1974, Italy/France**
Visconti is an actual member of the nobility. He has his own sensibility, and I'm not sure if we should chalk it up to his origins, or if it comes from how he was brought up. I met him several times, but he wasn't very approachable. I've heard that if someone came on set during production, he would scream at them to get out, losing his temper in an imperious way. People say he was terrifying.

69 ***Godfather Part II*, Francis Ford Coppola, 1974, USA**
This is my favorite part of the Godfather trilogy. It's palpable, how intense that family is, and their ruthlessness; the music keys into the violence and really works on your emotions.

70 ***Sandakan No. 8*, Kumai Kei, 1974, Japan**
I had dinner with Kumai around the time he made this film. He's such a gentle and serious person, and I got used to his works taking on some kind of social issue. I was surprised how subtle he was with the life of this female protagonist. Tanaka Kinuyo was especially strong. She was also good in Kumai's *The Sea and Poison,* which is very well done. As a director, the theme of *Sandakan No. 8* would terrify me, but he does it really well; he must be a strong person.

71 ***One Flew Over the Cuckoo's Nest,* Miloš Forman, 1975, USA**
Such an abundance of talent in this cast. Even though the backstories of the various characters don't really come up, the acting was so good you could almost imagine the situations that landed them in the institution. I am in awe of the expressive skill it took to play these parts. The head nurse was phenomenal.

72 ***The Travelling Players,* Theo Angelopoulos, 1975, Greece**
Angelopoulos is a wonderful person, and it's like his films show the depth of his lived experience, the way they can pierce through everything, right to the bottom of your heart. This film in particular is the work of a mature director.

73 ***Barry Lyndon,* Stanley Kubrick, 1975, UK/USA**
Kubrick has many masterpieces to his name. I've heard that this one in particular was shot by candlelight using special film and lenses. This effect was great; it made for a very gorgeous image. He really pulled it off, this one.

74 ***Lullaby of the Earth,* Masumura Yasuzō, 1976, Japan**
This one is really well made, isn't it, especially Harada Mieko, who is outstanding. When I saw her in this film, I knew she was destined to do great things in the acting world. She played Lady Kaede in *Ran,* which went over very well abroad. She really did an amazing job.

75 ***Annie Hall,* Woody Allen, 1977, USA**
Woody Allen's films present him as a real intellectual. Mine are not so complicated, and not at all like his, so I thought he would have hated them. But Richard Gere told me he was a huge fan of mine, which pleased me very much.

76 ***An Unfinished Piece for Mechanical Piano,* Nikita Mikhalkov, 1977, Soviet Union**
Nikita is a guy who is very garrulous; he seems so lively, a big white bear of a guy, but in reality his films are very subtle. When you see him, it's hard to believe that the person in front of you shot films like *Dark Eyes.* He's just so full of vitality and talent.

77 ***Padre Padrone*, Paolo Taviani and Vittorio Taviani, 1977, Italy**

The Taviani brothers' images themselves are marvelous, and as harrowing as that memoir is, their adaptation, as you would expect of their work, interprets it in a very smart way. I'm not sure how to explain it, but their work has a power to it, so immense that it shakes you down to your very core. I really envy how the brothers combine their talents to make their directing broader and deeper in all the senses of "directing."

78 ***Gloria*, John Cassavetes, 1980, USA**

When I saw *Shadows* I wanted to tell Cassavetes how much I liked it, but he got shy and ran away. His works are very rarely screened in Japan, so I wondered what he had been up to, and seeing *Gloria* I was again struck by his talent. Gina Rowlands really did the performance of her career, I think. This is really one of my favorite works of his; he died far too young, and it's devastating that the world lost a true creative force.

79 ***A Distant Cry from Spring*, Yamada Yōji, 1980, Japan**

I've said this to Yamada himself, but I admire him the most for producing his Tora-san series over such a long time. He was able to do that because each of the characters in the series had its own stand-alone identity. This film is almost the Japanese version of *Shane*; it's really well made.

80 ***La Traviata 1985*, Franco Zeffirelli, 1983, Netherlands/Italy**

La Traviata 1985 transforms the original opera into a film, which is very difficult to do. Seiji Ozawa has tried to talk me into doing an opera. But I had to turn him down: I'm a film director, and I wouldn't be any good with that material. Zeffirelli is used to doing work for the stage, so his art direction, and lighting, and costuming are much better suited. It's a very beautiful picture.

81 ***Fanny and Alexander*, Ingmar Bergman, 1982, Sweden/France/ West Germany**

It's a pretty long film, but of course the camerawork and art direction are superb, and the color really lovely. It follows the goings-on of one night. The way he folds in concrete little details is so interesting, it makes me wonder if Bergman himself grew up in that setting. I also love his works like *Wild Strawberries* and *The Virgin Spring.*

82 ***Fitzcarraldo*, Werner Herzog, 1982, West Germany**
It's really too bad that so few people have seen this film. It must have taken a massive effort to trace back the Amazon to its source and actually haul that big steamship over the mountain. The energy it took to make that happen is visible on the screen. I have a story from the time I met Herzog. He's a very conscientious person. One day he came to introduce himself and said he had a book he wanted to give me, but he had to leave that very day. I was surprised when the very next day he cancelled his flight and brought the book over. Afterward when I saw his film, I could understand how that same tenacity made it possible for him to make a film like *Fitzcarraldo.*

83 ***The King of Comedy*, Martin Scorsese, 1983, USA**
Scorsese is, of course, known as a superb director, and an accomplished actor—but I most admire him as a human being. He's a great advocate: fighting for the production of stable color film stock; promoting film preservation and the awareness of deteriorating color film; and finding support for film industry people as they age. He's a ball of energy; it would be great if someone like that existed in the Japanese film world.

84 ***Merry Christmas, Mr. Lawrence*, Ōshima Nagisa, 1983, UK/New Zealand/Japan**
I've talked to Ōshima about all sorts of things, like directors' mutual support for each other. People talk about his short temper, but I've found him to be a straightforward and serious person. I've told him so many times as we've shared a meal together that I counted on him for the future of Japanese film. This film must have been really difficult, since he had to be on top of every detail of a complicated shoot. His casting was inspired; he is the real deal as a creative force.

85 ***The Killing Fields*, Roland Joffé, 1984, UK**
This is a story about the Cambodian civil war, which drew in even little children into its orbit. How terrifying that human beings can become

so detached from reality they don't know what they're doing. It's really frightening how people in wartime can end up normalizing things. Haing S. Ngor, the actor who plays the journalist Dith Pran, who translates and guides the American journalists, comes off as really natural; it's very well done, a terrific film.

86 ***Stranger Than Paradise,* Jim Jarmusch, 1984, USA/West Germany**

I've never met Jarmusch, but it was clear that someone really interesting had appeared, which made me very happy. I rented all his works and watched them on video. The one-shot/one-scene aesthetic was wonderful. I loved the way the scenes were strung together by patches of plain black screen—pure cinema. I'm looking forward to seeing what he comes up with next. By using old film and other resourceful tricks, he made a great film without spending a lot of money—which is its own kind of genius.

87 ***A Summer at Grandpa's,* Hou Hsiao-hsien, 1984, Taiwan**

Hou made the epic masterwork *City of Sadness*. If you don't know the history behind that film, you might get confused. But he's got such a sincere eye; he is an auteur of the highest caliber. This film recalls the era when Japanese filmmaking was actually good. I really like this work a lot; it's a really lovely piece. I'm looking forward to seeing where his talent takes him next.

88 ***Paris, Texas,* Wim Wenders, 1984, West Germany/France/UK/USA**

I did a *taidan* with Wenders around the time of *Rhapsody in August*. He forgot we were on the clock, doing the talk for publication, and had a long list of specific questions for me about how things work on the set. "Kurosawa, you're really good at shooting in the rain, how do you get that effect?"—things like that. To be honest, I like that line of questioning better than the philosophical ones, but the poor editor didn't get much of a magazine article.

89 ***Witness,* Peter Weir, 1985, USA**

I was very taken with Weir's earlier film, *Picnic at Hanging Rock*: such a mysterious and broody film. *Witness* depicts the very particular world of the Amish. It carefully depicts the reality of the characters' daily lives while being a compelling drama; Weir did justice to both these dimensions of the story world. It feels like a very solid film, due to the care taken representing the Amish world.

90 ***The Trip to Bountiful,*** **Peter Masterson, 1986, USA**
You can take a very "small" topic and make such a fantastic movie out of it. This film is a great example of how you can make a quality film without throwing a lot of money into it; I would love for young filmmakers to see it.

91 ***When Father Was Away on Business,*** **Emir Kusturica, 1985, Yugoslavia**
I was really bowled over when I first saw Kusturica's works. He's Yugoslavian and still quite young. Everything I have seen is really great, with a kind of cool aesthetic to it; he is very talented. People were saying the same thing at Cannes. We all agreed; there's so much talent coming from places all over the world, it really keeps you on your toes.

92 ***The Dead,*** **John Huston, 1987, UK/Ireland/USA/West Germany**
It begins with a black horse-drawn carriage, right, so the shadow of death is over it from the beginning. Huston shot the film while hooked up to an oxygen tank, so it's no wonder he worked as if he were possessed. I heard that as he was dying, he got furious at the studio management and screamed, "Where's a gun! Let's kill them!" And after saying that he died.

93 ***Where Is the Friend's Home?,*** **Abbas Kiarostami, 1987, Iran**
I met him, and just like all good directors, he was a very decent person. The people who appear in the film seem so normal, and they play their roles shockingly well. So when I asked him how he got them to play their parts, he explained, "Well, they are true amateurs, so they really did say they had to do their laundry and had homework to do."[7]

94 ***Bagdad Café,*** **Percy Adlon, 1987, West Germany**
My kids bugged me to see it because they told me it was good, and they were absolutely right; I really enjoyed it. The use of color is amazing. There's a lot we can learn from this film. The actors play

their parts in a really natural way, and at times it reminded me of my own *The Lower Depths,* and just: wow, now that is a real film. It was so interesting, I ended up seeing it twice.

95 ***The Whales of August,* Lindsay Anderson, 1987, USA**
I met the director when he was still a working film critic, when I was awarded a prize in England. He had a history of making nonfiction movies and had real powers of observation. I never imagined he would make feature films, but *if*.... was outstanding, and when I saw *Whales of August,* it was everything I was expecting; really powerful.

96 ***Running on Empty,* Sidney Lumet, 1988, USA**
There's a scene where the main characters leave town, and suddenly the door of their van pops open, and they leave their dog behind; it's amazing. Lumet was one of my closest friends; he was always smiling and such a nice person, but he could make serious hardboiled stories about New York detectives with the best of them. The blocks in New York are so big, he says, he wears roller skates to get around. There's a story about the assistant director jumping into a toy store to buy some skates in order to keep up with him. Then the second assistant tried the same thing, but the store had run out, so he had to run along behind. He had a lot of crazy stories like that.

97 ***My Neighbor Totoro,* Miyazaki Hayao, 1988, Japan**
This one is an anime, but I found it really moving. I was really taken with the Catbus. Who else could come up with such a thing? *Kiki's Delivery Service* brought me to tears. Honestly, all the talent I would hope to see in the film world has moved over to anime. The film world really has to step up its efforts. We need to make films that make young people want to be a part of this industry.

98 ***Buddies,* Furuhata Yasuo, 1989, Japan**
I've known Muraki Shinobu, the art director, a long time—since the days of the open sets when she and art director Yoshiro were an item and would sit side by side. Her art direction is really good. I get so nostalgic thinking about those times. Mukōda Kuniko wrote some very fine scripts.[8] It was so terrible, the way she died. The wife in *Buddies* reminds me a bit of my own wife [Yaguchi Yōko].

Beat Takeshi (Kitano Takeshi, director of *Fireworks,* the final film in the list) and Kurosawa in a 1993 *taidan*. Kurosawa is wearing a Lakers jersey.

99 *La belle noiseuse,* Jacques Rivette, 1991, France/Switzerland

I actually wanted to make that film; it's from a Balzac short story. An excellent painter can see things in the world that just pass the rest of us by. Directors like me tend to shoot things at a pretty fast pace, but Rivette's method is really different. People like him are never satisfied because they see so many more things than other people. He does an excellent job with this very subtle material.[9]

100 *Fireworks* (HANA-BI), Kitano Takeshi, 1997, Japan

I knew Kitano was really talented from the moment I saw *Violent Cop* (1989). In their early works talented people want to do a lot of experimenting, and the experiments don't always get integrated into the film smoothly. That's because the raw ideas are all coming out at the same time. It's great to see him acting so decisively and jumping in with both feet; it's a real joy to watch. In this film, he got across the distinct presence of each actor, which was amazing.

Farewell, Papa (1998)

Kurosawa Kazuko

This essay reminisces about Kurosawa's last days and unfinished projects. Kazuko discusses her years as her father's caretaker, insights into their family life, being surrounded since childhood by the Kurosawa-gumi (the long-running group of cast and crew), and how she entered the film industry working as a costumer.

Three years ago, in 1995, my father slipped and fell in a ryōkan in Kyoto, fracturing a vertebra. That was two or three days before the Aum sarin incident took place.[1] He was with Koizumi Takashi, his chief assistant director, and I was worried, so I set out for Kyoto. I told him not to drink too much, and he was a bit chagrined: it's okay, don't worry about it, he assured me. It was clear that unless he healed completely, he would never be able to set foot on location for the next film, so he ended up recovering in the hospital for two or three months.

Apart from his fractured vertebra, there was nothing wrong with him physically, so he just rested while waiting for his bone to knit back together. He had always been one of those people who hated hospitals, and he said he wanted to come home as soon as possible, so he returned home to his house in Seijō and continued to live his normal life.

In Kyoto, he had been in the middle of writing another script. He had finished a draft of a film called *The Sea Is Watching,* the financing was secured, and they were poised to head into production; but first they needed to find a very large pool for a swimming scene.[2] There is only one pool in Japan big enough for that scene, and when their request to shoot was turned down, the whole thing fell through. To shoot without that scene would have really taken away from the film. So, he decided to move on, and that's why he ended up in Kyoto.

That script had only three pages to go before it was finished, but his mood changed while he was in the hospital. "The more time passes, the more bored I get with this one, so I think I'll get to work on another," he said. And once he went home, he spent his time reading books and doing various kinds of background research.

It didn't seem as if he were sad or suffering because he wasn't able to make that film. He took his situation in stride, as a "vacation from the gods," and watched a lot of movies on video, as well as the American football that he adored on TV. If he felt inclined to appear in public, he was able to. He said he didn't mind going around in a wheelchair, and he wanted to keep taking interviews. But when I suggested he shoot his film from the wheelchair, he really hated that idea, and in his words it just didn't look right. I suppose that had something to do with his aesthetic sense in general.

It probably would have been no big deal for someone who was more slight of build, but my father was 180 cm tall, and quite big at over eighty kilos. His strength had diminished because of his sedentary lifestyle. Even so, he ate delicious food and drank his whiskey until the very end.

Two weeks before he died, he had a bit of an irregular pulse, but that's something that happens to you at the age of eighty-eight, and usually doesn't raise an eyebrow, so he stayed calm about it. In any case, he said that under no circumstances did he want to go back into the hospital. That was the very least I could do, I thought, and I could promise that much.

On the morning of September 6, I received word from my father's caretaker that his complexion had gotten pale, and I ran over to his house. When I asked him, "Papa, are you okay?" he replied that he was. The doctor who had been making house calls every day said that he had probably had some small amount of internal bleeding, so he needed a transfusion. We got a call from the nurse saying that the blood had arrived and she would be right over. Around that time, the assistant director Koizumi, who had been coming by every day, without knowing anything, told my father he'd come to see him, and then just thirty minutes later, as if he were sleeping, he slipped away. He died painlessly.

The people present at his deathbed were me, my oldest son, and Koizumi. My brother, Hisao (head of Kurosawa Productions), had been on his way to formalize paperwork for building the Kurosawa Memorial Hall in Kyushu, but turned around mid-flight to get back to Tokyo. After my father's fall, my brother had picked up my father's share of work and was running around, though with the nagging feeling that he might not be able to be present at his father's death. I myself probably lived with the thought deep in my heart that at some point that day would come, but because we lived together, the whole fabric of daily life changed when my father died. Even now when I go to my father's house, I have a feeling that he is still there.

What Did You Dream Last Night?

Last year was the thirteenth anniversary of my mother's death. She first fell ill and collapsed a couple of years before that. So for about fifteen years, I did the cooking every day, and my father and I would have dinner together every night. I kept notebooks listing every meal we ate together. I had started keeping notes to give to the helper so that they could do the shopping and just kept going. You could see all the kinds of things we ate by looking at those notes—the major Japanese, Western, and Chinese dishes—but what really stands out is the number of meat dishes. He really liked to eat good things.

In time, I ate the same things my father did every day along with him. He once remarked that our musings about the next day's meals would surface at the same time, because our stomachs were in sync. [*laughs*] I could intuit those feelings, and when I would make up the day's menu, he would often say, "Oh, that's just what I wanted to eat!" The parent–child connection is a mysterious thing.

Even when my father died, I was never able to cry. I was so busy and had so many obligations to cover. The other day, I went to the usual market I used to go to, looked at the shelf, and all of a sudden I burst into tears. For fifteen years, day in and day out, I had thought about what to make for my father to eat.

It was more than just a daughter going to her father's place to cook dinner for him. As we ate, it was fun to talk about all kinds of things, and we would drift toward a particular topic. In fact, we usually had a special theme each week. It could be stories from the film shoot he was working on, or Russian literature, or politics. If things headed into some esoteric area, it could be difficult to keep up with him. If I didn't go home and spend a fair bit of time reading, I would soon fall behind.

Often the conversation would turn to dreams. Every day he would ask me, "What did you dream last night?" So even when I had slept it was hard to rest, since I had to remember it all. I had to try with all my might to remember and arrange things in my head before we ate dinner together. So while on one hand I was rejoicing—thinking he'd be in a good mood since I made something nice for him to eat—I had to also get my story together. [*laughs*] I would tell him "Papa, this is what I dreamed," and I might tell the story of a dream I had when I was a child. He in turn would start to tell me his own dream. That theme went on for several months. And out of that came the film *Dreams.*

I was really happy that we could transfer those dreams from the dinner table to the film set. I was encouraged to work on *Dreams* by Nogami-san, the production manager, and Koizumi-san. Then my father asked me, "Why don't you join me and the crew?" My background was in fashion, so it made a lot of sense to assign me to work on costumes. When I accepted, I went to Wada Emi-san's place to introduce myself and tell her I had been sent to help with costumes. I was my father's daughter, but, in fact, I was fairly new to the industry. I vowed to work ten times as hard as anyone else on the crew. I was happy that the people in the Kurosawa-gumi encouraged me so, calling me "princess" and telling me that I had been a member of the Kurosawa-gumi ever since I was born. I wasn't a complete novice, and given that I grew up hearing all sorts of backstories about film production, I didn't feel out of place. Of course, my father at home and my father at work are two completely different beings, and indeed the transition took a lot of getting used to.

I was assigned to locate some old-style *nora-chaku* indigo jackets for the "Village of the Waterwheels" episode and went exploring all around Aomori and Akita with just a backpack. I went many times to visit with collectors and finally I had enough material. Then I was assigned to find a sort of old farm hat called a *ba-ori.* My father had apparently seen these when he was working as assistant director on his mentor Yamamoto Kajirō's 1941 film, *The Horse.* When I finally turned them up, my father was so delighted, almost like a child. That made me very happy by association.

Apart from that, I volunteered to help with anything and stuck closely by my father's side. When he got mad, his anger would land on the person right in front of him. I was right in front of him fairly often, so even when he was actually mad at some other part of the production, he would yell at me. [*laughs*] Then it came about that I would convey whatever he was mad at to the unit in question. Going the other way, when the assistant directors or the prop masters had something to ask the director, they would turn to me instead, and I would help them as best as I could. It was a bit of a gamble when to ask my father anything, and the staff told me that they wish I had been brought into the production much earlier. [*laughs*] People tell me that my father started to calm down around *Kagemusha,* but he was still a pretty scary figure as a director.

Primal Memories of the Kurosawa-gumi

I was born when my father was forty-four. He died when he was eighty-eight and I was forty-four. Half his age. The day I was born was the same day as the wrap party for *Seven Samurai.* The staff all joke that it wasn't just the production of *Seven Samurai,* it was also the production of me, his daughter. [*laughs*] At that time, before I got there, it seems that all the children of Kurosawa-gumi were boys. It seems it was a major event when out of the blue a girl was born and added to the team.

Given the circumstances, it is not surprising that my first memory is also of Kurosawa-gumi. I think it must have been when I was around three. Every night the Kurosawa-gumi used to have a big spread on the second floor of the house in Komae, in suburban Tokyo. I remember I used to sit on the laps of Kurosawa-gumi staff, as they sat in a circle, being passed around to sit on each of the actors' laps, as they told me goodnight. I also remember bringing beer around to everyone at the dinners. At the beginning I could only hold two at a time, but my child's mind aspired to hold four, and then it became six, counting higher as I grew older.

All everybody talked about was the movies. So afterward, when I finally saw my father's works, they overlapped with my experience as a child, at home in that world. I always heard stories like about how that day's shoot on *High and Low* went well.

I began to see things in real time with *Red Beard* in 1965. I saw a press screening, then went home, and my father sat down in front of me and asked me how it was. When I said I liked it, he asked me if I understood it. When I said that of course I did, I remember him laughing and saying he would be a bit shocked if I actually had understood everything. When I see it today, I know how many complex things are wrapped up in the story. My father, as a parent, must have been a bit taken aback when my school-age self announced that I understood it all.

When I see works made before I was born, like *Seven Samurai,* I have complicated feelings, as I see how young my father was, and I see parts of him I don't recognize.

The movie *The Most Beautiful,* starring my mother, never played in the theater when I was young and was never available on video while she was

Yaguchi Yōko calibrates a lens in the wartime film *The Most Beautiful,* Kurosawa's first directorial effort.

alive. It was only after she died that I was able to see it at the Namiki-za repertory theater in Ginza.

It's the story of young girls drafted to work in a factory during the war. It's not sad, but because that was the first of my mother's movies I was able to see, I cried to myself, alone, all the way through. People all around me kept staring at me as if I were losing my mind.

When my father got out of the hospital that time, he came home and watched *The Most Beautiful* with his grandchildren on video. It was one of the rare times when I saw tears in his eyes. His grandchild—my son—asked why his own mother (me) was in the movie. It seems he mistook my face for hers. At other times, I look like my father. When I was little, people told me that they knew they had arrived at the Kurosawa house because I would be standing out in front—looking just like a Kurosawa. Even today, everybody tells tell me I look like my father when I glance sideways, or when I yell at my kids. [*laughs*]

When my mother got married, she became a complete stay-at-home wife and committed herself to supporting my father so he could best make movies. I was meticulously trained in domestic matters by my mother. Before she entered the hospital and died, even when her memory was fuzzy, she kept murmuring, "I've got to go home, I've got to get home," or "Papa is on location, I need to go make his bento." She would be running from morning until night, from the fish market to preparing the end-of-day dinners for the whole crew. She used to make the bento not only for my father but for all the staff. She came to the relationship as an actress, but rolled up her sleeves right away. As a director's wife, she needed to know how to cook, and she rose to the challenge—I can just imagine her saying there was no way she would let him outshine her in craft and perfectionism.

She was a cheerful person and would support the crew while looking after the family; everyone called her their "godmother." She was a small woman, short, but she was probably the only person who my father never towered over. Until she died at the age of sixty-three, she seemed really youthful and often laughed uproariously. My father had a drier personality, so I imagine he liked that about her.

One time she made fun of my father, asking him what kind of person (woman) he liked, and he said he was smitten with Audrey Hepburn. My mother, with her short hair, actually looked like that type, so it seems he did like that kind of woman. Probably my mother was actually a bit more "manly" than my father was.

Because my mother never made my father do anything, and took care of all his needs herself, my father never knew anything but movies. [*laughs*] I remember one point in elementary school or middle school. He would ask me once a year if I was a middle school student yet. After a while I eventually got married, then got divorced and came back home. He asked me, "Are you a Kurosawa these days, or still a Katō?" [*laughs*]

In some sense, once you reach a certain stature the people around you do everything for you. So he didn't know things like how to make a call on a public phone. [*laughs*] He thought maybe you folded a thousand-yen bill into the slot where you're supposed to insert a ten-yen coin. He really puzzled over that one. [*laughs*] He was really awkward on the phone, so when a call came to the house it was a mess. My brother made fun of him, saying it was like watching a chimpanzee dial the phone.

He didn't really know how to deal with money either, and would hand over ten thousand yen to the izakaya where he was a regular, which flummoxed the master who owned the place. This is a really old story, but my mother asked him to pick up some beans, since he was going to Shinjuku, and gave him ten thousand yen. And he came home hauling a huge sack, like a big bag of rice, in both hands. He had spent the whole ten thousand yen. My mother was completely stupefied and had to tell him that most people just ask for a few hundred grams. When he went overseas and brought my mother back an *omiyage,* he would buy her these huge clothes, and she would marvel that he had lived with her for decades but still had no idea what size she wore. His head was full of information, but only about movies, you see.

Rashomon in Real Life

The accounts of how my father and mother came to be married are very different depending on whether you ask my father or my mother. I wonder if perhaps there isn't one more truth, rather than one or the other being right. It's exactly like *Rashomon* in real life.

My father writes about this in his memoir *Something Like an Autobiography,* but as the war was intensifying, people didn't know if they would live or die, so as he writes, he thought it was not a bad idea to see what married life was all about.[3] Since his producer Morita Nobuyoshi had warned him that it would be good to match with someone as strong-willed as he was himself, he married my mother. According to my mother, my father wrote her a lot of letters, imploring her to marry him. But the stories my grandfather and grandmother tell are completely different. So there's really no way of telling which is true.

In my mother's version, my father made more of an effort than she did. Once they were married, when she saw my father from behind as he was sitting, she saw for the first time that the top of his head was balding. "He was so tall, I couldn't see the top. I was tricked!" she said. [*laughs*]

Apparently they fought a lot during the shoot of *The Most Beautiful.* My mother was really strong-willed, and she would snap back at my father, you see. For my father's part, he too realized she was quite a strong-willed young lady. So at that time, there was definitely no romantic kind of feeling between them. Although my mother had no feelings for him, she was cajoled into marriage, as she tells it. Neither of them is here anymore to clear up even this point, leaving us forever lost in the bamboo grove.

Another thing we don't really understand is the reason for my father's suicide attempt. Even my mother said that she had no idea. It's possible he got depressed and acted on impulse. When that happened in Shōwa 46 (1971), I was still a high school student. I remember the scene that day as vividly as any movie I have ever seen.

I was asleep in my bedroom and a maid dashed in very upset, saying, "Your father, your father!" I got up, and my mother was saying, "Papa, Papa!" Soon an ambulance arrived. The way I was raised told me to stay calm and keep myself together in the face of tragedy, and my brother and I took charge of dealing with the press. People were climbing on to the roof and sticking their feet in the door to keep us from slamming the door on them. I had to tell them that we would soon be having another press conference and to please give us some space. Where these lines came from, I have no idea, but at the time there was no choice but to go on this way. My mother took to her bed due to the shock. I remember dealing with the chaos of it all without having any idea what was going on.

About a week before that, my mother told me that she had seen him sitting and staring at the garden, which was unusual for him. People have different theories about what she said, but most likely he was brooding over the responsibilities that weighed on him. How he felt about the decline of the Japanese film scene, how he felt he was working against the wind. But just a few days after he was out of the hospital, he was going about things just like usual. [*laughs*] He was someone who was able to shrug anything off. He really was not someone who was dragged down by the past.

What was actually harder was the time around *Dersu Uzala*. I went to visit the set a number of times, but apparently there was always one sort of crisis after another. After that, my father would always walk around wearing a Russian fur hat. If you'd ask him why, he would say, "I survived such a terrible shoot as that, and that reminds me that no matter how terrible the shoot is, I will make it through."

He is wearing that hat in his coffin, along with his much-loved sunglasses. My father did the editing of his own films, and his eyes were quite bad, and it seems that he had been told by the doctor to protect his eyes from the light by wearing sunglasses. He always said that he wasn't wearing the sunglasses just for effect.

Kurosawa the *Benshi*

If you pay attention to his movies, or the impressions he gave off in public life, the image of my father was very masculine, but I didn't really have an awareness of him as a father or a man per se. This is because when I was a child, I was told that our daily life was structured to supporting my father's moviemaking—to me, he was the Director Akira

Kurosawa through and through. But I should say, he was a very sensitive person. In his private life he was a lot less guarded. When he was at home, he was very naive, almost childlike; he would get overjoyed by little tiny things. He was someone who cried while watching *My Neighbor Totoro.* [*laughs*] Really, just like a child. I never really thought of him as a paternal figure. I don't really have any memory of being clingy with him in that kind of a way.

From time to time we would go to see movies together, the two of us. We would get on the train and go to the theater just like a regular father and daughter. On the way home he would ask me what I thought, and we would talk about it. One I remember even now is the time the two of us went to see *The Exorcist.* In the middle of the night my father stuck his head into my room, it must have been four or five times, and when I asked him if everything was okay, he said, "After seeing that scary movie, I was worried your head might be spinning round and round." [*laughs*] He did have a part of him that worried, just like a child.

In his later years, he used to watch his own films a lot on TV and on video as well. He watched the works of other directors, too, and then when he saw his own work again, he would say that as time passed they seemed like someone else's work.

When I watched my father's movies with him, he would comment and tell me the backstories behind the productions. It was a lot of fun, like listening to a live broadcast. There were a lot of behind-the-scenes stories. I think it was the black market scene in *Stray Dog.* He told me, "Those legs aren't Mifune-chan's. They're actually Honda-kun's." Or this was the image he had in his head during the shot. Anyway, he told me a lot of stories like that.

He had a lot of things to say about other people's movies as well. Especially when we went to see older movies by Mizoguchi or Naruse, he was very subdued. When I asked him what was wrong, he would say, "You know, when I see Naruse-san's movies I feel like I'm there with him."

About Mifune-san, he said that there was no other Japanese actor working who could get up to speed on a part so quickly; this quality of Mifune's was amazing. If it took a typical actor several minutes to get the part down, Mifune had it down in a matter of seconds, which was amazing. After Mifune-san split off and formed his own production company, Mifune Pro, my father seemed to think that "Mifune-kun has his own world now. We were able to work together through *Red Beard* and experience so many things." And he would often talk about how they had done everything under the sun together that you could do in making a film.

My father was never one to look back, and only kept moving forward, thinking ahead. It was the same until he died. He often said, "Young people often use the phrase '*mae-muke*' [face forward], right. But humans are built to face forward, so there's nothing special about that." [*laughs*]

And he would often go to see works by young directors. When he heard that Abbas Kiarostami was coming to town, he said he had to see all of Kiarostami's works before meeting him because he's such a sincere person, and also a bit of a perfectionist. When he learned that Kiarostami would be arriving the next week, he did everything he could to see them all. Early on after seeing Kitano Takeshi's movies he thought that Takeshi was going to be one of the new leaders of Japanese cinema. My father didn't just like films that were of the same stripe as his. He often said that he found good points in all kinds of movies.

We went overseas together around the time *Ran* came out. There was nothing different about him per se, but it was only when we went overseas that it would hit me that Akira Kurosawa was actually important. When we got to the airport, there would be a limousine waiting to pick us up. We got a message from the publicity people that there were so many interviews packed in that they didn't know if we would have time to change clothes in between. Every evening, there would be a party. Every time there was a dinner, a car would arrive to take us. We went together to Paris, Amsterdam, Los Angeles, Cannes, and many other places, but we never had a chance to take a walk together, escaping the cars. [*laughs*] When it really got claustrophobic, we'd open the windows of the hotel room and stick our heads out, breathing in the fresh air of whatever place we were in. Feeling beset by interviews, and so busy, he said, "We're like goldfish." But he really liked the hotel where we stayed in Antibes, the Hôtel du Cap-Eden-Roc, and was always happy to be there. The rooms were so big, and the view was amazing; the hotel was so wonderful I had hoped to be able to come year after year, but in the end we went only three times.

Sleep Is Food

He used to drink alcohol, until the very end. He liked whiskey, and when he was working with Mifune, the two of them would empty three

Kurosawa and daughter Kazuko visit Cannes for the last time Courtesy of Kurosawa Production Co., Ltd.

bottles every night, and then show up for the shoot the next day. Until he slipped and broke his vertebra, he would drink half a bottle every time a guest would come over. When he came home from the hospital, every day he would drink between three and five glasses. I don't really drink, but I would often stay up all night with him, socializing. I loved when he would tell stories, and he could keep it up until five or six in the morning. All the while eating.

It's not just me; my brother also doesn't really drink. Neither do the grandchildren. When he would say in disbelief, "You all don't drink?!?" they would retort back, "Papa drinks enough for three generations, so no one else needs to."

Then there was how focused he would get on things. When I was an elementary school student, my father got really caught up in *shodō* calligraphy, and bought a lot of books about it: he would practice tracing different characters and how to write them. Anyway, he was so immersed in it that he would forget to come to dinner. He told me I should practice it with him, and I sat next to him practicing writing. My mother scolded us, saying, "You two get so wrapped up in it, you're going to fall over from forgetting to eat." It was just as she said; he would get immersed in everything. Food was the same way. Nogami-san gave him the nickname of *hanjuku-tamago* (perfect soft-boiled egg). If he got obsessed with one dish, he could go on eating it for six months straight.

One time he was told to draw a suit of armor, and he obsessed over that as well, saying he had to draw it with *nihonga* mineral pigments on *washi* paper, and it took him over a month to finish.[4] All the while complaining that it gave him eyestrain. Whatever it was, he would throw himself into it fully.

Before he would begin shooting a film, he would always sketch out a storyboard. When you asked him why he did this, my father would say that showing everything graphically means that you've accounted for everything in the process. If you don't know the form of things, or what color they will be in, you can't draw them. He said he writes these storyboards because he figures out a lot during the process; also, it's important for directing, since you can plan out how the filmmaking will have to unfold from every level. So while he even wrote in his memoir that he was naive, and a humanist who cried from time to time, part of him could be very businesslike when he needed to think concretely and make things happen artistically.

When he was beginning to make a film, my father said that he would always start off by thinking what it might be like to use that script to make a silent film. Then after that exercise, he would turn back to the main project.

When you get to be eighty years old, you do start to have a philosophical edge, don't you? When his great old friend Honda-sensei died, I was worried my father would be depressed, as everyone around him was thrown into a tizzy, but in fact it was quite the opposite. He chided all the crew to stop fretting. When he heard that Mifune-san passed away last year, all he said was, "Ah, is that so?" and seemed to take the news indifferently.

When my mother died it was similar: he didn't get distraught, nor did he cry. That was around the time they were shooting *Ran*. The Kurosawa-gumi parked a camper van at the Juntendō hospital. My father put on his usual jeans, stuck his army cotton work gloves in his pocket and wandered up and down the hospital corridor, sometimes stopping to think, just like on a movie shoot. It seems that Juntendō was built on the site where my father's old middle school, Kyōka Middle School, had been. He stood, now a grown man, and looked at the facade: "What a strange link of fate." My brother and I asked him what kind of funeral we should have for our mother, and the only thing he said was, "Make it a funeral that's not like a funeral." He never liked to put those kinds of feelings out in public.

One thing my father often said was, "You can't just stay feeling sad forever. Anyway you have to get things done for those who are living." After that line would come, "Okay, let's eat and go to sleep."

Even though he was feared as the "devil of film," he doted on his grandchildren and whiled away the hours with them. The youngest is still small, and seeing his face every day brought him no end of joy till the very end. No matter what, he would murmur approval, smiling, smiling. Just looking at my son's face he was overjoyed. Just following with his eyes seemed to delight him.

He was kind of self-conscious, and when he learned that my oldest son, Katō Takayuki, was going to make his debut as an actor, he just said, "Hmm," in a satisfied way. [*laughs*] We had decided to send out postcards marking the occasion on August twenty-fourth, and my father wrote a line of inscription. "He's a sentimental humanist, just like me" and added that his only worry about my son was that he might get overshadowed by his own image and treated unfairly. I realized for the first time how highly my father thought of my son. Showing his emotions would have made him feel awkward, and he had never said a word.

The day before my father died, we did the photo shoot for the postcards. I rushed in to show him the Polaroid: "Look Papa, look what came out. Now you have to hang in there." But it was already the end. He saw it, but I wonder if he understood.

Farewell, and Well Done

More than thirty-five thousand people came to pay their respects at the memorial service we had at Kurosawa Film Studios in Yokohama. We were grateful for that, but even more, without any prompting at all, his fans each laid down 1,800 yen. Instead of incense, they offered 1,800 yen in loose change: the price of a movie ticket. That made me so happy. My father was grateful for his fans because their laughter and tears make the movies emotionally alive, so he held them in great esteem. It was fitting that they bid their farewells with such a stylish tribute.

The altar at the memorial was made on the motif of *Ran,* the last production that the Kurosawa-gumi had all worked on together; they poured their heart and soul into making it. I'm sure this too made my father extremely happy. My father always felt extremely grateful for the crew of Kurosawa-gumi. He said, "I'm called a genius; they call me the 'emperor' of movies and everything, but my films were really made possible because of all the crew." Of course, there were all the crew whose names are in the credits, but also it was thanks to the crew whose names are never known, like the guy who scatters sand on the set; the films were all made thanks to their work. While my father was alive, he was awarded a lot of prizes, which delighted him, but he always saw himself as receiving on behalf of everyone, as their delegate.

After the general condolences ended, we shut the shutters, and all the Kurosawa-gumi crew gathered, and once again laid flowers by the altar. And then, just like when a shoot was going well, everyone clapped, and my father's bones were sent off to my brother's house. At that point my brother broke down and cried for the first time and greeted them: "The Akira Kurosawa you knew was because of all of you, thank you so much."

I was happy that so many fans told us that they wished my father had more time to make more movies. But my father hated neat endings. He made thirty films all together, a neat number. It's not the old man from

The venue prepared for Kurosawa's memorial service, attended by many fans as well as colleagues. Courtesy of Kurosawa Production Co., Ltd.

the "Village of the Waterwheels" episode of *Dreams,* but he did his work well. I want to think that gave him a feeling of satisfaction. I'd like to send him off with "Well done" and "Congratulations."

It was my father's habit to say these words: "You can't just stay feeling sad forever. Anyway, you have to get things done for those who are living. Okay, let's eat and go to sleep." So I said it myself, and it gave me strength.

Edited by Tanaka Masumi

Dreaming It Forward (1999)

Introducing the Kurosawa-gumi

Kurosawa Kazuko

This essay details Kazuko's daily life with her father on the set and introduces the artisans who made up the Kurosawa-gumi. She touches on the tribute of making the film ***After the Rain*** with a Kurosawa script and the long-standing Kurosawa-gumi.

I saw my father in a dream the day before the shoot began on *After the Rain,* the movie based on my father's last script.

My father was on a set, with its dimly lit retro rooms and well-kept old wooden doors, his physical body outsized as usual. He was giving instructions: "There's no way to move the camera back, so we'll need to make the wall removable." He went back and forth to the adjacent room, slouching to bow out through the doorframe, and wandering around as he did when he was alive.

In the dream, he was giving orders about everything—from the set, to the camera, to the actors. I woke up just as he was telling me, "If you can't work it out yourself, come find the director or cinematographer."

The script my father left, *After the Rain,* is the last script he ever wrote. He collapsed two days before he was slated to finish it, leaving three pages to go. On September 6, 1998, he passed on to the other world.

An idea came to my older brother, Hisao, the day of my father's wake. He thought it might be nice to make Koizumi Takashi the director of *After the Rain* to acknowledge all he did for our father. After all, Koizumi-san had worked all those years for our father and was devotedly by his side every day until he died.

On the day of the memorial service, on September 13, after the mind-boggling number of thirty-five thousand mourners had left, we closed the shutters. The Kurosawa-gumi once again gathered and people made offerings of flowers, one by one. My brother addressed them: "I don't really know how to repay Koizumi-san. When our father was alive, he said he wanted to keep working as assistant director, and never shot films of his own. Now that our father is no longer here, we sincerely hope Koizumi-san can direct *After the Rain.* Even if he says no at first, I hope he changes his mind. Everyone in the Kurosawa-gumi, please give him all your support. The Kurosawa-gumi has supported us for so long. Thank you." This appeal by my strongheaded brother, crying all the while, launched the production. Preparations started three months later and five months after that shooting began.

I looked up at my father's photo and said, "Well, you're not working today, but maybe you can at least take care of the weather?" We were lucky and were blessed with good weather, and even location shoots that we had thought would take a month went quickly, so we were able to get back to Tokyo three days earlier than planned.

Every day was a joy to work with the new Koizumi-gumi on the set, the place my father loved most in the world, surrounded by many friends. In reality my father was not there, but his presence lived on through them.

Day by day things passed in a daze, and everyone on the new team, now without my father, worked with all their might. Every night at dinner people would tell stories about my father getting mad at them, and all sorts of other memories about him. One night, Koizumi-san mused, "The reason we can tell all these stories about Sensei is because all these amazing people have been on the crew for so long. That alone is something to be grateful for."

During the long days of shooting that month, we brimmed with the joy of forming a new team even more than we felt the loss of my father who was no longer there. Before we knew it the shoot was over.

The last location was on the Izu peninsula. I drove back alone and passed by the waterfall at Jōren Falls; it had been a location for *Rhapsody in August.* At that moment, I suddenly burst into tears that just wouldn't stop. Even more than missing my father, I was just so happy that all the old Kurosawa-gumi—now the Koizumi-gumi—had joined their forces and were working together, going all out, even though my father wasn't there. I remembered how much he loved being on set and I remembered the *Rhapsody in August* set where he had been so happy, but this time he wouldn't be there with everyone, and a feeling of terrible sadness came over me.

I was used to seeing him working in a frenzy in the middle of the night on his storyboard, moving between shelves and the wall, the result of which was getting painting and drawing materials all over himself, then heading over to the set early the next morning for the real thing, pacing around from the morning on.

The crew would be busy making preparations on the set. They would want us to come a little late; so as to kill some time, I would make coffee, set out some tea, catch up with people before diving in, but my father would say, "Okay, time to go." I tried to stall him with some juice, but he told me to drink it fast so that we could go. I tried desperately to bring up topics that I knew interested him: "Now that you mention it, the big battle . . ."

"Let's go."

"Wait, your shoes aren't polished. Aren't those socks uncomfortable?"

"I'll just wear sneakers. Let's go." He would stand up.

We would call the staff room to say we were on our way, and they would tell us to take our time as much as possible, and I would drive the car as slowly as I could. If we poked along my father's mood would get worse, but if we got there too fast, the staff would be unprepared; it was just like the delicate balance of making salt plums.

He would holler out, "Nooooow, start!" and then his reaction would be displayed on his face for all to see. If the scene was spot-on, a big smile would break out, and he would look supremely happy. If the part displeased him (though he himself wrote it), his expression would be a disgusted contempt unbearable to see. Some actors were certain he hated them because of this expression. At some point later, they would be told, "You played that really well!" and the misunderstanding would clear up, and they would wonder what had gone on at all. If it was a battle scene, he would be caught up like a child playing director, and with twinkling eyes would shout, "Stab him!"

I just adored seeing my father working with such pleasure, such joy, and each time there was a take, I made it a point to look at my father's face. The next day when I heard several crew members, as I expected, say, "When we see him working so happily, it makes the exhaustion disappear." I was very thankful for everyone's feelings.

Actually, my father used to say, "I take a look at the crew's faces, and I can gauge if that scene came off as I wanted." The crew's expression became a very good barometer of how the directing went. That's because the crew were all amazingly beautiful people. My father, who loved movies so much, thought so highly of the crew, thought of them as a gift.

The Kurosawa-gumi

Here I would like to introduce the wonderful members of the Kurosawa-gumi. I have been a part of the Kurosawa-gumi since I was born. But because it was only with *Dreams* that I began working with my father making films, sometimes I was too young to remember well, and I wasn't able to work with some of the crew who were very important to my father's work. It might be rude, but in this section I will limit myself to writing about the crew since the time of *Dreams,* remembering some things my father explicitly said.

Director Koizumi Takashi of *After the Rain* was born in 1944 and was assistant director on all the productions since *Kagemusha.* This simple summing-up expresses the feeling of trust my father had in Koizumi: "Koizumi is really a good man; you will never find a man as good as he is." After my father had his health crisis, until the very day he died, he would come to my father's bedside and massage his feet; he would sit quietly by his side and look after him; he really contributed. Because he was such a kind person, many of the crew made a huge effort to support him because they knew it was his first film as a director.

Nogami Teruyo was born in 1927, and first joined the Kurosawa-gumi as a screenwriter with *Rashomon.* She worked as the director's right-hand person on the set of *After the Rain.* When he talks about her, my father's eyes wrinkle up as if he is a child telling a story: "When she first joined up with Kurosawa-gumi as a young girl, she was still in braids. Of course, now she's come into her own as an independent person. She's done me the favor of working with me over so many years. When we were editing, and we would worry that it just didn't seem to flow, I would know that she would be standing behind me, encouraging me, even if I couldn't actually see her." When he talked about his crew, my father would always seem happy. These days Nogami-san is like the godmother of our team, supporting us all even if my father is not there. She herself has said she is the "wet nurse of the team," which has been acknowledged widely, as far as French newspapers.

The art director Muraki Yashirō was born in 1924 and has been with the Kurosawa-gumi since *Drunken Angel*: "When Muraki would drink, he had a tendency to bite people's heads off. He would go to great pains to make an amazing set and if you didn't show off every corner to its advantage, you might also make him mad. It does make sense, I have to admit. We knew each other for such a long time; we would scream at each other, we knew each other so well, and worked together for so long." When Muraki-san's anger reached a certain point, he would lash out at my father. But then it would soon blow over and he would say, "Once I've gotten it off my chest, I feel so much better." Other crew members would, of course, say, "This is just t-t-t-too much," though. My father said, "I'm used to Muraki's blowups, so it doesn't really bother me. I've gotten used to it," and it didn't seem to faze him at all. When you see the two of them together, you think it's good to have good friends who understand each other.

The cinematographer Saitō Takao was born in 1929 and was attached to the Kurosawa-gumi beginning with *Record of a Living Being*. [My father would say,] "Oh yes, Taka-bō. He was always such a gentle person. It was really striking how he would suddenly get very decisive when he picked up a camera. Sometimes I wouldn't be able to see him, and I would say, 'Taka-chan, is everything all right?' and he would say, 'Fine,' and I would be confident he was holding it down." It seemed that he put his utmost trust in him. If I were to borrow my father's words, Saitō had been working with him even before he was of age, so that's why he still called him Taka-bō, even after he was sixty years old. "Dammit, I called him that stupid name again!" he would think afterward.

The cinematographer Ueda Masaharu was born in 1938 and has been with the Kurosawa-gumi since *Kagemusha*: "When Ue-chan is on the set, it's always lively. He's very sturdy both mentally and physically, and somehow it always feels refreshing to be around him. He's classically masculine, and at first glance he looks a bit rough, but he is really the nicest of them all. Someone just like that would make a good husband, you know!" He's always full of energy. I wonder how much he's spent running around here and there. One of these days I'd like to put a pedometer on him and see how the steps add up. When my father used to tell stories about Ueda-san, he spoke with such a gentle expression it was as if he were talking about one of his grandchildren. When I heard from my father the story I just recounted about marrying Ueda-san, he was already married, which was a real shame.

The lighting designer Sano Takeji was born in 1930. He worked at Shōchiku until 1965 when he quit to go freelance and joined up with the Kurosawa-gumi: "When I'd hear Sano-chan's voice, I'd know that, ah, pretty soon we'd be shooting, and I would start to get excited. His voice would really carry very well. In tune with his voice, his crew would all work efficiently. It was really a marvel. They were fast. Even now, they're the ones who set the pace for the team. In any case, we waited to start until the lighting was completely in place, and we'd get the signal to start, '*Hai, dōzo.*' " My father would often talk to me about lighting. How you would use red lighting to make the darkness stand out, or how to create the most vivid green by shifting the light, or how to work with reflections. He would be full of pride, as if it were he himself who had done such a good job. My father said, "When another unit would be slow for some reason, Sano-chan would help them out, by telling them to move that lower light over to the right, things like that. And all the while Sano-san would be attending to the other crew, he would pretend not to know what's going on, even though he would be really satisfied with the attention Sano-san was giving and would be laughing."

Miwano Isamu, born in 1928, was in charge of special equipment and was with the Kurosawa-gumi since the days of *Seven Samurai*: "When I would see Miwano-kun's face on set, I would feel like, now, *this* is a movie set; it would make me feel at home, you know. He was like an old-time moviemaker, and always complaining about something, but you could feel his affection for cinema."[1] He could handle anything in the way of equipment and was the kind of person any movie studio would prize. He was a dandy and indispensable to the Kurosawa-gumi as a true adept of wind and rain. According to my father, because he was the key to these particular techniques, he was often a topic of conversation at mealtime. Even so, since it was rumored he was born in the late 1920s, I was shocked to see him on this shoot clambering up the stone steps of the castle holding his gear under the hot sun. His passion for film no doubt makes that nimbleness possible. May you always keep working in good health.

Minawa Ichirō, in charge of sound effects, was born in 1918 and worked with the Kurosawa-gumi on twenty-two films beginning with *No*

Regrets for Our Youth: "Minawa-kun was always a quiet man. When we were working on the sound editing he would be silent standing in the back. I would be watching, and just when I would think, 'Here's what we should do,' I wouldn't even have time to turn around before Minawa would say, 'Got it' and would vanish to go fix it exactly as I had imagined. It's a detail-oriented job that takes a lot of attention, but the power of films is made up of the work of people like that, you know." Whenever he talked about his crew like this, my father's gentleness came out, like a child who is proudly sharing his favorite things.

The sound operator Benitani Kenichi, born in 1931, worked on *Dreams* and *Rhapsody in August* after retiring from Nikkatsu in 1980.[2] "On set, Beni-yan would be off in a corner, with headphones on looking like he was deep in thought. Ah, he was adorable to watch. He would get so worked up about little noises that the rest of us didn't even notice." [*chuckles*] These funny stories were a running commentary of my early life, and wrapped up in them was the message of the crew's value. My father was always keeping an eye on the staff, their whereabouts, and their well-being.

Hamamura Kōichi, born in 1923, was in charge of the interior design and props on the set and was with the Kurosawa-gumi since *Drunken Angel*. "Whenever I see Hama-chan's big, good-humored face smiling on the set like some guardian deity, I feel a huge sense of relief. It makes me feel like, ah, I'm so happy to be able to shoot another film." I think that for my father, seeing Hama-san embodied the happiness that came from being together with the rest of the Kurosawa-gumi making his own film.

Aimi Tameyuki, born in 1926, was a specialist in *chonmage* hair styling as well as makeup, and was part of the Kurosawa-gumi beginning with *Yōjimbo*. "He was a bit of an odd duck, but he was intense about his work and really good at it. In the old days of filmmaking there were a lot of people with their own eccentric styles, and it was a lot of fun." He loved magic tricks and was an extremely funny person. Back then there were a lot of people on the crew with their quirks, like the guy who was crazy about trains, or the one who hung from the rafters like a cicada and even sang like a cicada. It could be hard to wrangle them, as they were so offbeat, but it was such an interesting world, and they would tell such great stories.

Tsuboi Kazuharu-san, born in 1953, of the set construction crew, joined the Kurosawa-gumi with *Ran*. "He always had a hammer hanging from his belt. The women would go mad over him whenever he would clamber up someplace high and work away up in the rafters." Guys like him had many admirers. You could yell out, "Hey, Tsuboi!" and he would clamber right down and fix whatever you needed. In the old days, there were many like him. These are the people whose skills make a film possible. My father kept an eye on every corner of that set. He knew the name of every person on a set, down to the last part-timer, and he kept his eye on everything. He constantly told me that a film was made thanks to the effort of each of these many people.

Kumata Masahiko, born in 1946, has been with the Kurosawa-gumi since *Ran*. He had a rather unique role in production as the person specially designated for Kurosawa to get mad at. As my father said, "Kuma messes up anything you give to him, but you can't hold a grudge against him. Just having him around takes the pressure off. He's so easy to get along with, his presence on set is always a plus." As well as acting as a buffer for my father, he helped look after him on set, from making sure he ate to making sure my father's coffee was just the way he liked it. He was just constantly taking the heat from my father getting mad, a kind of "wife" role, as they used to say. Even as my father was hollering about "that idiot," you could always find them together, even outside of work. He was a wonderful caretaker, so I am sure my father was really thankful to him.

Ōtsubo Ryūsuke, born in 1951, the editing assistant, worked with the Kurosawa-gumi beginning with *Kagemusha*. As my father remembered him, "He was always grinning and not very talkative; he was a lovely man. In his editing work, he was very diplomatic, and he could look at my expression and key right in, doing exactly what was needed at the time. Most of the time he didn't speak, except to chuckle, but he was a very skilled editor." My father was fairly clumsy, but always took pride in the one thing he could actually do with his hands, which was film editing. Ōtsubo, who had silently helped my father on the difficult finishing touches of many films, took on the job of editing *After the Rain*, but unfortunately, only a couple of weeks into the shoot, he passed away suddenly. I'd like to think he's up there in heaven with my father, silently smiling, sharing a drink, perhaps toasting to the good fortunes of *After the Rain*. I'm so grateful to him for all his work; thank you.

There are still many wonderful old members of the Kurosawa-gumi I would like to introduce, but it's such a big tent that I will now bring it to a close.

No matter how terrible a mood he was in, my father would without fail brighten up and smile when I brought up stories about the Kurosawa-gumi. That's one more proof of how valuable his crew was to my father.

"I Am Not a Panda"

When my father was still "himself" enough to carry on a conversation, these were the last things he talked about. He was concerned that everyone in the Kurosawa-gumi would have a proper job. He hoped the day would come when the film industry was back on its feet, so it could once again support directors in making films that were truly their own. And after watching *The Trip to Bountiful,* he talked about how it was possible to make a good film even without a vast sum of money. And that was the end of the stories.

In interviews I would often be asked what kind of a person my father was at home, but waking or sleeping, film film film was all my father thought about. At one point my father got fed up with this line of questioning, and he laughed: "Well, it's not like I am some exotic specimen like a panda and I go around eating bamboo all day. You are really curious about my habitat, aren't you!"

Still, everyone wanted to know all kinds of things about my father. After he died, I got many requests from publishers to write something about him.

At that time I hesitated because it didn't sit well with me to be thought of as profiting off my father's death, and anyway I had too many memories in my head to get down on paper neatly, and I didn't know how to put a lot of things into words because they were just too important.

After a while, one of the Kurosawa-gumi crew came to me and asked me to write everything down while it was all still fresh. So I thought it was time to finally commit to writing and I said I would give it a try, and I finally replied to Hirao-san and Terui-san of *Bungei shunjū.* At this moment I am right in the midst of composing it, and today I am regretting it a little.

Today we had the closing party for *After the Rain.* We all got together and had a grand time—the director, of course, and all the cast and crew. *After the Rain* is an homage to my father by the former Kurosawa-gumi, now the Koizumi-gumi. Everyone tried their utmost to use the training they got from my father. This movie is meaningful in so many ways: as a heartfelt tribute to "Maestro Kurosawa," as a joint effort with the next generation, working together and passing on their know-how for making good films, and, of course, as Koizumi Takashi's debut film as director.

The protagonist was played by Terao Akira, one of my father's favorites. He said it was a hard role for him: playing a seemingly weak character who couldn't stand up to his wife, but was in reality strong—on top of his first sword-fighting scenes. But as usual he lived up to the challenges of the role.

The Lord Nagai role was played by Mifune Toshirō's eldest son, Shirō. I've known him ever since he was young, and he played the role with as much grace as he possesses in person, and he is a real presence.

I have been talking up the film by telling how the two of them supported each other, and were bolstered by the whole crew of highly unique actors. It's a wonderful film; please go and see it! (Sadly, despite my best efforts, Yodogawa Nagaharu won't be able to join!)

The story of the good-natured rōnin Mizawa Ihei—who's lost his job in hard times—and his wife, Tayo, will give the frazzled people of today something to cheer them up, and get them back on their feet. I continue to be amazed at how shrewdly my father was able to size up contemporary life and shape it into a story.

The day my father fell was just a few days before the Aum sarin incident, and from his sickbed he said, "This has become a very strange era. In these times we need to reach out to children's hearts rather than forcing them to study and then study some more all the time and take exam after exam. Philosophy is more important; we need that kind of learning now more than ever." He watched the horrifying accounts on the news day after day, in grief, lamenting that "we have to give kids the time to do what they want, to get lost in their imaginary worlds."

Judging from his comment that "the only way we have to express ourselves is by making films," I gathered that he was frustrated at being stuck in bed, not being able do his work.

Through the process of making *After the Rain* with everyone, I was able to pick myself up and march on ahead, knowing that the clouds had lifted and we too had our work cut out for us, our own era to tend to.

Living as Akira Kurosawa's daughter for forty-four years was difficult at times, seeing he had such a large presence. His larger-than-life nature could be a burden, but it was also a huge gift. From this point on, it's all up to me to put this gift into practice as a human being and as my own kind of artisan.

Now and again my father will appear to me in my dreams. They always take place on a movie set. He's just smiling there, not saying a word, but it makes me so happy that he's looking approvingly on me, as I work away on a movie, and makes me commit all the more.

Most of the chapters in this book have appeared as interviews and *taidan* in the monthly magazine *Bungei shunjū,* along with writings I compiled and edited in time for publication on the first anniversary of my father's death.

Originally I had planned to publish the book I mentioned above, with my new preface, on September 6, but the start date for shooting *After the Rain* was decided, and once we got into production that alone was enough to more than preoccupy me. There's a saying that the child of the frog is also a frog—or the apple doesn't fall far from the tree. I have to confess that just as my father often pushed back his deadlines, I had to ask for indulgence on the deadline and get an extension.

I was asked by *Bungei shunjū*'s Terui-san to write a loooong afterword, and I agreed immediately. But right at the height of the shoot the deadline was upon me before I could get things together. The night before the party I felt anxious about the deadline and fell asleep. And then I had this dream.

The chief editor of *Bungei shunjū,* Hirao-san, has been a precious friend for a long time. She kept chasing me down along with Terui-san, who asked me to write a loooong afterword, which I pared down to a merely looong afterward. Hirao-san played the part of a fashionable young Edo-period woman, while Terui-san was an elegantly appointed samurai in formal dress.

I suddenly turn around, and Hirao-san has changed clothes. In real life, I am in charge of costumes in the Kurosawa-gumi. *After the Rain* was set in the Kyōhō era (1716–36), so perhaps the traces of the costumes from the production remained in my head.

Oh no, that's not it. Hirao-san's young Edo-ite costume has a stripe pattern that didn't yet exist then. No, that won't do. And wasn't the way the *obi* was tied different then as well?

Terui-san's *kamishimo* outfit looks like it has a proper dyed crest. It's summer, so he should be wearing hemp, but the fiber looks different. No, that's hemp. Hemp usually gets all wrinkled if you walk around a lot, so the continuity is going to be difficult. I'd better steam it out or put some water on it to smooth it out again. No, wait—a book editor doesn't do physical work, so he's not going to be running around a lot . . . it'll be all right.

While I was thinking all these strange thoughts, Terui-san, dressed as a samurai, came at me in slow motion. Just as he was about to strike me with his sword, my mind screamed, and my eyes opened.

Dreams are really a kind of inspiration. In their dreams, anyone can become a genius.

The things are all in your mind: things you know, and things that are just on the verge of being known, sentiments that jumble and rush out in full force; your thoughts expressing themselves without any rules, freely.

Dreams make you able to face tomorrow, when the events of the day weigh upon you.

My father reminded me that "there are so many things you should learn from dreams."

That is indeed true, Papa. I learn from my father who always held on to *his* dreams, and am encouraged by the memory of my father to learn from my dreams.

So, it's time to get to work, with all our hearts, those of us who are left.

Edited by Tanaka Masumi

TRANSLATOR'S ACKNOWLEDGMENTS

Many thanks to earlier readers of this manuscript who offered suggestions and their own stories of work in the realms of film and translation. With much gratitude to Paul Anderer, Julia Alekseyeva, Joanne Bernardi, Helena Čapková, Ryan Cook, Sarah Frederick, Earl Jackson, Chika Kinoshita, Markus Nornes, Kyoko Ōmori, John Pinson, Sharif Shakhshir, and Christophe Thouny. I could not have navigated the complexities of Kurosawa's speech-in-print without the linguistic and cultural knowledge of Uchiyama Shōta and Yokoyama Yusuke. Thanks for assistance from Ariel Acosta, Ken Shima, and Kerim Yasar in helping me get my hands on texts as this project came to a close. Librarians at University of California, Riverside and elsewhere helped me obtain materials that would otherwise have remained out of reach. Thanks to Sahra Missaghieh Klawitter and Sabrina Simmons at UC Riverside; Alfonso Huertes at the Art Center College Library; and Alanna Quan at Occidental College Library. I am also indebted to the knowledge of Maura Spiegel and Kenna McKenna with respect to Kurosawa's myriad encounters with the Hollywood studio system. All mistakes and unreceived dreams are, of course, my responsibility.

CHRONOLOGY OF AKIRA KUROSAWA

1910 Born in the Tokyo neighborhood of Ōi-machi (now, Higashi Ōi-machi, in Shinagawa), the last of four brothers and four sisters. Blood type B. His father, Isamu, from Akita prefecture, was forty-five at the time of his birth, had worked as an instructor at a military school belonging to the army, and was the head of the Ebara middle school. His mother, Shima, was forty at the time of his birth, the daughter of a merchant family in Osaka.

1916 In April, enters the kindergarten attached to the Morimura Gakuen school, in Shinagawa.

1917 In April, enters the Morimura Gakuen elementary school.

1918 In August, the family moves to Nishi edogawa-machi in Koishikawa-ku (now Suidō 1-chōme, in Bunkyo-ku). In September, transfers to Kuroda Primary School. In the same grade is future screenwriter Uesaka Keinosuke. Is awakened to painting by teacher Tachikawa Seiji.

1923 In March, graduates from Kuroda Primary School. In April, begins at Keika Middle School.

1924 In July, publishes essay "The Lotus Dance" in a school magazine.

1926 In July, publishes essay "A Certain Letter" in a school magazine. His older brother Heigo begins work as a film "explainer," or *benshi,* under the name of Suda Teimei at the Cinema Palace in Kanda.

1928 In March, graduates from Keika Middle School. Aspiring to be a painter, applies to art school, but is not accepted, and begins attending a painting academy. In April, a still life painting is accepted to the Nikkaten art exhibition. Around that time, the family moves to Meguro and then to the Ebisu neighborhood in Tokyo.

1929 Joins the Japan Proletariat Artists' League. In December, exhibits watercolors and oil paintings at the Second Proletarian Arts Exhibition.

1930 In April, takes the physical exam for entrance into the military, but is exempted, thanks to his doctor being a former student of his father. In December, exhibits posters in the Third Proletarian Arts Exhibition, but they are withdrawn.

1933 On July 10, his brother Heigo commits suicide in the onsen town of Izu-yugawara at the age of twenty-seven.

1934 In May, moves to the neighborhood of Nagayato-chō in Shibuya (now, Ebisu-nishi 1-chōme).

1936 Applies and is accepted for position of assistant director at PCL Studios (later folded into Tōhō). Works as third assistant director on films by Yagura Shigeo, Yamamoto Kajirō and Fushimizu Osamu.

1937 In September, four companies, including PCL Studios and JO Studios, merge with Tōhō Studios, founded the previous month. Works as chief assistant director (then called production manager) on the production of Yamamoto Kajirō's *Beautiful Hawk* (October).

1938 Works as chief assistant director on Takizawa Eisuke's *Mining Town* (February); and Yamamoto Kajirō's *The Love of Tōjūrō* (May), *Composition Class* (August), and *The Surprising Life* of Enoken (December).

1939 Works as chief assistant director on Yamamoto Kajirō's productions of *Enoken's Winning Age* (January), *Chūshingura* (April), and *Carefree Alleyway* (September). In October, shooting begins on Yamamoto's *The Horse*. Over the course of the shoot, a love affair transpires between chief assistant director Kurosawa and the lead actress, Takamine Hideko.

1940 Works as chief assistant director on Yamamoto Kajirō's productions of *Enoken Has His Hair Cropped* (March) and *The Monkey King* (November).

1941 Works as chief assistant director as well as second unit director on Yamamoto Kajirō's production of *The Horse* (March). In December, scenario for the film *A German at Daruma Temple* is published in *Film Criticism.*

1942 Writes the scenario for Fushimizu Osamu's *Currents of Youth* (February), released by Tōhō. Scenario for *All Is Quiet* wins second prize in the Ministry of Information's Citizens' Film Competition in February and is published in *Japan Film.* In April, scenario for *Snow* wins first place in the Japan Magazine Council's contest for propaganda (kokusaku, 国策) films, is published in *New Cinema.* Cowrites with Toyama Benpei the scenario for Yamamoto Kajirō's *Song of Winged Victory,* released in October by Tōhō.

1943 First directorial effort, *Sanshirō Sugata,* is released on March 25. Wins the Yamanaka Sadao Prize, along with Kinoshita Keisuke's *Port of Flowers.* In June, scenario for *Three Hundred Miles through Enemy Lines* is published in *Film Criticism.*

1944 Writes scenario for Marune Santarō's *Sumo Festival,* released in March from Daiei. Writes a scenario for *A Story of Wild Horses. The Most Beautiful* is released on April 13.

1945 Writes scenario for Saeki Kiyoshi's *The Admirable Ishin Tasuke,* released in January from Tōhō. In February, marries Katō Kiyo (the lead actress in *The Most Beautiful,* stage name Yaguchi Yōko), with Yamamoto Kajirō as matchmaker. Moves to the Soshigaya neighborhood in Setagaya-ku. On May 3, *Sanshirō Sugata II* is released. A film that Kurosawa was slated to direct, *Silvering Spear,* had to be scrapped due to a lack of horses. Screening of *The Men Who Tread on the Tiger's Tail,* shot during and after the war, prohibited by GHQ. Premieres the play *Talking* at the Yūraku-za, performed by the New Life Shinpa troupe. On December 20, son, Hisao, is born.

1946 In March, the first general strike takes place at Tōhō studios. The film *Those Who Make Tomorrow,* codirected by Kurosawa, Yamamoto Kajirō, and Sekigawa Hideo, is released on May 2, but due to the concessions to the labor union during production, Kurosawa strikes the film from own list of credits. *No Regrets for Our Youth* is released on October 29.

1947 Writes the scenario for "First Love," the first episode of a four-part omnibus film, *Four Love Stories,* directed by Toyota Shirō (Tōhō). *One Wonderful Sunday* is released on July 1. Writes the script for and edits Taniguchi Senkichi's *Snow Trail,* released by Tōhō in August.

1948 Father, Isamu, dies at age eighty-three on February 8. Joins the Film Art Association in February, formed by Yamamoto Kajirō and Motoki Sōjirō, along with other directors, including Naruse Mikio and Taniguchi Senkichi. *Drunken Angel* is released on April 27. Writes the scenario for Kinoshita Keisuke's *The Portrait,* released by Shōchiku in August.

1949 Cowrites the screenplay for Oda Motoyoshi's *Lady from Hell* with Nishiki Motosada, released by Tōhō in March. *The Quiet Duel* is released on March 13. Cowrites screenplay for Taniguchi Senkichi's *Jakoman and Tetsu,* directed by Taniguchi and released by Tōhō in July. *Stray Dog* is released on October 17.

1950 Cowrites screenplay for Taniguchi Senkichi's *Escape at Dawn,* directed by Taniguchi and released as a Film Art Association/ Shin Tōhō production in January. On April 30, *Scandal* is released. Writes scenario with Tanada Gorō for Kosugi Isamu's *Tetsu Does the Jitterbug,* released by Tōyoko Films in August. Also in August, writes scenario for *Swordmaster Danpei,* directed by Makino Masahiro for Tōyoko Films. On August 26, *Rashomon* is released.

1951 Cowrites scenario for Taniguchi Senkichi's *On the Other Side of Love and Hate* with Taniguchi, released in January by the Film Art Association / Shin Tōhō. On May 23, *The Idiot* is released. Around this time, writes the screenplay for *The Captain of the Coffin-Ship*. In June, writes screenplay for *The Den of the Beasts,* directed by Ōsone Tatsuo and released by Shōchiku. On September 10, *Rashomon* wins the Golden Lion at the Venice International Film Festival. On December 26, *Rashomon* is released in New York by RKO.

1952 Moves from Chitose-funabashi in Setagaya-ku to Komae city. On March 20, *Rashomon* is named the twenty-fourth Best Foreign Film at the Academy Awards. On April 24, *The Men Who Tread on the Tiger's Tail* is released. In May, cowrites scenario for Inagaki Hiroshi's *Sword for Hire,* directed by Inagaki and released by Tōhō. *Ikiru* is released on October 9. Mother, Shima, dies at eighty-two on November 4.

1953 With Taniguchi Senkichi, writes screenplay for *My Wonderful Yellow Car,* directed by Taniguchi and released by Tōhō in January.

1954 *Seven Samurai* is released on April 26. Daughter, Kazuko, is born April 29. In June, *Ikiru* wins the Silver Bear Grand Jury Prize at the Berlin International Film Festival. *Seven Samurai* wins the Golden Lion at the Venice International Film Festival in September.

1955 With Kikushima Ryūzō, cowrites *The Disappearing Squadron,* directed by Mimura Akira (Harry) and released by Nikkatsu in January. Contributes to screenplay and editing on Horikawa Hiromichi's October release from Tōhō, *Tomorrow I'll Be a Fire-Tree*. On October 15, the composer Hayasaka Fumio dies at the age of forty-one. On November 22, *Record of a Living Being* is released.

1957 *Throne of Blood* is released on January 15, followed by *The Lower Depths* on September 17. In October, invited to the first London Film Festival. With Oguni Hideo, cowrites the scenario for Mori Kazuo's *Secret History of the Russo–Japanese War: Three Hundred Miles Through Enemy Lines,* released by Daiei in December.

1958 *The Hidden Fortress* is released on December 28.

1959 Founds Kurosawa Productions in April. Polishes a screenplay by Yamanaka Sadao, directed by Sugie Toshio as *Saga of the Vagabonds* and released by Tōhō in August.

1960 In August, visits Europe for the second time. The initial plan called for a site visit to the Rome Olympics in preparation for shooting a documentary film about the Tokyo Olympics. On September 4, *The Bad Sleep Well* is released.

1961 *Yojimbo* is released on April 25.

1962 *Sanjūrō* is released on New Year's Day. In September, moves to the Matsubara neighborhood in Setagaya-ku. A remake of the scenario for *Swordmaster Danpei* is released in September, directed by Mizuho Shunkai.

1963 *High and Low* is released on March 1.

1964 Cowrites with Taniguchi Senkichi a remake of *Jakoman and Tetsu,* directed by Fukasaku Kinji and released by Tōei in February.

1965 Wins the Asahi Culture Prize in January. In March, *Red Beard* is released. Contributes to screenplay and editing for a remake of *Sanshirō Sugata* by director Uchikawa Sei'ichirō, released in May by Kurosawa Productions and Tōhō. Donald Richie's book *The Films of Akira Kurosawa* is published by University of California Press in August, the first real critical appreciation overseas of Kurosawa as a director.

1966 Starts legal action after realizing that Sergio Leone's 1965 film *A Fistful of Dollars* plagiarized from *Yojimbo.* A settlement is reached stipulating that Kurosawa and Tōhō receive the take from distribution in Japan, Taiwan, and Korea, compensation of $100,000, and fifteen percent of the remaining worldwide box office returns. In June, announces a coproduction with U.S.-based Embassy Pictures for *Runaway Train,* but it is canceled. Around the same time, writes the script for ... *And Then...*

1967 Announces plans for *Tora! Tora! Tora!* on April 28, coproduced by Twentieth Century–Fox and Kurosawa Productions.

1968 Starts production on *Tora! Tora! Tora!* at Tōei's Kyoto studios, but shooting is abruptly stopped.

1969 In January, production of *Tora! Tora! Tora!* by Twentieth Century–Fox and Kurosawa Productions is called off. Kurosawa Productions steps away from the production. In June, Satō Tadao's *The World of Kurosawa Akira* is published by San'ichi shobō, marking the first real critical appreciation in Japan of Kurosawa as a director. In July, forms the Four Knights Club with Kinoshita Keisuke, Ichikawa Kon and Kobayashi Masaki; the four collaborate on the script of *Alley Cat.* In August, *Seven Samurai* screens with five other films as the Works of Director Kurosawa Akira series on TBS television.

1970 On October 31, releases his first color film, *Dodes'ka-den.*

1971 Receives the Order of the Yugoslav Flag from Yugoslavian President Tito.

1972 In October, moves to the Ebisu nishi neighborhood in Shibuya-ku.

1973 Finalizes deal on March 14 to make *Dersu Uzala,* produced jointly with Mosfilm.

1974 Contributes the original idea for a remake of *Stray Dog,* directed by Morisaki Azuma, released by Shōchiku in September. Yamamoto Kajirō dies on September 21, at the age of seventy-two.

1975 *Dersu Uzala* is released on August 2 in Japan, and in the Soviet Union in September. Wins the Golden Prize at the Moscow Film Festival. Publishes the book *Subtle Like a Demon, Bold Like an Angel* through Tōhō.

1976 On March 29, *Dersu Uzala* wins the Academy Award for Best Foreign Language Film. Kurosawa is selected as a Person of Cultural Merit by the Agency for Cultural Affairs on October 26.

1977 In April, the series "Kurosawa Akira's Selected Works" screens at the National Film Center of the Tokyo National Museum of Modern Art. Moves to the Irima neighborhood in Chōfu city. Writes scenario for *The Masque of the Red Death.*

1979 The book of *Kagemusha,* including images and the script, is published by Kōdansha in November.

1980 *Kagemusha* is released on April 26. On May 23, wins the Grand Prix at the Cannes International Film Festival.

1981 Japan Society in New York presents a series of twenty-six films as a Kurosawa retrospective, with Kurosawa in attendance.

1982 Shimura Takashi dies at the age of seventy-six on February 11. Receives a special award for services to cinema during the thirty-fifth anniversary of the Cannes Film Festival in May. In September, *Rashomon* is awarded a Career Golden Lion on the fiftieth anniversary of the founding of the Venice International Film Festival. NHK Hall screens Abel Gance's *Napoleon,* presented by Kurosawa and Francis Ford Coppola.

1983 Kurosawa Film Studios is founded in the Kirigaoka neighborhood of Yokohama city, Midori ward.

1984 Named an officer of the French Légion d'honneur in May. In June Iwanami publishes the memoir *Something Like an Autobiography.* A hardcover book of *Ran,* including images and the script, is published by Shūeisha in October.

1985 Kurosawa's wife, Kiyo, dies on February 1 at the age of sixty-three. On June 1, *Ran* is released. In June, a set of four lithographs featuring scenes from *Ran* is published by Arubo. In June, receives the honor of Commandeur, the highest rank of the French Order of Arts and Letters. On November 3, receives the Order of Culture (Japan). Chris Marker's documentary film *A.K.* is released in December.

1986 On March 24, Kurosawa attends the Academy Awards, where *Ran* is nominated in four categories; designer Wada Emi wins the costume category. Serves as a presenter along with Billy Wilder and John Huston. On March 27, is awarded the first Akira Kurosawa Prize at the San Francisco Film Festival. In June, *Runaway Train,* inspired by an idea by Kurosawa, is directed by Andrei Konchalovsky and released in Japan by Canon, distributed by Shōchiku-Fuji.

1987 The *Collected Works of Kurosawa Akira* is published by Iwanami in November.

1990 Wins a special honorary award at the sixty-second Academy Awards and is recognized on the occasion of his eightieth birthday by the entire audience, including many filmmakers. A hardcover book of *Dreams,* including images and the script, is published by Iwanami in April. *Dreams* is released on May 25.

1991 *Rhapsody in August* opens on May 25. A long interview with director Hara Masato, *Kurosawa Akira Speaks,* is published as a book by Fukutake.

1992 In September, a volume of storyboards and sketches titled *Graphic Works of Kurosawa Akira* is published by Tokyo FM.

1993 Honda Ishirō dies on February 28 at the age of eighty-one. A hardcover book of *Maadadayo,* including images and the script, is published by Tokuma in April. Beginning in April, a series of twenty-one of Kurosawa's Tōhō-era works is released on laser disc. On April 17, *Maadadayo* is released. In August, Kurosawa's set of dialogues with Miyazaki Hayao is published by Tokuma as *What Is Cinema?* Starts work on the script for his next film, *The Sea Is Watching,* based on a short story by Yamamoto Shūgorō. Gets ready to send it to the printers on December 1 to enter production but is hampered by money problems. On December 19, childhood friend Uekusa Keinosuke dies at the age of eighty-three.

1994 Receives the Tenth Kyoto Prize.

1995 Collapses in his ryōkan in Kyoto's Nakagyō-ku while writing the scenario for *After the Rain,* based on a Yamamoto Shūgorō story of the same name. Is hospitalized for three months due to a lower spine compression fracture and related injuries, and will be confined to a wheelchair.

1996 On February 5, Oguni Hideo dies at the age of ninety-one. On October 1, receives honorary title from the city of Tokyo.

1997 On December 10, the photo book *Kurosawa Akira Chronicle* is released by Sony Magazine publishers. Mifune Toshirō dies on December 24 at seventy-seven.

1998 At forty-five minutes past midnight on September 6, Kurosawa dies of a stroke at his home in Seijō 4-chōme, in Setagaya-ku. On September 8, a private funeral takes place at the family home. On September 13, a memorial service takes place at Kurosawa Film Studios. On October 1, receives the People's Honor Award from the prime minister of Japan. On October 25, remains are interred at Kamakura's Anyōji temple, and a posthumous Buddhist name is conferred.

1999 In May, *After the Rain* goes into production based on Kurosawa's scenario, directed by Koizumi Takashi and assisted by many staff of the Kurosawa-gumi. Filming finished in July.

Compiled by *Bungei Shunjū* editor Terai Yasuo,
with assistance from Ogata Toshirō

TRANSLATOR'S NOTES

Translator's Introduction

1 For a rich and detailed account of Occupation film policy, see Kyoko Hirano, *Mr. Smith Goes to Tokyo. Rashomon* actually showed almost a year earlier in Honolulu than it did in New York and was noted in the Japanese American press well in advance of its appearance in the mainstream U.S. press.

2 Yoshimoto, *Kurosawa: Film Studies and Japanese Cinema*, 188.

3 See Kurosawa, *Something Like an Autobiography.*

4 For a good selection, see Satō 佐藤忠男 and Kishigawa 岸川真, *The Era of "Film Criticism"* (「映画評論」の時代).

5 Keathley, *Cinephilia and History*, 39.

6 Given Kurosawa's deep knowledge of Noh theater, discussed in this collection, it is possible he is aware of the status of the word in Noh discourse as set out by Zeami, its early theorist and the author of many plays. Zeami saw this quality of "omoshiro" as the lowest stage of revelation of an ultimate aesthetic experience, a trajectory not unlike Eisenstein's theory of intellectual montage, an upward cascade of awareness that begins with attraction. In Zeami's case, it is the "moment when conscious awareness of the event" of aesthetic contact sparks an entire process. See Thornhill, "The Goddess Emerges."

7 My title also echoes the simple "adjective + noun" structure of many of Kurosawa's favorite films and those adjacent—*Broken Blossoms, The Big Sleep, My Darling Clementine, Vanishing Point, The Travelling Players, The Killing Fields,* and so on.

8 Though it is beyond the scope of this brief introduction, Kurosawa's toolbox from silent film transposed into "talkies" resonates strongly with discussions of film and realism that occurred in many sectors of film journalism and criticism from the 1920s through the 1950s, including André Bazin's realism, Sergei Eisenstein's montage, and Satyajit Ray's depiction of "off-screen" world-historical events.

9 The phrase here is from *Something Like an Autobiography*, 6. For discussions of cinemas and modern entertainment districts in an era of state and civilian/journalistic moral surveillance see Gerow, *Visions of Japanese Modernity.* While older, Donald Shively's article "Bakufu Versus

Kabuki" gives fascinating historical background on the cat-and-mouse game of kabuki regulation that would have specified different art forms for different classes—here, samurai.

10 Hyakken-sensei wrote about this song in his essays on the Maadakai reunions. See Uchida Hyakken, 内田百閒, *Maadakai* (まあだかい).

11 *Benshi* are storytelling movie orators who during the silent era functioned something like human dubbing tracks or commentators to interpret films through vocalization and narrative. There is a voluminous literature on the *benshi*, its star systems, and the rise of automated soundtracks. One of the most interesting depictions of a *benshi* occurs in the 1929 proletariat novel *The Crab Cannery Ship*, by Kobayashi Takiji. The *benshi* arrive aboard a ship of indentured workers to provide entertainment as a safety valve but end up commenting on the awful living and working conditions (the book will ultimately end in mutiny). Four useful pieces of scholarship on *benshi* in English, in addition to Gerow's *Visions of Japanese Modernity*, are Dym, *Benshi*; Fujiki, "Benshi as Stars"; Ōmori, "Narrating the Detective"; and Raine, "No Interpreter, Full Volume." Raine, in particular, notes that *benshi* "became the central figures in industrial actions that were billed as a struggle against machine civilization" (127), in tune with Solovieva's note, paraphrasing Yamano Ichirō, that "the most painful aspect of this defeat was the fact that the higher professional class of narrators were hired back whereas the lower-class staff of ushers, janitors, and ticket vendors with whom they had joined ranks in solidarity lost their jobs permanently" (Solovieva, *The Russian Kurosawa*, 78).

12 See Kurosawa's description in *Something Like an Autobiography*, 71–72. Nate Shockey's *The Typographical Imagination* discusses the explosion of one-yen series in depth.

13 Solovieva, *The Russian Kurosawa*, 6.

14 Kurahara, "Translator's Introduction" to Fadeyev, *The Rout*, 1.

15 The language in these three quotations is from page 158 of Kurahara's essay "On Fadeyev's Novel *The Rout*," published in his 1929 collection of proletarian art criticism, *On Art* (芸術論). In later passages of that essay, Kurahara remarks that Fadeyev is commonly judged to have been influenced by Tolstoy, but finds this work less deferential to fate and less romantic about the spontaneous rebellion of peasants and farmers, as well as departing from the tendency to homogenize the will and motivations of the various partisans. These features resonate with Kurosawa's

interpretation, though he draws on Tolstoy's thinking about art, without attributing its forces to religious transcendence as Kurahara does.

16 The version Kurosawa refers to is probably volume 7 of the World Socialist Literature Collection 世界社会主義文学叢書, referenced in note 14. *The Rout* was published several times: first as part of the World Socialist Literature series, and again as the first volume of *Selected World Proletariat Revolutionary Novels,* 世界プロレタリア革命小説選集 (1930), and volume 4 of the *Contemporary Soviet Literature Collection,* 世界プロレタリア革命小説選集 (1939). Kurahara would continue to publish interpretive essays on Fadeyev, this novel, and other proletarian works. Some of his writings are available in English in Bowen-Struyk and Field, *For Dignity, Justice, and Revolution.* The reference to Fadeyev occurs in Kurosawa's handwritten creator's notes on *Seven Samurai* and is referenced in the catalog to a 2022 exhibition on Kurosawa at the National Film Archive of Japan, Makita 槇田寿文 and National Film Archive of Japan, eds., *Akira Kurosawa, Screenwriter* (脚本家黒澤明).

17 Shiga Naoya (1883–1971) was a fiction writer strongly associated with the "I-fiction" mode who burst onto the literary stage with a story about an affair with his family's maid, published under a pseudonym. He frequently used digressions and embedded narratives, adding to the complexity of a first-person story. Kurosawa misremembers this passage as being more straightforward than it actually is. In the Shiga story, the boy's anecdote is less of a joke with a punch line and comes from the embedded narrative of a boy's school composition that is considerably shorter—and less like the *rakugo*-esque version that Kurosawa remembers. The story "Bear" is part of a triptych of very short sections found in the story "The Blind Turtle and the Floating Tree" (盲亀浮木), referencing a Buddhist didactic tale. A Shiga story is also the base text of the fourteenth film on Kurosawa's list, *Capricious Young Man.*

18 Fujii, "Who's That Man? Mifune at 100." Later in her essay, Fujii refers to the scene discussed in this volume by Kurosawa and how Tarkovsky, too, was riveted by Mifune's ass: he "would take a shot at a theory of Mifune's lower half in *Seven Samurai*—why it affects him so—though he's more indirect about it: 'the samurai,' he wrote, wears a 'garment that leaves most of the leg bare, and their legs are plastered with mud. And when one samurai falls down dead we see the rain washing away the mud and becoming white, as white as marble . . .' I wanted more clarity."

19 Abel, *French Film Theory and Criticism,* 124.

20 The emphasis on micro movements of consciousness might seem to undercut readings of *Rashomon* by scholars such as Solovieva and Mike Sugimoto as an allegory of the legal system in 1950 during and after the Tokyo War Crimes trials—decentered, lacking in authority, and quite possibly illegitimate. My point is actually compatible: that elaborating the "individualism" of each character with the same complexity means that Kurosawa attributes the same amount of complexity to the bandit, if not more in this scene, and does not exempt him as a "primitive" character who can be dismissed as an essential criminal.

21 Cardullo and Kurosawa, " 'I Am Simply a Maker of Films,' " 172–73.

22 In "*Broken Blossoms:* The Art and the Eros of a Perverse Text," Dudley Andrew notes that the institutions that sprang up around the French Impressionist movement fostered demand for more "elite" films, whereas Griffith's money and prestige linked "art" to more populist genre films. This relatively more highbrow group of narratively driven films inaugurates Kurosawa's list, suggesting roles for both experimentalism and genre in the cinema he appreciates. Though Kurosawa likely did not see the film until a year or two later, in 1919 the flagship magazine *Kinema jumpō* (Cinema times) was launched, and debates about "pure film" and its status as art thrived. See Gerow, *Visions of Modernity* for discussions of the Pure Film movement.

23 This use of art in the service of proximity and empathy is Tolstoyan in the extreme. See Solovieva, *The Russian Kurosawa,* especially chapter 2. Kurosawa's spin is to situate the encounter in the theater and to extract the formal mechanism's attachment to affect without bringing along the (racialized) contents. This is especially evident in his use of formal devices from Griffith and Ford.

24 Anderer, *Kurosawa's Rashomon,* 94.

25 Nornes, *Cinema Babel,* 38.

26 Zahlten, *The End of Japanese Cinema,* 162.

27 It is common in scholarship and popular writing about Kurosawa to segregate him from avant-garde and New Wave filmmakers. But a look at the themes of the ATG (Art Theater Guild, a distributor that later produced many remarkable small-budget, indie films) pamphlet series that introduced many foreign films to Japan in the 1960s and 1970s reveals many names from Kurosawa's list. These include Cassavetes, Anderson, Truffaut, Bergman, and many more. Clearly Kurosawa's knowledge base of film meshes intimately with and actually depends on the work of ATG,

the premiere distributor and later producer of independent, experimental film.

28 Ishikawa Takuboku 石川啄木, *Clouds Are Forms of Genius* (雲は天才である).

29 See Konishi's *Anarchist Modernity* for discussions of how "worldis[t]" thought (sekaishugi, 世界主義) deeply in dialogue with Russian sources was transposed through Japanese translations, writings, and publications. In his account, worldism is "a popularly circulated imagination of world order . . . in early twentieth-century Japan that was distinct from notions of world order and international relations centered on the nation-state that held sway in the twentieth century" (261) and had close ties to mutual aid and anarchist movements.

30 The filmmaker is Kawase Naomi, who won the prize for *Suzaku* in 1997.

To Spark a New Golden Age

1 The star production system refers to productions made by stars who founded their own companies. *Jidai-geki* star Bandō Tsumasaburō established the model in the silent era by founding his own production company and building the first sound stage in Japan. He was followed by actors such as Hayakawa Sessue and, later, Katsu Shintarō and Mifune Toshirō.

2 The area has been redeveloped, but 1970s Shinjuku would have been the crossroads of many subcultures: theater, gay nightlife, bohemians, and outlaws of all kinds. Although it is in black and white, Wakamatsu Kōji's 1970 *Shinjuku Mad* captures the dissonance between these two realities exquisitely.

3 The Big Five refers to the five major studios that signed a contract in 1953 stipulating common terms for the studios' use of actors and directors: Shōchiku, Tōhō, Tōei, Shin Tōhō, and Daiei. Though Nikkatsu would sign on in 1958, the "Big Five" name stuck. The goal was to stop the studios from poaching from each other.

4 In this sentence, as in many others in these dialogues and interviews, Kurosawa uses the final particle *yo* to conclude his statement. In conversational Japanese, this particle is both an opening to his interlocutor, and a strong suggestion that Kurosawa is saying something the interlocutor should either wise up to or should agree to. It's a declarative particle that I have translated as "right," without a question mark, because it is more an assertion than a question. In some other cases, Kurosawa ends declarative statements with a slightly softer particle, *ne*. This, too, assumes

agreement, but is less forceful; I have similarly translated it as "right," because it, too, expects agreement rather than asking a question.

5 Yonki no kai was founded in 1969. It produced the Kurosawa-helmed *Dodes'ka-den* but disbanded in 1970 after the film's box office failure.

6 John Frankenheimer (1948–2002) directed thrillers such as *The Manchurian Candidate* (1962) and *Seconds* (1966), as well as neo-noir melodramas like *I Walk the Line* (1970).

7 Several of the major weekly magazines, both cinema-specific and general news, printed running chronicles of the production's "splendors," "miseries," and problems. *Runaway Train* and *Tora! Tora! Tora!* were intended to be Kurosawa's first forays into Hollywood. *Runaway Train* was based on an article about a runaway locomotive in New York State published in *Life* magazine and translated in *Bungei shunjū*. The film had been intended as a coproduction between Joseph E. Levine's Embassy Pictures and Kurosawa Productions and would have been Kurosawa's first film made entirely in color, with a large budget and an almost all-American cast and crew. The Kurosawa team quickly holed up as usual and drafted a screenplay. But Kurosawa's dissatisfaction with the rewrite into English, among other things, led him to ask for shooting to be postponed; Levine canceled. A film based on the amalgamated script was ultimately directed by Andrei Konchalovsky in 1985. *Tora! Tora! Tora!* was brought to Kurosawa as *Runaway Train* was falling apart and was designed as a coproduction between Kurosawa Productions and Twentieth Century-Fox about the Japanese bombing of Pearl Harbor. The film, directed by both Kurosawa and Richard Fleischer, with much oversight by studio people, was ultimately canceled after production started, ostensibly on the pretext that Kurosawa's ruined health made it impossible for him to continue. For the longer saga, see Tasogawa's *All the Emperor's Men*. Tasogawa traces the processes of writing and financing, as well as the major historiographical differences between the U.S. script and Kurosawa's; namely, though both had Yamamoto as the main character, the U.S. script (credited to Larry Forrester) emphasizes the surprise nature of the attack (which overlapped with preexisting Orientalist thought), whereas Kurosawa's portrays Yamamoto as down to earth, even comic at times, while framing Yamamoto's involvement in the overall saga as a tragedy. Parts of this paragraph and the next two draw on language from Tasogawa's discussion on page 288.

8 This and other conversations with Kurosawa are transcribed in a way that allows the features of his distinctive speaking style to come to the fore and maintains aspects of the conversation that are decidedly oral. In the original publication and in the translation, ellipses allow for pauses, transitions, jumps in topic, and time spent thinking or reaction by one person, or between interlocutors. They are a typographical reminder that the participants are not just giving us content; they are taking each other's words in, reflecting, and responding, with a spontaneity that is referenced by the ellipses.

Reading John Ford

1 This conversation took place between Kurosawa and the editor of *Bungei shunjū* on the occasion of the translation of *Pappy* by Ford's grandson Dan into Japanese by Takahashi Chihiro.

2 *Chambara* films were a subgenre of *jidai-geki* period drama that featured what Yamamoto Ichirō (307) defines in "The *Jidaigeki* Film *Twilight Samurai*—A Salaryman–Producer's Point of View" as "choreographed and stylized, stagey sword fighting," usually at the climax of the film. The name *chambara* dates from the silent era and is said to have come from the sound made by the clashing swords in the spectacular fight scenes.

3 The scene is described in Ford, *Pappy*, 86, from which the quotations are taken.

4 Frankel recounts the incident more fully in *The Searchers*, 2.

5 Actually it was three years, from 1948 to 1951.

6 The anecdote is on page 264 of *Pappy*, with more detail.

7 Kurosawa's paraphrase draws on page 125 of *Pappy*.

8 The language is quoted in Ford, *Pappy*, 128.

9 Ford, *Pappy*, 315.

10 Ibid., 315.

The Artisans of *Maadadayo*

1 Hyakken-sensei refers to writer Uchida Hyakken (1898–1971), the writer fictionalized in the film. Hyakken-sensei did not sing the song, but he wrote about it in his essays on the Maadakai reunions. The song is a rowdy call-and-response exchange between Hyakken-sensei and his partying students at their annual banquet. It's based on a familiar song sung

by strolling medicine peddlers, veterans of the Russo-Japanese War in the Meiji era who would wear old military uniforms and sing the refrain while walking and playing an accordion. The film treats the song as a *kaeuta* (changing song, 替え歌)—a parody that swaps out parts of a song's lyrics with topical references, while keeping the melody. Song, of course, plays roles in other Kurosawa films, including *Ikiru* and *The Lower Depths.*

2 Subjectivity (shutaisei, 主体性) was the focus of many debates about wartime fascism and potential agents of change in immediate postwar Japan. Debates went beyond advocating that characters should be individuals and individuated; "subjectivity" referred to ideological and moral complexities intensely articulated in political-philosophy circles between 1946 and 1948, and later by filmmakers such as Ōshima Nagisa, Matsumoto Toshio, and Masumura Yasuzō. They worked to engage with similar ideas about how to transform individual interiority in relation to social reality. Kurosawa's citation of his 1947 film retrospectively locates the film in the thick of the political-philosophical debates, though film historians typically begin the film-related timeline with the *taiyōzoku* (sun tribe) films that began in 1956 with Nakahira Kō's *Crazed Fruit.* Kurosawa's choice of 1947 grounds debates on subjectivity in a different set of political concerns.

3 This word *hiroba* comes up frequently in Kurosawa's discussions of film exhibitions and screenings. It literally means something like public square or plaza, but Kurosawa tends to use it to describe an ideal experience of participation and observation on the part of filmgoers, one that mixes epistemological features (about generating awareness) and affective features (about feeling in common with characters, all at the same time). While the word refers literally to a space, it also conveys associations to the activities imagined taking place in such a space—exchange, accidental encounters, competing discourses, empathetic communication, etc. An example of a famous *hiroba* is the plaza outside Shinjuku station where protests occurred in the 1960s. While the commercial dimension of the built environment is acknowledged, as in a movie theater, the focus is on the activity of those dwelling in the space.

4 Kurosawa uses the phrase "earth age" or "planetary age" (chikyū jidai, 地球時代), which emerged in the 1970s along with discourses of environmentalism and pollution. Kurosawa issued strong warnings about human damage to the environment in interviews around this time. For

example, his focus is air pollution in a 1992 interview with Bert Cardullo (Cardullo, " 'I Am Simply a Maker of Films,' " 180), but the post-blue marble invocation of a cosmological scale in this village setting suggests that multiple Anthropocene-related issues are interconnected.

5 It might be tempting to read this section on negating national borders as a defanged globalization discourse that promotes commercial exchange above all and ignores the inequities such exchanges can perpetrate. But Kurosawa's background in specific humanist thought, including the art pedagogy he experienced as a child and the Russian literature he prized that valued one-worldism, opens up other framings through which we can historicize his utopianism, especially the role that the aesthetic plays in popular empathy outside a nation-state framework.

6 The theaters Kurosawa mentions here are *yose*, popular venues strongly associated with *rakugo*, a comic storytelling art of wordplay and shaggy-dog stories often thought of as a traditional popular art. As discussed in the introduction, *rakugo* performance consists of a series of sketches performed by a single person sitting on the simply outfitted theater stage with a few standard props, putting the attention on virtuoso performance.

7 One of Ray's last films, *Agantuk* (The stranger, 1991), features a bourgeois family who receives news a long-lost uncle is coming to visit after decades abroad. The family fears he is there to dupe them, and the story of two vastly different systems of value plays out over one week of the family's awkward meetings with friends and consultations with lawyers, as the visiting uncle spins yarns of his life as cabin boy, anthropologist, and partisan of indigenous ways of life in both the United States and India. The uncle's postcolonial stance of living with anticolonial tribes presents a different point of entry to indigenous life than does Kurosawa's earlier confrère, John Ford. Elsewhere, Kurosawa refers to Ray's film *Ashani Sanket* (Distant thunder, 1973) as one of the two most antiwar films he knows; the other is *Johnny Got His Gun*, number 63 on his list of one hundred.

8 *Tansu* are wooden storage chests with drawers and sometimes cupboards. Today *tansu* are often used like chests of drawers, for kimonos and other textiles, but in the Edo period medicinal *tansu* were often covered in lacquer and contained many drawers that held medicine, like the medicine chest here.

9 Tokoro Jōji is a popular TV personality, also noted for being one of the rare actors that Kurosawa never blew up at.

10 Azumino is a small city in Nagano prefecture, in the foothills of the Japanese Alps. The waterwheels in *Dreams* were built at the intersection of the Yorozuigawa and the Tategawa, the rivers that run through the area.

11 Ukiyo-e were popular pictures of the "floating world" and a huge part of the mass culture of urban Edo, in the popular media of the day that linked together printers, painters, publishers, and writers. At the time, though, works by Utamaro, Hokusai, and Hiroshige were seen as throwaway pieces of mass culture, very much a part of this media ecology, and only accrued autonomous "artistic" value when "discovered" by painters such as Picasso and Dégas and writers like Émile Zola.

12 The Hibiya Chanté (now the Tōhō Cinemas Chanté) is a movie theater located in Yurakuchō, a neighborhood that was a major reference point of postwar ruins-to-recovery. Kurosawa's laughter probably comes from the fact that the film deals with corporate and political corruption. Kurosawa mentions that he got postcards from readers who assumed that the off-screen man on the telephone speaking to the villain Iwabuchi was then-Prime Minister Kishi Nobusuke.

13 The idea of Japan as an "island country," *shimaguni*, was often invoked in the late twentieth century to explain how isolated—sometimes deliberately—Japan was from the rest of the purportedly more modern or sophisticated world.

14 This sequence unfolds in a series of shots that emphasize restricted vision, both literal and figurative. Hyakken and his wife move into a small hut, the former dwelling of a gamekeeper on an aristocrat's estate, featuring an outhouse with no roof. The shots are tight and include a close-up of a lively, rescued bird in a cage. It is only when visitors arrive, and Hyakken points it out, that we see the hulking ruin of the mansion adjacent to the hut. Uchida is glad the hut *(koya)* was spared and likens it to the famed hut of thirteenth-century writer Kamo no chōmei. *Hōjōki* (An account of my hut, 1212) is a classic of recluse literature, a mix of Buddhist worldliness and reflection on impermanence whose spareness and destitution grafts well on to the barely postwar context. In the film, *Hōjōki* is the only book Hyakken carries when fleeing his bombed-out house; the real-life Hyakken published in 1947 an essay-memoir called *New Hōjōki*. A true child of Edo, he quips that where Kamo no chōmei had the delicate

sound of mountain water flowing nearby, the only water sounds in urban Tokyo are men passing by who piss on the wall next to the hut.

15 Shōsōin is a part of Tōdai-ji temple in Nara, built in the eighth century from "diverse documents and courtly treasures," "the elegant accoutrements of Nara court life" donated by an eighth-century emperor; it is the oldest repository of material culture and texts detailing life and ritual in Japan, but according to Hayashi also marks contacts with China, Korea, Iran, and India. Objects include old tax registers, Buddhist objects and sutras, textiles and clothing, furniture, games and weaponry, and instruments like lute-like biwas, flute-like shakuhachis, and zither-like kins used for Buddhist rituals, not to mention musical scores, "whistling arrows with turnip-shaped heads," and panpipes modeled on T'ang dynasty instruments (Hayashi, "Restoration of an Eighth Century Panpipe," 18, 24). The sound of such instruments, along with their dimensions and materials, could evoke a range of now-forgotten or erased soundscapes. Given that the Shōsōin is owned by the Japanese state and is part of the national heritage system, its offerings are predisposed to enable isolated national histories. However, Kurosawa's interpretation focuses on the range of expressions that made up a premodern soundscape and how that archive might be used by modern storytellers. He mentions the Heian and not the Nara period, so he perhaps didn't dig enough into these histories to know the collection (it is open only two weeks per year, with select artifacts on exhibition), but according to Hayashi, a survey of instruments was conducted in 1949–50.

Seven Samurai, Redux

1 Both popular actors were trained in kabuki and then made the transition to film, specializing in *jidai-geki* and appearing in over three hundred films each. *Shinpa* is a style of late nineteenth-century theater that, along with kabuki, was the basis of many early films. Inoue seems to see *Seven Samurai* as a modernist film, a truly modern *jidai-geki* extending the line of thought felt by Pure Film movement critics who saw theater as unrealistic and full of anachronisms and tried to purge film of theatrical traits, foregrounding purely visual elements such as light, camerawork, and montage. See Gerow, *Visions of Japanese Modernity.*

2 Maeda Seison (1885–1977) was a famous painter of *nihonga,* modern paintings that used themes and materials historically used in Japan, as opposed to so-called Western styles and themes.

3 The *habutaé* is a silk head covering that goes on top of the actor's head to cover up their actual hair and give a surface for the wig, with its period-specific hairstyle. *Habutaé* refers to a lightweight woven silk but has come to also mean the head covering made from this kind of silk.

4 Toraya is a well-known purveyor of traditional sweets, including yōkan jellies. These are sweets in the shape of rectangular bars made out of azuki beans, gelatin, and sugar, sometimes flavored according to the season. A *chonmage* is a hairstyle for men in period dramas, usually samurai, of the Edo period. The top of the head is smoothed over by a silk covering, the *habutaé*, to simulate a shaved pate, and the remaining long hair gathered into a ponytail and folded back over to rest on the bald pate. If not arranged properly, because of the pomade applied, the topknot can have the look of a wobbly rectangular blob with a patina on top just like a yōkan.

5 Screenwriter Hashimoto Shinobu recounts in his memoir (32) that the original title was *A Day in the Life of a Samurai* (Samurai no ichi-nichi, 侍の一日).

6 Hashimoto describes, in that memoir, how the filmmaking staff were acutely aware of both Kurosawa's shift from Japanese to "the world's Kurosawa," as well as the indeterminacy of the historical record about key details of meals that would have a big ripple effect on the plot. Most notably, after talking to over twenty historians and novelists, they still did not know whether a samurai on castle duty in the early Edo period would bring his own bento for lunch, an event that would impact the drama of the whole story. So what might have been a drama of daily life in the Edo period was revised into the story of a righteous battle in the Sengoku period.

7 The Sengoku era, the era of warring states, was a period of constant upheaval and war that lasted from the mid-1400s, as the former feudal regime crumbled, through the establishment of the Tokugawa *bakufu* military government around 1600. Kurosawa's choice of the Sengoku era, and not the later Tokugawa era, is unusual for *jidai-geki* films; he repeated this choice with *Kagemusha*'s setting.

8 *Twenty-Four Eyes* is Kinoshita Keisuke's 1954 melodrama about an idealistic female teacher (played by Takamine Hideko) stationed on the island of Shōdoshima from 1928 to 1946: before, during, and after the war. The "eyes" belong to the twelve first-grade students she meets, teaches, and coexists with through the rise of militarism and the war's end.

9 The Self-Defense Forces (SDF) are Japan's standing military. While forbidden by Article 9 of the Constitution to pursue aggressive wars, they conduct training and dispatch troops to peacekeeping and antiterrorist operations.

10 *A Brief Account of the Combat Arts in Our Land* is a 1704 book that contained what Hinatsu Shigetaka calls "short biographies that recount the histories and deeds of great warriors" (261), or what translator John Rogers describes as "[how] an educated reader of the mid-Edo period regarded the martial arts," when their "mythology and lore" were first put down on paper (417). Hashimoto regarded it as the one source for tales of Edo-period swordsmen and used it to develop the characters for *Seven Samurai.* He used its source material—its portraits of lone heroes—in his initial plan of an omnibus story of storied swordsmen including Miyamoto Musashi and Sakakibara Kenkichi, but Kurosawa returned it to him to be reformatted as a *kishōtenketsu* narrative, with a story-driven introduction, development, twist, and conclusion, resulting in the third and final version that became the film.

11 The Kōdōkan is the building that houses the world headquarters of judo. The Four Guardians are four men who were of samurai origin and were early and exceptional students of judo founder Kano Jigorō, who transformed martial arts into a modern form.

12 Kurahara was a stalwart of proletarian literature and a translator of Fadeyev.

13 Like a piece of tempura, where the batter covers a vegetable or a shrimp, the tempura student is enrobed in an outer covering, his uniform, that hides what is on the inside. In other words, he is an imposter. Masumura Yasuzō's 1960 film *Fake Student* (Nise gakusei, 偽学生), based on a story by Ōe Kenzaburō, is one such story.

14 *Fundoshi* are a kind of traditional underwear, resembling a loincloth tied out of a single piece of fabric, leaving the wearer's bottom mostly exposed, as the case of Mifune here. Men commonly wore *fundoshi* through the wartime era, as underwear and as swimsuits, but they are less common today.

15 These lines of dialogue are taken from the elegant subtitles of the Criterion edition DVD.

16 A National Treasure (Kokuhō) is an art object or a historical building whose current incarnation is designated under the Law for the

Protection of Cultural Properties (1951). The law's goal is both to preserve the object and to prevent the object from being exported.

17 Misora Hibari (1937–1989) was a wildly popular star, whom Christine Yano calls "Japan's premiere diva of popular song" (96). Renowned for her precociousness in an era of war orphans as well as her singing and acting, she made her film debut when she was only eleven and reached stardom with her box office hit in the 1949 film *Sad Whistle* (Kanashiki kuchi-bue, 悲しき口笛), her fifth. The title song features Hibari's enka stylization as a set piece in a cabaret, strolling among the tables in elegant top hat and tails. Hibari became an icon of the postwar nation's resilience, optimism, and recovery. In her teenage years, she starred in a number of transmedial works, dancing and acting in a number of *jidai-geki*, sometimes cross-dressed as a young sword-fighting man in Tōei genre films. See Yamazaki, "Calico-World in Rainbow Colors," for a discussion of these lower-budget works; the films had pop elements that attracted a new, younger, and more female audience than Tōhō *jidai-geki* audiences. The updated Tōei films remained largely geared to domestic audiences and were not marketed on the international art circuit like Kurosawa films. "Sad Saké" (Kanashii sake, 悲しい酒) is a later song, a cover Hibari released in 1966. With its classical guitar and spoken-word sections about loneliness and lost love, Hibari's blockbuster rendition of drinking away her sorrows is regarded as one of the sadder songs in a generally melancholy genre.

18 Tani Akira (1885–1966) had a long career, primarily in side roles in TV dramas and at Tōhō; he also appeared in *Throne of Blood* and *Yojimbo*.

19 Takahara Toshio (1923–2000) was trained in theater, under Tokugawa Musei, among others, and had a long career working for all the Big 5 studios as well as TV.

20 All three of these actors had careers that stretched over decades, often in supporting roles and often in period dramas. Tōno and Yamagata had theater backgrounds, while Kamiyama spent time in silent-era Hollywood and had parts in various Orientalist dramas like *The Thief of Baghdad* and *The Chinese Parrot*, where he starred as Charlie Chan.

21 A *chōchin* baba is an old woman who has many horizontal wrinkles, like a *chōchin* paper lantern; a *kasa* or umbrella baba is an old woman with vertical wrinkles, like an old-style umbrella folded up.

22 See my Translator's Introduction for more on Fadeyev as an important proletarian writer who interested Japanese readers and critics because

of his craft as well as his politics. He was a war correspondent for *Pravda* between World War I and World War II, and became known for *The Rout* as well as *The Young Guard* (1946). Later he became a powerful literary bureaucrat who rose to the position of secretary-general of the Writers' Union and member of the Central Committee under Stalin; Fadeyev ended up signing the arrest warrants of many distinguished writers and friends. He committed suicide in 1956.

23 A *saru-mawashi* act was a kind of street performance that featured a trained monkey; the name also refers to the trainer. In medieval Japan, monkeys were seen as intermediaries to the gods and had a ritual function of warding off illness from horses and cattle for aristocratic owners. Over time, in the Edo period, *saru-mawashi* became a street performance, one of the popular arts, in the pleasure quarters or public areas; performers exchanged stories and tricks for alms. *Saru-mawashi* nearly vanished by the 1960s and underwent a small revival in the 2000s.

24 *Sewa-mono* are domestic melodramas set in the everyday life of townspeople in the Edo or early Meiji period; *wagoto* and *aragoto* are two different styles of kabuki acting: *wagoto* is more subdued and "gentle," and is thought to be realistic, whereas *aragoto* is wilder and more brashly stylized in *kata* set forms rather than naturalistic action. *Seven Samurai* characters were more along the lines of *aragoto,* and Yamada applies these styles—realistic, contemporary versus stylized and period drama—to the genre focus of the respective studios.

25 Here Kurosawa invokes a comparison with Ozu, who often overmodestly compared himself to a tofu maker—putting out the same product time after time, working away as a rather austere, humble, local artisan.

26 Andrei Bolkonsky is a character in Leo Tolstoy's *War and Peace.*

Pure Films of Broken Nature

1 Kurosawa tells a slightly different version of the story in a 1992 interview (Cardullo, " 'I Am Simply a Maker of Films,' " 168). In that version, it is Hyakken's grandson, and an essay rather than a short story. But regardless, the message is consistent that film is its own creature made of many autonomous parts.

2 Here Inoue describes the topography of the kind of stage and main characters as they appear in *mugen* Noh, a phantasmal as opposed to realistic genre. A typical play involves a *shite,* the lead character of the play, whose story is drawn out by the *waki,* or supporting character, who

always appears first in a *mugen* Noh play. Where the *shite* character is often some sort of unreal being who presents a past to the secondary character, the *waki* is often a traveler to whom the *shite* appears. In this episode, the "I" character draws out the story of the ghostly soldier who refuses to go to the land of the dead in a landscape that transposes the major landmarks of a Noh stage into the dreamlike setting right after the war.

3 *Kitsune* are folkloric, fox spirits that can take on many forms and feature in many local legends as well as Shintō beliefs. In some regions of Japan, shape-shifting weather such as atmospheric ghost lights or sun-showers is referred to as a *kitsune* wedding.

4 *Jigoku-e* are vividly painted scrolls that were popular beginning in the Heian based on Buddhist texts that depict hell as part of Buddhist pictorial storytelling practices called *e-toki* (picture decipherment). Priests, and later itinerant entertainers, explicated the hell pictures to draw out specific meanings and give a guided tour to listeners of the kinds of suffering in store for those who transgress and land in the hell reserved for their particular category. The demons, physical torture, and bubbling red pools of blood in episode 7 are familiar images from this line of *jigoku-e* (interpretation). See Saka, *Datsueba the Clothes Snatcher*, 12–40, and Sekiyama, *Deciphering Pictorial Images*.

5 A "Dersu village" is thus in theory a concept that might be transposed to Japan. The name comes from the village on the *taiga* in Kurosawa's Siberian film, *Dersu Uzala*. Inoue is probably interpreting the village in *Dreams* as aligning with the values of *Dersu Uzala*. In context it may sound sentimental, especially when viewed through the festivity and bright colors. But *Dersu Uzala* is also a film about retrospection, in which the protagonist, based on explorer Vladimir Arseniev, visits the village where he met his guide, the indigenous Dersu, who is later killed as a result of his exchanges with Arseniev. As we see from the relation to Tarkovsky, the film narratively positions the village at the end of a life story, but as part of a cosmos of children, water, flowers, and ex-lovers at the same time. It is a deeply relational account of multiple life cycles, dynamic at all levels, rather than one human being's immersion in a fixed idea of "nature." Inoue's comment raises the question of how Kurosawa's views of nature and cosmological belonging draw in historical relations of grief and colonial violence as part of a general critique of modernity. See chapter 6 of Solovieva, *The Russian Kurosawa*.

6 The ashura statue is a National Treasure, a Nara period work whose figure has six arms and a head with three faces facing different directions. The ashura is a type of supernatural being, one of the eight guardians of the Buddha. This type of being is sometimes associated with rage and conflict, but this statue's expressions seem more youthfully vexed than violent, more proximate to viewers than many Buddhist statues. It is worth noting that the critique comes via an object that, in the twentieth century, was seen as an aesthetic object rather than an exclusively "religious" object. Kurosawa picks up on the popularity of the aesthetic Buddhist statue and makes the connection to popular entertainment with an ethical critique of privatized institutional wealth. His use of the ashura resonates with the 1924 poetry collection *Spring and Ashura* (春と阿修羅, Haru to ashura) by another Tolstoy-influenced writer, Miyazawa Kenji, as well as experimental filmmaker Matsumoto Toshio's 1971 film *Shura*. The meeting points of Buddhism and modernism are beyond the scope of this translation, but Shields offers some frameworks in *Against Harmony*, as does Konishi's *Anarchist Modernity*.

7 In Kyoto, temples (and other religious corporations) are exempt from paying taxes on offerings, which has allowed them to accumulate substantial wealth, even as the city of Kyoto has often struggled financially. This roundtable appeared shortly after a small tax was imposed in 1985 on visitor admissions to some major temples, provoking strikes, including at temples that Kurosawa mentions.

8 *Bota-mochi*, as in this scene, are homemade rice balls covered with sweet red bean paste, often eaten around the Buddhist equinox holiday of *higan*, which marks a phase of contemplation vis-à-vis the other world (higan, 彼岸). In the story world of *Dreams*, the mention of *bota-mochi* seems to act as a signal for the soldier to soothe his suffering and retire to the world of the dead, rather than haunting the earthly world.

9 The Tsukiji Little Theater was founded in 1924 as an alternative to prevailing theatrical styles. It produced many experimental and creatively left-leaning productions, including proletarian productions by Japanese creators, as well as translated adaptations such as Karel Čapek's *R.U.R.*

10 The second play was based on a *rakugo* story by San'yūtei Kimba the Third (1894–1964).

11 In *Something Like an Autobiography* (196), Kurosawa names Saitō Takao (1929–2014) as one of the only two cinematographers in Japan capable of understanding the diagram he uses to coordinate a film shoot with his

customary three cameras. The other is Nakai Asakazu (1901–1988), who also worked on Kurosawa films from *Stray Dog* to *Ran.*

12 Sano (1930–2011) worked on several of Kurosawa's later films, including *Kagemusha, Ran, Dreams, Maadadayo,* and *Rhapsody in August,* as well as the posthumous *After the Rain.* Sano began work attached to the Kyoto *jidai-geki* section of Shōchiku, where he worked on many period dramas before going freelance; he brought with him a repertoire of extensive work in *jidai-geki* as well as melodramas and mid-century experimental narrative works. These include Ōshima Nagisa's New Wave classics *Japanese Summer: Double Suicide* (1967) and *Three Resurrected Drunkards* (1968); *Mujō* and *Mandala,* two of the three films known as Jissoji Akio's Buddhist trilogy, produced by Art Theatre Guild; Shinoda Masahiro's *Silence* (1971) and *MacArthur's Children* (1984); and Yoshida Kiju's *The Eighteen Who Stirred Up a Storm* (1963) and *Woman in the Mirror* (2001).

Kurosawa's One Hundred Films

1 The Kurosawa-gumi is the crew of long-term members that Kurosawa assembled over the course of his career, both at the Tōhō studio and in his independent productions.

2 As there is no lighthouse in the Buñuel film, it's possible that Kurosawa has confused *Un chien andalou* with the 1929 surrealist film *Les gardiens du phare* (The lighthouse keepers).

3 Uchida Hyakken (1889–1971) was a writer of short stories and *zuihitsu* essays, as well as a diary of his life living in the ruins of bombed-out Tokyo. Hyakken was the model for the main character in Kurosawa's last film, *Maadadayo,* and his 1948 story "The Sarasate Disc" (Sarasāte no ban, サラサーテの盤) was the inspiration for Suzuki Seijun's 1980 film *Zigeunerweisen.*

4 This film is tenth on Kurosawa's list of one hundred films.

5 Kurosawa is likely referring to the long stream-of-consciousness scene that happens near the end of the film. Schubert had fallen in love with a young aristocrat, Countess Esterhazy, who laughed impertinently during a performance he gave for his patroness, Princess Kinsky. The laughing countess and Schubert fall in love, after she reveals herself to be an accomplished singer, but her family insists she marry a safe suitor from her own class. In the sequence Kurosawa refers to, Schubert arrives in the middle of the wedding and is ushered in to play for the hall. He begins playing, and their shared memories of her dancing, singing,

and kissing are montaged in as a stream of consciousness from his point of view. When the performance reprises the symphony and reaches the moment where the countess had broken into peals of laughter, she tears up, faints, and is carried out. She recovers, and after a tête-à-tête in which he reveals that the symphony was for her, she bids him farewell. He tears the symphony to shreds in recognition of their unfinished love.

6 Henri Langlois (1914–1977) cofounded the Cinémathèque française in 1936, beginning a long career of film collecting and programming. He saved many films from Nazi hands, was responsible for screenings of many midcentury auteurs like Mizoguchi Kenji, Ingmar Bergman, and Kenneth Anger, and for creating the conditions for the cinephilia that in turn fostered the French New Wave.

7 According to Kurosawa's longtime collaborator Nogami Teruyo, Kurosawa and Ford met in London in October 1957. See Nogami, *Waiting on the Weather*, 277–79.

8 This is the film Kurosawa was shooting at the time of the surrender; SCAP is the Supreme Command of Allied Powers, an infrastructure given the mandate to "democratize" Japan, which included supervising film production. *The Men Who Tread on the Tiger's Tail* would ultimately be banned by U.S. Occupation censors and not shown to Japanese audiences until the end of the Occupation in 1952. Period dramas were thought to be connected to popular sympathy for fascism when censors interpreted historical themes, regardless of content or critique, as endorsing premodern loyalty, which they thought both prefigured and endorsed fascism. For a detailed account of the topics and historical tropes banned under the Occupation, see Hirano, *Mr. Smith Goes to Tokyo*, 47–103.

9 The Sanno Hotel was known as one of the top-tier luxury hotels in Tokyo. At the time of Ford's visit it was leased by the government of Japan for the use of U.S. forces under the provisions of the U.S.–Japan Security Treaty.

10 In twentieth-century Japanese, a "boy" referred to a male service worker, often on a ship or in a hotel or café, who regardless of actual age performed the duties of a porter, waiter, or other related service job.

11 The film contains several scenes of horses riding in formation, in choreographed order: silhouettes against a sky, being led through a swamp, traveling through Mississippi. Thematically the backdrop is a vast nature, where the composition emphasizes the mobility and connection of varied but coordinated abstract forms of horse and rider. For

an in-depth analysis of motion and form in Ford's oeuvre, see Hasumi Shigehiko, *On John Ford*. A related, earlier piece was translated and published as "John Ford, or The Eloquence of Gesture."

12 Lumet adapted the successful 1959 Broadway version of *Rashomon*, written by Fay Kanin and Michael Kanin, into a television drama in 1960. After *Ran*, Lumet would lead a successful campaign to get Kurosawa a Best Director nomination for the film in 1985.

13 Kurosawa and Honda initially worked together under Yamamoto Kajirō at PCL, the Photo Chemical Laboratory, a lab-turned-studio that was integrated into Tōhō after the war. As assistant director, Honda shot the renowned Surrealist black market sequence of Kurosawa's *Stray Dog* (1949). Honda and Kurosawa had a falling-out but later reconnected, and Honda shared a producer with Kurosawa and served as right-hand man, a kind of associate director, on five late Kurosawa films: *Kagemusha*, *Ran*, *Rhapsody in August*, *Dreams*, and *Maadadayo*.

14 *Kagemusha* was released in the United States in October 1980; the TV appearance was likely on Dick Cavett's show on October 20 and 21, 1981.

15 As representative directors of the Golden Age of the 1950s, Mizoguchi and Naruse worked more in the genre of melodrama, particularly those featuring female protagonists.

16 Kurosawa started his assistant director career at PCL under the director Yamamoto Kajirō (1902–1974) with the film *The Horse* (Uma, 馬, 1941); he worked under Yamamoto for seventeen films altogether. Yamamoto directed the renowned wartime "national policy" film *The War at Sea from Hawai'i to Malaya* (Hawai-marē oki-kaisen, ハワイ・マレー沖海鮮, 1942) as well as many genres including melodrama, comic *jidai-geki*, and two adaptations of novels by Natsume Sōseki. In Kurosawa's eyes Yamamoto was also an advocate for daydreaming and against overwork, and an example of how the older studio system created a structure for assistant directors to rotate through all the departments on a set, giving them a holistic set of tools and the experience to be skilled directors.

17 The context Lucas seems to have in mind is the legal actions Kurosawa and his studio took toward director Sergio Leone after the epoch-making *A Fistful of Dollars* was released. An employee of the producer/distributor Tōhō saw Leone's movie—with its Japanese title, *Kōya no yojimbō*. In an exchange with Leone, Leone wrote that he had sent several letters to Tōhō inquiring about a remake and decided that six months

without a reply meant he had permission. Tōhō wrote a letter of protest on behalf of Kurosawa and screenwriter Kikushima Ryūzō. According to Galbraith in *The Emperor and the Wolf,* a settlement was reached that gave Kurosawa 15 percent of worldwide receipts with a minimum of $100,000. Nishimura writes that the Italian studio gave rights to Japan, Taiwan, and Korea to the Kurosawa side, and instead of getting worldwide distribution rights, the Kurosawa side would get $10,000 and 15 percent of the distribution (87–88). Later, Lucas, along with Francis Ford Coppola, would be instrumental in Kurosawa's return to the global stage, as they helped secure funding for *Kagemusha* (1980), the first of the series of Kurosawa's late films made possible with support from non-Japanese directors.

18 The television period drama of *Red Beard* ran on NHK for almost a year during 1972 and 1973.

19 Matsumura also starred in *Maadadayo,* but the role of Watanaka Kyōta in *Dodes'ka-den* was his first Kurosawa film.

20 Shimura Takashi (1905–1982) was a regular in Kurosawa productions, appearing in twenty-one films from 1943's *Sanshirō Sugata* to *Kagemusha* in 1980. He is also one of the small stable of actors who worked for Kurosawa and on Yamada Yōji's *It's Tough Being a Man* (Otoko wa tsurai yo, 男はつらいよ) series.

21 Hidari Bokuzen (1874–1971) played in *Ikiru* (1952), *Seven Samurai* (1954), and *The Lower Depths* (1957). In *Ikiru,* his drunken outburst during a banquet celebrating the life of the main character, Watanabe, blows away the pretensions of Watanabe's coworkers at city hall. The fragmented bureaucratic territories enforced by the functionary coworkers had sidelined Watanabe's grassroots efforts at building a pocket park much loved by its neighbors.

22 Gillett was a film critic, programmer, and film historian. He was a long-time staff member at the British Film Institute (BFI), and programmed Japanese filmmakers, including Ozu Yasujirō and Naruse Mikio, at the National Film Theater. In 1994, he was awarded an Order of the Sacred Treasure by the Japanese government.

23 Yamanaka Sadao (1909–1938) died young in Manchuria after making twenty-two features between 1932 and 1937, mostly *jidai-geki,* all of which were lost but three. Although in entry no. 13 Kurosawa rails against Japanese studios for failing to preserve Yamanaka's films,

firebombing during the war would also have been a major issue. Naruse's films played in New York, Los Angeles/Santa Monica, Chicago, and other art houses in the 1980s to wide acclaim among film critics.

24 *Cuore* (Heart) was an Italian film serial (1915–1916) based on the best-selling children's book by Edmondo De Amicis, which was a best-seller in Meiji-era Japan. In his memoir, Kurosawa reprises an episode in which a boy gives his spot on a lifeboat over to a young girl. Kurosawa was born in 1910, so must have seen the films—about boys a few years older than he—not long after they came out.

25 Yodogawa Nagaharu (1909–1998) was a hugely popular film critic who began his career as an editor but established a televisual presence introducing Hollywood and European films on a long-running weekly series. He not only made American blockbusters accessible with his commentaries, but traveled extensively to film festivals abroad, including a trip where he attended the Academy Awards ceremony on behalf of *Rashomon.*

26 Tokugawa Musei (1894–1971) was the most famous of the *benshi* and worked for high-end theaters that showed Euro-American films as well as more avant-garde Japanese films such as *A Page of Madness* (Gerow, *Visions of Modernity,* 264). Kurosawa's older brother Heigo was a protégé of Musei. Heigo worked in major theaters and enjoyed a following as a *benshi* in Kanda and Asakusa. See Anderer, *Kurosawa's Rashomon.*

The List

1 Shimazu (1897–1945) worked his way through the ranks at Shochiku's Kamata studios, moving to Tōhō after the sound era began. He was an innovator in the burgeoning middle-class family film as well as the "women's film." *Our Neighbor Miss Yae* is the quintessence of what Mitsuyo Wada-Marciano calls a "cheerful" modernism: its young heroine thoroughly at ease in modern city life and emblematic of a signature Shochiku studio style of modernist film distinct from Hollywood.

2 In *Something Like an Autobiography* (187), Kurosawa attributes this submission to the "angel," Giuliana Stramigioli.

3 My translation is adapted from a translation of the same passage from Honda's memoir *Godzilla and My Movie Life* (*Gojira* to waga eiga jinsei, 『ゴジラ』とわが映画人生) in Ryfle, Godziszewski, and Honda-Yun, *Ishiro Honda,* xxiii.

4 *Rakugo* is a one-person type of vaudevillian storytelling dating from in the Edo period popular in *shitamachi* entertainment districts. The performance is a comic monologue, but usually involves a panorama of social types and a story full of wordplay, twists, and digressions. In this story, Saheiji is a kind of grifter who is unable to pay his bill at a pleasure house in Tokyo, but he makes himself so indispensable to its staff and the prostitutes that the owner finally lavishes him with gifts and pays him handsomely to go away.

5 Ichikawa's film was criticized by its sponsors for focusing on the delicate quotidian movements of audience members and athletes, and not celebrating Japan's athletes or the new architecture and infrastructures enabled by its postwar recovery. In the end the Japan Olympic Committee enlisted producer Taguchi Suketaro and journalist Kawamoto Nobumasa to recut Ichikawa's massive body of footage into a completely different, shorter film called *Sensation of the Century* (1966).

6 Fujiwara Katamari, or Kama-san, was renowned for not always learning his lines properly.

7 Kiarostami had a long association with Japanese art-house cinema, working since the 1990s with Japanese festival organizers, crew, and actors. He explicitly paid homage to Ozu Yasujirō with his 2003 film, *Five Dedicated to Ozu;* his 2012 film, *Like Someone in Love,* was shot in Tokyo with an all-Japanese cast.

8 Mukōda was an accomplished writer of TV screenplays and short fiction. A set of short stories won her the Naoki Prize for best popular fiction in 1980. Her short story "Meeting Again" appears in the collection *Tokyo: A Literary Stroll* (2002). She died in a plane crash in 1981 in Taiwan just as she was solidifying her career as a fiction writer.

9 Rivette's film is based on Balzac's short story "The Unknowable Masterpiece" (Le chef d'oeuvre inconnu). The "trickiness" probably refers to the sexual politics of the film, in which a young artist offers his own lover to an aging painter to respark his genius, a redo of a painting of his own wife that he abandoned earlier. The film dwells on the artistic process and the sacrifices it demands, while showing the complicated desire of all parties to use the body of the young model to its fullest powers—painter, his wife and former model, the young painter, and the new muse herself.

Farewell, Papa

1 Aum was a techno-millenarian Buddhist sect whose members acted under the leadership of Asahara Shōkō. The sect conducted an attack with the poison sarin gas on several subway trains connecting stations near finance and political buildings in Tokyo during morning rush hour on March 20, 1995, killing multiple people and injuring many.

2 The film was directed by Kumai Kei and released in 1992. It was based on a 1951 short story by Yamamoto Shūgorō, whose works were also the basis of Kurosawa's *Sanjurō* (1962), *Red Beard* (1965), and *Dodes'ka-den* (1970). The story is a period piece set in an Edo-period brothel, and unlike other Kurosawa *jidai-geki* it features a love story at its center.

3 In his 1982 memoir *Something Like an Autobiography* (137–39), Kurosawa describes the ceremony, as well as a melodrama of courtship in which the very person supposed to plead his case as a go-between sabotaged the union by writing many letters slandering Kurosawa.

4 *Nihonga* is a modern mode of Japanese painting whose artists used mineral pigments, ink, and shell white, rather than oil paints. The color relied on an alchemical mix of natural materials, glues, and other liquids in reaction to the *washi* paper, so the mixing process might require a lot of experimentation to get it right. Given that *nihonga* works with what Chelsea Foxwell calls "references to past masterpieces and strategies for adapting 'tradition' (that loaded word) to modern spaces" ("The Painting of Sadness?" 28), the fixation on using materials proper to *nihonga* to develop his own style is consistent with Kurosawa's often experimental use of tools to represent past historical materials in film.

Dreaming It Forward

1 The term *katsudō-ya* (活動家) was used earlier in the century to refer to "moviemakers"; it seems old-fashioned, retro, because the word "katsudō" was used in the earlier era to mean something like "moving pictures." A person in charge of special equipment would be in charge of things like the rails for camera movement, high-speed fans, rainmaking equipment—the infrastructure enabling the shoot to take place.

2 A sound operator (ongaku gishi, 録音技師) is an overall director of sound, in charge of recording, mixing, and editing the entire acoustic dimension of the film, including music and sound effects.

BIBLIOGRAPHY

English

Abel, Richard. *French Film Theory and Criticism*, vol. 1, *A History/Anthology, 1907–1929*. Princeton, N.J.: Princeton University Press, 1988.

Anderer, Paul. *Kurosawa's Rashomon: A Vanished City, a Lost Brother, and the Voice Inside His Iconic Films.* New York: Pegasus Books, 2016.

Andrew, Dudley. "*Broken Blossoms*: The Art and the Eros of a Perverse Text." *Quarterly Review of Film Studies* 6, no. 1 (January 1981): 81–90.https://doi.org/10.1080/10509208109361080.

Cardullo, Bert, and Akira Kurosawa. " 'I Am Simply a Maker of Films': A Visit with the Sensei of the Cinema." In *Akira Kurosawa: Interviews.* Conversations with Filmmakers Series. Jackson: University Press of Mississippi, 2008, 166–81.

Bowen-Struyk, Heather, and Norma Field. *For Dignity, Justice, and Revolution: An Anthology of Japanese Proletarian Literature.* Chicago: University of Chicago Press, 2016.

Dym, Jeffrey A. *Benshi, Japanese Silent Film Narrators, and Their Forgotten Narrative Art of Setsumei: A History of Japanese Silent Film Narration.* Lewiston, N.Y.: Edwin Mellen Press, 2003.

Emmerich, Michael, and Daisuke Miyao, eds. *The World of the Benshi.* Los Angeles: Yanai Initiative for Globalizing Japanese Humanities, 2024.

Farris, William Wayne. "Pieces in a Puzzle: Changing Approaches to the Shōsōin Documents." *Monumenta Nipponica* 62, no. 4 (2007): 397–435. https://dx.doi.org/10.1353/mni.2007.a230264.

Ford, Dan. *Pappy: The Life of John Ford.* New York: Da Capo Press, 1998.

Foxwell, Chelsea. "The Painting of Sadness? The Ends of Nihonga, Then and Now." *ARTMargins* 4, no. 1 (February 2015): 27–60. https://doi.org/10.1162/ARTM_a_00104.

Frankel, Glenn. *The Searchers: The Making of an American Legend.* New York: Bloomsbury, 2013.

Fujii, Moeko. "Who's That Man? Mifune at 100." The Criterion Collection (April 3, 2020). https://www.criterion.com/current/posts/6879-who-s-that-man-mifuneat-100.

Fujiki, Hideaki. "Benshi as Stars: The Irony of the Popularity and Respectability of Voice Performers in Japanese Cinema." *Cinema Journal* 45, no. 2 (Winter 2006): 68–84. https://dx.doi.org/10.1353/cj.2006.0016.

Galbraith, Stuart. *The Emperor and the Wolf: The Lives and Films of Akira Kurosawa and Toshiro Mifune.* New York: Faber and Faber, 2002.

Gerow, Aaron. *Visions of Japanese Modernity: Articulations of Cinema, Nation, and Spectatorship, 1895–1925.* Berkeley: University of California Press, 2010.

Hasumi, Shigehiko. "John Ford, or The Eloquence of Gesture." *Rouge,* no. 7 (2005). Translated by Adrian Martin. http://www.rouge.com.au/7/ford.html.

Hayashi, Kenzō. "Restoration of an Eighth Century Panpipe in the Shōsōin Repository, Nara, Japan." *Asian Music* 6, no. 1/2 (1975): 15–27. https://doi.org/10.2307/833840.

Hinatsu Shigetaka. "Honchō Bugei Shōden." *Monumenta Nipponica* 45, no. 3 (1990): 261–84. https://doi.org/10.2307/2384903.

Hirano, Kyoko. *Mr. Smith Goes to Tokyo: Japanese Cinema under the American Occupation, 1945–1952.* Washington, D.C.: Smithsonian Institution Press, 1992.

Keathley, Christian. *Cinephilia and History, or The Wind in the Trees.* Bloomington: Indiana University Press, 2006.

Konishi, Sho. *Anarchist Modernity: Cooperatism and Japanese-Russian Intellectual Relations in Modern Japan.* Harvard East Asian Monographs 356. Cambridge, Mass.: Harvard University Asia Center, 2013.

Kurosawa, Akira. *Something Like an Autobiography.* Translated by Audie E. Bock. New York: Vintage Books, 1983.

Nogami, Teruyo. *Waiting on the Weather: Making Movies with Akira Kurosawa.* Translated by Juliet Winters Carpenter. Berkeley, Calif.: Stone Bridge Press, 2006.

Nornes, Markus. *Cinema Babel: Translating Global Cinema.* Minneapolis: University of Minnesota Press, 2007.

Ōmori, Kyōko. "Narrating the Detective: *Nansensu,* Silent Film Benshi Performances and Tokugawa Musei's Absurdist Detective Fiction." *Japan Forum* 21, no. 1 (April 2009): 75–93. https://doi.org/10.1080/09555800902857070.

Raine, Michael. "No Interpreter, Full Volume: The Benshi and the Sound Transition in 1930s Japan." In *The Culture of the Sound Image in Prewar Japan,* edited by Michael Raine and Johan Nordström, 127–56. Amsterdam: Amsterdam University Press, 2020.

Rogers, John M. "Arts of War in Times of Peace: Swordsmanship in Honchō Bugei Shōden, Chapter 5." *Monumenta Nipponica* 45, no. 4 (Winter 1990): 413–47. https://doi.org/10.2307/2385378.

Ryfle, Steve, Ed Godziszewski, and Yuuko Honda-Yun. *Ishiro Honda: A Life in Film, from Godzilla to Kurosawa.* Middletown, Conn.: Wesleyan University Press, 2017.

Saka, Chihiro. *Datsueba the Clothes Snatcher: The Evolution of a Japanese Folk Deity from Hell Figure to Popular Savior.* Brill's Japanese Studies Library 371. Leiden: Brill, 2022.

Shields, James Mark. *Against Harmony: Progressive and Radical Buddhism in Modern Japan.* Oxford: Oxford University Press, 2017.

Shively, Donald H. "Bakufu Versus Kabuki." *Harvard Journal of Asiatic Studies* 18, no. 3/4 (December 1955): 326–56.

Shockey, Nathan. *The Typographic Imagination: Reading and Writing in Japan's Age of Modern Print Media.* Studies of the Weatherhead East Asian Institute. New York: Columbia University Press, 2019.

Solovieva, Olga V. *The Russian Kurosawa: Transnational Cinema, or The Art of Speaking Differently.* Oxford: Oxford University Press, 2022.

Sugimoto, Mike. "The Fifty Year War: *Rashomon, After Life,* and Japanese Film Narratives of Remembering." *Japan Studies Review,* no. 7 (2003): 21–41.

Tasogawa, Hiroshi. *All the Emperor's Men: Kurosawa's Pearl Harbor.* Montclair, N.J.: Applause Theatre and Cinema Books, 2012.

Thornhill, Arthur H. "The Goddess Emerges: Shinto Paradigms in the Aesthetics of Zeami and Zenchiku." *Journal of the Association of Teachers of Japanese* 24, no. 1 (April 1990): 49–59. https://doi.org/10.2307/489229.

Wada-Marciano, Mitsuyo. *Nippon Modern: Japanese Cinema of the 1920s and 1930s.* Honolulu: University of Hawai'i Press, 2008.

Yamazaki, Junko. "Calico-World in Rainbow Colors: The Aesthetics of Gender in 1950s Toei Jidaigeki." In *A Companion to Japanese Cinema,* edited by David Desser, 130–48. Hoboken, N.J.: John Wiley and Sons, 2022.

Yamamoto Ichirō. "The *Jidaigeki* Film *Twilight Samurai*—A Salaryman-Producer's Point of View." In *The Oxford Handbook of Japanese Cinema,* edited by Daisuke Miyao, 306–26. Oxford: Oxford University Press, 2013.

Yano, Christine R. "From Child Star to Diva: Misora Hibari as Postwar Japan." In *Diva Nation: Female Icons from Japanese Cultural History,* edited by Laura Miller and Rebecca Copeland, 95–114. Berkeley: University of California Press, 2018.

Yoshimoto, Mitsuhiro. *Kurosawa: Film Studies and Japanese Cinema.* Durham, N.C.: Duke University Press, 2000.

Zahlten, Alexander. *The End of Japanese Cinema: Industrial Genres, National Times, and Media Ecologies.* Durham, N.C.: Duke University Press, 2017.

Japanese

Fadeyev, Alexander アレクサンドル・フアヂエーエフ. *The Rout* (壊滅). In World Socialist Literature Collection 7 世界社会主義文学叢書 7. Translated by Kurahara Korehito 蔵原惟人. Tokyo: Nansō shoin, 1929.

Hashimoto Shinobu 橋本忍. *Compound Cinematics: Akira Kurosawa and Me* (複眼の映像: 私と黒澤明). Tokyo: Bungei shunjū, 2010.

Hasumi Shigehiko 蓮實重彥. *On John Ford* (ジョン・フォード論). Tokyo: Bungei shunjū, 2022.

Ishikawa Takuboku 石川啄木. *Clouds Are Forms of Genius* (雲は天才である). Aozora bunko. https://www.aozora.gr.jp/cards/000153/files/4097_9491.html.

Kurahara Korehito 蔵原惟人. "Translator's Introduction"「訳者序」to ファヂエーエフ・ア Fadeyev, Alexander, *The Rout* (壊滅) 世界社会主義文学叢書 7. Tokyo: Nansō shoin, 1929.

Kurahara Korehito 蔵原惟人. "On Fadeyev's Novel *The Rout*" (ファヂエーエフの小説「壊滅」に就いて」). In *On Art* III (芸術論 III), 157–66. Tokyo: Shin Nihon shuppansha, 1966.

Makita Toshifumi 槙田寿文 and National Film Archive of Japan, eds. *Akira Kurosawa, Screenwriter* (脚本家黒澤明). Tokyo: Kokushokan kōkai, 2022.

Miyazawa Kenji 宮澤賢治. *Collected Poetry: Spring and Ashura* (春と修羅: 詩集). Tokyo: Nihon kindai bungakukan, 1969.

Satō Tadao 佐藤忠男 and Kishigawa Makoto 岸川真. *The Era of "Film Criticism"* (「映画評論」の時代). Tokyo: Catalog House, 2003.

Sekiyama Kazuo 関山和夫. *Deciphering Pictorial Images* (絵解き). Tokyo: Yūseidō, 1985.

Shiga Naoya 志賀直哉. "The Blind Turtle and the Floating Tree" (盲亀浮木). In *The Ashen Moon/A Red Chinese Platter* (灰色の月・万暦赤絵), 291–304. Tokyo: Shinchōsha, 1978.

Tasogawa Hiroshi 田十川弘. *Akira Kurosawa vs. Hollywood: The Saga of "Tora! Tora! Tora!"* (黒澤明 vs. ハリウッド:「トラ・トラ・トラ!」その謎のすべて). Tokyo: Bungei shunjū, 2010.

Uchida Hyakken 内田百閒. *Maadakai* (まあだかい). In *Uchida Hyakken Collected Works* 10 (内田百閒集成 10). Tokyo: Chikuma shobō, 2003.

Uchida Hyakken 内田百閒. *New Hōjōki* (新方丈記). Tokyo: Shinchōsha, 1947.

INDEX

AKIRA KUROSAWA (1910–1998) was among the most significant and influential directors in the history of cinema. His career began as assistant director at PCL Studios, the predecessor to Tōhō, where he wrote screenplays in multiple genres and worked under directors including his mentor, Yamamoto Kajirō, and Naruse Mikio. Beginning with the 1936 debut *Sanshirō Sugata,* Kurosawa directed thirty films, including one set in Siberia, and traveled to festivals worldwide, following the Grand Prix for *Rashomon* at the Twelfth Venice International Cinema Festival in 1950. Among his films are *The Most Beautiful, One Wonderful Sunday, Rashomon, Seven Samurai, Red Beard, The Hidden Fortress, Dodes'ka-den, Kagemusha, Ran,* and *Dreams.*

KUROSAWA KAZUKO is a costume designer, the daughter of Akira Kurosawa and actress Yaguchi Yōko. She supervised costumes on her father's productions beginning with *Ran.* Her other productions include Kitano Takeshi's *Zatoichi,* Koreeda Hirokazu's *Shoplifters,* and the NHK prestige drama *Segodon.*

ANNE MCKNIGHT is associate professor of Japanese and comparative literature at University of California, Riverside. She is author of *Nakagami, Japan: Buraku and the Writing of Ethnicity* (Minnesota, 2011).